On the Condition of Anonymity

THE HISTORY OF COMMUNICATION

Robert W. McChesney
and John C. Nerone, editors

A list of books in the series
appears at the end of this book.

On the Condition of Anonymity

Unnamed Sources and the Battle for Journalism

MATT CARLSON

UNIVERSITY OF ILLINOIS PRESS

Urbana, Chicago, and Springfield

© 2011 by the Board of Trustees
of the University of Illinois
All rights reserved
Manufactured in the United States of America
C 5 4 3 2 1
∞ This book is printed on acid-free paper.

Library of Congress Cataloging-in-Publication Data
Carlson, Matt
On the condition of anonymity : unnamed sources
and the battle for journalism / Matt Carlson
p.   cm. — (The history of communication)
Includes bibliographical references and index.
ISBN 978-0-252-03599-9 (hardcover : alk. paper)
1. Attribution of news.
2. Reporters and reporting—United States.
3. Journalism—Political aspects—United States.
4. Journalistic ethics—United States.
I. Title.
PN4781.C38   2011
070.4'3—dc22   2010035388

To my wife Curtis,
with unanonymous love

Contents

Acknowledgments

Writing a book seems quite deceptively to be a solitary undertaking. In reality, I owe an enormous amount of credit to the many smart and supportive people surrounding me over the past six or so years.

I am forever grateful for the education I received from the Annenberg School for Communication at the University of Pennsylvania as both a master's and doctoral student. I offer my sincere thanks to the faculty, staff, and students. Specifically, Michael Delli Carpini and Carolyn Marvin provided key insights at different stages of this work. I also benefitted from discussions with Eran Ben-Porath, Carrie Brown, Nicole Maurantonio, and Monroe Price. Above all, this work exists because of the guiding hand of Barbie Zelizer. I am proud to have been her student.

I am fortunate to have received useful feedback in making this text into a book. In particular, Carolyn Kitch and Claire Wardle offered fantastic advice during the prospectus stage of this work. Much of the writing was completed at Saint Louis University. At SLU, Kathleen Farrell offered her enthusiasm and support for this book from the moment I stepped on campus. Caroline Jack and Jason Peifer were indispensable in helping me through final revisions. At University of Illinois Press, John Nerone, Tad Ringo, and Kendra Boileau helped me make this the best book that it could be.

Finally, I want to thank my family for their support: my mother Judy and father Gary, my brothers Eric and Dave, and sister Barbie. And then there is my new family: my wonderfully perceptive and encouraging wife Curtis and, most precious of all, my daughter Lizzie.

I offer my sincere gratitude to everyone for making this book a reality.

The Problems—and Promise— of Unnamed Sources

> Journalists have to be careful about making promises to conceal the identity of sources. Information delivered without acknowledging its source can shake public confidence in the information. But confidentiality can also be essential to unearthing important news, news that people in power don't want you to have.
>
> —*Chicago Tribune* editorial

Readers of the May 26, 2004, *New York Times* opened their papers to find an unusual note from editor Bill Keller on page A10. Fourteen months after the invasion of Iraq, the newspaper took itself to task for having bungled its reporting on the buildup to what was then in 2004 an increasingly unpopular war. Keller's note called attention to the harm caused by competitive news pressures coupled with the difficulty of reporting on sensitive and secretive topics. But it was also an admission that unnamed sources—those known to the reporter but confidentially kept from readers—posed serious problems for journalism and, in turn, the public by failing to reveal what they were supposed to reveal: that the evidence of an imminently dangerous Iraqi arsenal was not as sound as public claims by the Bush administration made it out to be.

Keller's note was not the coda the newspaper had hoped it would be, nor was the newspaper alone in confronting problems due to anonymity. Rather, an astonishing series of news controversies involving unnamed sources followed in 2004 and 2005 at *Newsweek, Time,* the *Washington Post,* and *60 Minutes.* The incidents culminated in the 2007 trial of vice presidential aide I. Lewis "Scooter" Libby for obstructing the investigation into who leaked the identity of CIA analyst Valerie Plame in 2003. The journalistic community witnessed the uncomfortable spectacle of elite journalists spilling details about their relationships with unnamed sources while administration officials described their strategies for anonymously planting favorable news items. During this era, reporters relying on anonymity faced a slew of charges, including harboring political biases, being too close to sources, and placing professional status above the public interest. As controversies accumulated at prominent U.S. news outlets, so did questions on such topics as how the news should cover politics, the impact of elite news in a changing media world, the growing clout of journalism's critics, and the close ties between reporters and sources.

Why did all these incidents happen? And what do they mean for journalism? Or, more importantly, how do they influence the meaning of journalism? These questions require an understanding of how anonymity alters the underlying relationship among news sources, journalists, and audiences. In contrast to conventional attribution, the absence of a source's identity leads to unique risks and rewards that prove difficult to disentangle. Both arise from the bargain struck when a journalist grants anonymity: the identity of the source is withheld to obtain and distribute otherwise unattainable information. The warnings of journalism textbooks aside, this is not an unusual condition sources place on their information, but a regular and often repeated practice. Journalists justify hiding their practices from news audiences by linking this arrangement to their stated goal of holding society's institutions accountable. However, the loss of transparency exposes journalists who rely on unnamed sources to challenges over the accuracy of the information provided and the intentions of all those involved. What emerges is a set of extremes as unnamed sources contribute to journalism's greatest triumphs and its most shameful episodes. To bring into relief these complexities, this book tackles issues that arise when attribution disappears.

More precisely, each chapter illuminates how controversial incidents involving unnamed sources expanded into a wider interpretive struggle. The spark of controversy ignites a public competition in which journalists and others slug it out to define what happened, what (if anything) went wrong, and—most crucially—what should be done differently. Isolated diagnoses of mistakes are eclipsed by scrutiny taking aim at core news practices and deep-seated journalistic norms. By breaking from the unexamined flow of news, these ruptures expose the deep fissures of conflicting needs and pressures underlying newsgathering. Previously taken-for-granted practices face public reconsideration of their very viability. These squabbles deserve attention as a struggle to dictate what journalism should be.

Given this broader focus on the meaning of journalism, this book avoids either a straightforward defense or dismissal of unnamed sources. To do so would oversimplify the inherent problems posed by the loss of attribution whenever anonymity is granted or ignore their worth in providing valuable information to the public. Instead, this book seeks to understand the contradictions of unnamed sources through a cultural analysis of discussions and circumstances that arise when their use proves contentious. This focus on the symbolic tug-of-war erupting around unnamed sources grants us a view of the discursive means by which journalists and their critics compete to define what is acceptable and what is objectionable in the news. This is not merely a struggle over words, but one with real stakes for our expectations of the news and the tools available to achieve them.

Autonomy, Authority, and News Sources

This book proceeds from the premise that there is much to be gained in recognizing journalism as inextricable from the myriad societal institutions, cultural forces, economic conditions, and political contestations in which journalistic work is embedded. It is immediately noteworthy that this assertion strikes at the heart of claims journalists make about their detachment from the world they profess to represent. Autonomy remains a touchstone for journalism—a defining facet ardently defended through invoking the First Amendment as a legitimating document. The protestations of journalists aside, emphasizing context enhances our understanding of how journalism works. In moving away from accepting journalism as autonomous, self-contained, and self-determining, we place ourselves in a better position to examine how various flows of influence and power connect to and shape the news. Journalism should be recognized, in the terminology of Pierre Bourdieu, not as an autonomous entity, but as a heteronomous field inextricably intertwined with adjoining fields—namely politics and economics.[1] Journalism is embedded in and reliant on its environment, which means it can never truly be the independent observer it claims to be. This is not to excoriate the usefulness of journalism; it is only to recognize how the news fits within larger circuits of power and influence, as well as shared cultural values, beliefs, norms, and histories.[2]

Viewing journalism as a field overlapping—sometimes tensely, sometimes amiably—with other fields alerts us to a key problem for journalism: it can never be assured of its cultural role. Just as journalism's autonomy is always compromised, its authority to prosecute the news is always problematic and never guaranteed. It must continually reproduce and renegotiate this role.

What's more, this is not an uncrowded endeavor. Journalists constitute only one of the parties—and a complicated and contradictory one at that—seeking to define journalism in a public arena crowded with outspoken critics and stakeholders. This being the case, to deny journalism a fixed cultural position and to focus on its operation within a complex of social relations attunes us to the constant definitional tension surrounding journalistic practice.

Journalists continually address notions of who is a journalist, what journalism is, and what journalism should do against competing notions from others aiming to transform, minimize, stifle, or redefine news practices. Through attending to these questions, journalists seek to sustain their cultural authority to provide veridical stories about the important happenings of the world. This position is never guaranteed, however. Instead, journalists must actively advocate their social value. As David Eason writes, "The history of journalism is, in part, that of establishing, repairing, and transforming the authoritative base for accounts of 'the way it is.'"[3] Journalism cannot be adequately understood only from the inside, but must be considered in conjunction with its broader context. Barbie Zelizer defines journalistic authority as "the ability of journalists to promote themselves as authoritative and credible spokespersons of 'real-life' events."[4] This active effort by journalists to promote their authority encounters disputes on the inside and assaults from the outside.

Nowhere does journalism's quest for authority and its insistence of autonomy appear more fraught than the routinized exchanges between journalists and sources.[5] Decades of critical attention have given us many perspectives for assessing the impact of this relationship, variously posed as "inextricably intertwined" in a mutually beneficial relationship,[6] as enforcing propaganda,[7] as vesting sources with the power to be primary definers,[8] as setting news frames,[9] as providing "structured access" for particular sources at the exclusion of others,[10] and as dominated by an onslaught of public relations practitioners.[11] Others have suggested the relationship between sources and journalists is marked by "complexity and contingency,"[12] or, as Herbert Gans describes it, "closer to a tug of war" than a chummy alliance.[13] Nonetheless, critiques of journalistic practice have continually focused on questions of who speaks through the news and who does not.[14]

The power granted to sources to speak through the news places them in a prominent interpretive position. Leon Sigal poignantly highlights this arrangement: "The news is not reality, but a sampling of sources' portrayals of reality, mediated by news organizations."[15] The power of sources arises in part because the provisions of objectivity stifle strong journalistic voices. As a result, sources normally supply evidence in journalistic accounts while the journalist moves to the background as an assembler of quotes.[16] But objectivity alone does not explain news sourcing patterns. It is only one structural constraint linked with others, including the continuous need for news organizations to generate stories as efficiently as possible, the likeness of news structures with other bureaucracies,[17] and homophily between elite journalists and the elite sources they cover.

What emerges is a hierarchy of importance; not all sources are given the same weight. This inequality of access reinforces the "authoritative apparatus of society" by reproducing and legitimating certain perspectives and not others.[18] In all these ways, the literature on sourcing strikes at journalistic notions of autonomy by signaling a disconnect between journalism's norms and the patterns that emerge in practice. Journalists base their authority on a normative independence activated through objective reporting standards. Yet, in practice, journalism relies on knowledgeable, authoritative sources to maintain its authority and to confront constraints on resources and time.

The gulf between the rhetoric of autonomy espoused by journalists and their actual sourcing practices creates a problem for journalism. David Eason uses the term "disobedient dependence" to describe journalistic efforts to negotiate the contradiction between journalistic independence and reliance on official sources: "Dependent upon governmental authority for its conventional coverage and disobedient to the same authority in its exposés, the press advertise[s] its own freedom and independence from government while remaining conventionally bound to that authority for the bulk of its news."[19] Journalism relies on official sources to construct an authoritative account of the world, yet it must simultaneously proclaim its independence from such sources through accentuating its watchdog role. Despite the centrality of autonomy to journalistic authority, it is endlessly problematic in practice.

Unnamed Sources: Promise or Peril?

Unfortunately, the special case of anonymity has received scant attention within the body of work examining news sources. In theorizing about how unnamed sources relate to problems plaguing news sourcing raised above, two possibilities present themselves. In one view, promise underlying the use of unnamed sources derives from the hope that by circumventing standard conventions, journalists can escape the bonds of their patterned relationships with sources. Pushing aside attribution allows journalists to challenge on-the-record claims or force out into the open guarded information. This revelatory perspective of unnamed sources allows journalism to break from its stale patterns to truly serve out its normative pledge of holding power accountable. And while this may sound overly normative, there are ample moments in which journalists have broken a news story of considerable political importance through the use of unnamed sources.[20]

Of course, it doesn't always happen this way. A perilous view of unnamed sources suggests that anonymity only magnifies problems accompanying journalist-source relations. Dashing hopes of enhanced accountability, journalists merely facilitate a flow of unattributed—and therefore unverifiable—claims into the news. With the newsgathering processes mystified, the audience meets only disembodied voices purported by journalists to be dependable and reputable. At its worst, the use of unnamed sources further entrenches the dominance of elite news sources capable of commanding anonymity from journalists hungry for stories and access. The fragile dynamic of disobedient dependence gives way to simply dependence, further eroding journalism's claims of acting as a detached observer and, therefore, its claims to cultural authority.

Given the potential for both promise and peril, unnamed sources deserve more attention than they have received thus far. In the chapters that follow, the practices underlying the use of unnamed sources are brought to light in the midst of controversial uses and challenges from inside and outside of journalism. But before delving into specifics, the culture of unnamed source requires further attention.

Journalism and the Culture of Unnamed Sources

An unnamed source is a common sight in U.S. journalism, particularly in the national affairs reporting of elite news outlets—a group comprising network and cable television news, news magazines, and a handful of influential newspapers with a national reach. The prevalence of unnamed sources persists despite internal guidelines stressing restraint and external criticism advocating transparency. Numerous studies document the extent to which unnamed sources appear in news content.[21] One study found rampant use of unnamed sources in national security reporting in major newspapers with 48 percent of executive branch sources and 32 percent of congressional sources going unnamed.[22]

While these studies provide numerical evidence documenting the number of unnamed sources, the interest here is not the quantity of anonymity measured over time and across news outlets, but the impact of a style of journalism that regularly relies on unnamed sources to report the news.

What does it mean to withhold the identity of a source in return for his or her information? What types of relationships develop between journalists and sources? How does it affect notions of acceptable journalistic practice and journalistic success? How does it alter how sources insert their messages into news? These sorts of questions are better answered through an approach that recognizes the culture of unnamed sources *as a culture*. This view steers an inquiry into unnamed sources away from frequency and implementation toward questions of shared meanings and patterns of collective interpretation among journalists, sources, and audiences. The granting of anonymity is not simply a matter of technique. Rather, it is an appeal to a particular way of imagining the relations between these three parties.

When introducing an unnamed source into a news story, the journalist implies that the value gained in making hidden information public outweighs the lack of transparency in withholding the source's identity. However, the opacity of unnamed sources prevents audiences from gaining additional information from which to make judgments about unattributed information. Unnamed sources require unseen news practices, which results in journalism's increased vulnerability to charges of hiding unacceptable biases or improper source–journalist relations. This becomes a problem for journalists when questions of motive and autonomy creep in. As Taegyu Son warns, "The more journalists grant anonymity to sources without verifying their bias, calculation, and purpose, the more often they sink to being government's managerial tool, putting journalists on slippery moral ground."[23] Son confronts the normative conception situating unnamed sources as a tool aiding journalists in collecting otherwise hidden information by suggesting that journalists primarily grant anonymity in exchange for access. By allowing sources to speak without accountability, journalists' claims of autonomy evaporate, leaving behind a pattern of privileging sources above audiences.

In the face of such problems confronting the practice of source anonymity, four sets of questions hover above any investigation into the use of unnamed sources in the news: Where did this culture of anonymity originate? What motives do sources have for seeking anonymity? What compels journalists to grant it? What do news audiences think of it all?

THE RISE OF THE CULTURE OF ANONYMITY

As long as the United States has had a federal government, it has had anonymous leaks. Since the administration of George Washington, unnamed sources have supplied the press with hidden information.[24] From the beginning, tensions between legislative secrecy and journalistic exposure boiled over into aggressive hunts to out leakers.[25] Throughout the 1800s, Congress conducted hundreds of leak investigations, even confining a *New York Herald* reporter to a room in the Capitol for leaking a still-secret treaty with Mexico in 1848.[26] These efforts to force journalists to identify leakers led to public debate over the function of anonymity in ways reminiscent of what occurred in the first decade of the twenty-first century. Yet as the nineteenth century wound to a close, reporters bristled—and often cooperated—with these investigations without drawing on a notion of the freedom of the press or of professional identity to avoid testifying.[27]

During the presidency of Theodore Roosevelt in the early twentieth century, authorized unnamed sources became a key tool of the White House.[28] Some years later, Daniel Boorstin labeled leaks a "well-established institution in American politics" and "one of the most elaborately planned ways of emitting information."[29] At the same time, unauthorized leaks led to frustrations and internal searches to root out disloyal officials. Most famously, Daniel Ellsberg's 1970 publicizing of the so-called Pentagon Papers revealed an internal history of American intervention in Vietnam that the Nixon administration would have preferred be kept secret.[30] The spectrum between authorized disclosures (planted items devoid of attribution) and uncontrolled revelations (whistle-blowers taking risks) continues to mark the complexity of unnamed sources, as we will see in this book.

Starting with Ellsberg, the 1970s became a pivotal time for unnamed sources. From this era emerged journalism's most famous unnamed source— Bob Woodward and Carl Bernstein's Deep Throat. The mythology surrounding Deep Throat is discussed in chapter 4, including the heralding of Deep Throat as the quintessential whistle-blower source abetting journalists in their quest to shed light on the secret actions of the government. In between Ellsberg and Deep Throat, the most significant development for anonymity emerged out of the 1972 Supreme Court case of *Branzburg v. Hayes.* The case drew together efforts by *Louisville Courier-Journal* reporter Paul Branzburg, *New York Times* reporter Earl Cardwell, and local Rhode Island television reporter Paul Pappas to avoid having to testify about their unnamed sources. In a 5–4 decision, the justices ruled that the First Amendment did not grant journalists a confidentiality privilege making them immune from being compelled to testify about their sources in court. However, the case did leave room for what has been labeled a "qualified privilege" due to the ambiguity of Justice Lewis Powell's concurring opinion.[31] The split decision in *Branzburg* resulted in journalists rarely being called to testify at the federal level.

With judges loath to exact sanctions against reporters refusing subpoenas, prosecutors have focused on other means of gathering evidence. At the same time, numerous congressional efforts to enact a federal shield law have been put forth only to fail to receive support.

Neither the *Branzburg* ruling nor failed legislative attempts to pass a shield law have dampened the use of unnamed sources by journalists. If *Branzburg* reminded journalists of the dangers they face in deploying source anonymity, Woodward and Bernstein showed them the professional glory to be had.[32] As they have for centuries, elite journalists cultivated access to top sources partly through granting anonymity. Sources, in turn, grew to expect the availability of going unnamed. These two forces strengthened the culture of anonymity pervading much of the news reporting emanating from the centers of American power at the start of the twenty-first century.

THE RELIANCE ON TRUST AND THE QUESTION OF MOTIVES

Withholding the identity of a source raises issues related to trust. Normally a virtue of named sourcing as an evidentiary strategy lies in allowing audiences to verify or corroborate attributed news statements. Journalists can be held accountable for their quoting practices through comparison with reporting in other news outlets or from the original source. With unnamed sources, however, journalistic practice becomes invisible to the public. Withholding a source's identity eliminates the verifiability of the information so that it cannot be independently confirmed or corroborated.[33] Tension arises from journalism's "unshared vision"—a privileged position to see what others cannot.[34] Journalism depends on its authority to provide such information out of sight of its audiences, and, therefore, faces strain when unnamed sourcing practices lead to controversy.

Because of this invisibility, the utilization of unnamed sources requires trust between the source and the journalist over confidentiality as well as between the journalist and the audience concerning the source's suitability. The reliance on trust exposes journalists to potential difficulty—as David Boeyink puts it, the "dependence on trust is the vulnerable jugular of journalism."[35] The outlet and the journalist incur risk that the source, who "speaks without accountability,"[36] will turn out to be incorrect or deceitful, and thus not worthy of having been unnamed. Boeyink raises an additional question of fairness when unnamed sourcing practices facilitate disguised attacks. In these cases, sources manipulate the news in an individually beneficial manner rather than in a way that provides a social benefit.

Another tension with unnamed sources involves sources' motives for requesting anonymity. Normatively, the anonymous source takes the form of a whistle-blower, using the news to expose wrongdoing when other avenues prove either blocked or ineffective. Through a journalist also pursuing the exposure of corruption, the whistle-blower finds a safe space to address these wrongs publicly and effectively. However, in practice unnamed sources are often highly placed officials using anonymity to leak or present information without attribution. Anonymity furthers a conception of news as a forum for elite sources, since, as Leon Sigal observes, "most unattributed disclosures in the news are not leaks from below deck, but semaphore signals from the bridge."[37] Leaks are a regular tool for officials to disseminate information in a manner that conceals a source's identity from the majority of outsiders, but not to the minority of insiders.[38] The use of anonymity to send messages among officials is an example of what Aeron Davis calls "inter-elite communications."[39] From this perspective, unnamed sourcing practices allow elites to hold a coded conversation through widely mediated channels. In addition, the system is perpetuated when officials in power, by virtue of their position, gain double access to the news as both named and unnamed sources.

The utility of anonymity for releasing unattributed public messages drives the preponderance of leaked information in news stories.[40] To demonstrate the range of motivations driving unnamed sources, Stephen Hess outlines a typology of Washington leaks: the "Ego Leak" used to make the source feel important; the "Goodwill Leak" used to establish a bond with a journalist for later use; the "Policy Leak" used to bring attention to an issue or agenda; the "Animus Leak" used to embarrass someone personally; the "Trial-Balloon Leak" used to gauge support for a possible proposal; and the "Whistle-Blower Leak" used to bring attention to wrongdoing.[41] This typology underscores the complexity of unnamed sourcing practices by highlighting the multiple ways leaks serve leakers' interests. Problematically, journalists do not always know into which category information they receive falls. The situation is worse for audiences who may be unsure of a leaker's motive because the journalist either is also not sure, or does know, but conceals these motives.

An additional difficulty for journalists arises from the lack of codified rules for handling leaks. Taegyu Son examined ethics codes from different news outlets and organizations and found only passing references to leaks instead of concrete policies.[42] Ethics codes avoided the topic, leaving journalists with individualized decision making. Rules governing unnamed sources are often idiosyncratic, flexible, and orally transmitted rather than fixed and codified.

REASONS JOURNALISTS RELY ON UNNAMED SOURCES

Despite the perils bound up in unnamed source use, journalists have compelling reasons to participate in this system. Granting anonymity to sources helps generate the material journalists require to continually churn out stories. But more than filling pages or airtime, journalists work to establish their status in a news organization as well as with the audience through cultivating relationships with high-ranking sources.[43] Access to prominent sources marks elite journalists and elite journalists mark elite news organizations. Certainly, this can be seen in the hierarchy of various news beats as well as in the prestige accorded to such venerated journalists as Seymour Hersh or Bob Woodward, who are known for their insider connections. In other cases, source contacts provide individual autonomy for Washington correspondents working away from their home outlet by highlighting their command of the beat.[44] Another reason journalists use unnamed sources is to make a story seem more important than it actually is. An unnamed source connotes something secret, which makes the journalist seem enterprising and connected.[45] Plus, inserting unnamed sources into less significant stories amplifies both the story and the journalist.[46] Ultimately, a journalist's stable of unnamed sources comes to symbolically represent her status while instrumentally helping her promote news stories to editors.

The promise of confidentiality between a journalist and an unnamed source encompasses several trust-related provisions. Through this pledge, and because of the individual credibility that they invest in an unnamed source, journalists may find themselves having to support an unnamed source even when the source becomes controversial. As Herbert Strentz notes, journalists protect their relationships with sources when their own success is tied to sources' continued legitimacy.[47] As a result, they may defend a source out of self-preservation. Such a slippery slope threatens to undermine the journalist when the source can no longer be supported. Journalists are also careful to protect their promises of confidentiality so as not to alienate present and future sources by appearing untrustworthy.

Confidentiality also raises specific legal issues for journalists intent on protecting source identities in the face of prosecutors desiring disclosure. While most states have shield laws to protect journalist-source confidentiality, no statute exists at the federal level. The unresolved legal aspects of unnamed sources came to a head with the subpoenaing of reporters Matt Cooper and Judith Miller, described in chapter 5. Their resistance raised deeper questions of whether journalists should be afforded special rights above nonjournalists.

The federal courts may claim that the public benefit of disclosure outweighs the bond of confidentiality, while journalists justify their need for special rights through presenting their work as a check on other public institutions. However, this latter argument is hampered when individual journalists come to be portrayed as self-interested rather than as working for the benefit of the public.

Given the potential benefits and pitfalls attached to unnamed sources, it is not surprising that journalists express a "can't-live-with-them, can't-live-without-them" dilemma.[48] Surveys of journalists regularly show a recognition of the problematic side of unnamed sources, but also an acknowledgement of their utility.[49] This division underscores the reality that unnamed sources can and do serve a useful purpose in bringing otherwise unavailable information to the public. Even with their potential pitfalls, unnamed sources remain a central part of journalistic practice, especially in national affairs reporting. Anonymity should be respected for this function, but also recognized as a vehicle for spreading misinformation or opinions without reprisal. In the end, this is the true difficulty of unnamed sources that journalists throughout this book struggled with: anonymity provides undoubtedly useful information informing the watchdog function of the press while simultaneously undermining this function through its gratuitous application. For this reason, the rewards and punishments for journalists using unnamed sources are stark—they lead to both the highs and lows of the profession.

UNNAMED SOURCES AND PUBLIC OPINION

In the triad of unnamed source–journalist–audience, the audience occupies a precarious situation. It seeks information about the workings of society's public institutions, and in this regard benefits from the insider perspectives made possible through anonymity. Yet news audiences increasingly express wariness over the accuracy of news reports, a condition not helped by the rampant use of unnamed sources. Surveys of public opinion at the time of the incidents in 2004 and 2005 revealed anxiety regarding unnamed sources with divided perspectives ranging from cautious support to utter suspicion.

The range of opinion on unnamed sources was clear in an ABC News/ *Washington Post* poll following *Newsweek*'s retraction of its story on Koran desecration at Guantanamo Bay, Cuba, in May 2005 (at the midpoint of the incidents being examined in this book). When told "journalists sometimes get information by agreeing not to identify their sources by name in the story," 53 percent approved and 43 percent disapproved. With regard to the frequency of unnamed sources, the same survey found nearly evenly divided assessments: 33 percent of respondents considered unnamed sources to be used too often, 40 percent deemed their use about right, and 33 percent thought that they were used too infrequently.[50] Opinion was not uniform, but segmented.

How survey questions framed the stakes of unnamed source use impacted responses. When the Pew Research Center offered a contrast between the positive of audiences "find[ing] out important news they otherwise wouldn't get" and the negative that unnamed sources "can sometimes lead to inaccurate reports," 52 percent considered them "too risky" while 44 percent approved.[51] By injecting the risk of inaccuracy into the question, Pew found inverse results from the ABC News/*Washington Post* poll above. Paradoxically, Pew conducted its poll shortly after the unveiling of Deep Throat led to widespread praise for unnamed sources. Even when presented with what was often dubbed an ideal case, wariness emerged in public attitudes toward source anonymity.

When broken down by political party and ideology, the Pew survey findings showed widely differing opinions on unnamed sources. Republicans and conservatives expressed far greater concern over the use of unnamed sources than Democrats and liberals. While 51 percent of Democrats and 61 percent of liberals considered unnamed sources to be acceptable, only 36 percent of Republicans and 33 percent of conservatives agreed. By contrast, a full 63 percent of conservatives judged the practice to be too risky.[52] This result may owe to the poll's timing; it was taken a month after the *Newsweek* Koran desecration story criticizing a Republican administration and shortly after Deep Throat's revelation, which was connected to the resignation of a Republican president. These two adjacent stories involving unnamed sources may have contributed to low opinions of unnamed sources, along with a general conservative mistrust of the press. However, this divide along ideological and party lines demonstrates the importance of attending to the political questions that arise when unnamed sources are used to report on those in power.

Despite the disdain for unnamed sources evident in the Pew survey, 76 percent considered the occasional use of confidentiality acceptable. This finding was consistent over time, with 79 percent approving the occasional use of unnamed sources in 1989 and 78 percent in 1985. In 2005, only 19 percent of respondents asserted that reporters should "always reveal" their unnamed sources.[53] This finding suggested the acceptance of unnamed sources in principle, but a concern over their misapplication in practice—a tension running through this book.

In sum, the results of these surveys indicated an overall willingness to view anonymity as a tool for the press to provide valuable information to the public, but tempered by a strong sense of irritation at the misuse of unnamed sources. This was not a homogenous attitude, as the Pew data also exposed differences linked to political and ideological backgrounds. This range of opinion is important for understanding the contextual constraints journalists face in conducting their work in a polarized political environment with an increasing number of sites for news scrutiny. Journalists deploying anonymity encountered a public ranging from skeptical to adversarial. All of this underscores the importance of embedding unnamed sources in the conditions of their use and reception—the context of news at the beginning of the twenty-first century.

Journalism in Crisis

This book does not seek a universalized model to explain the tensions that surround the use of anonymity by reporters. Such a task would be uselessly abstract and disconnected from the world journalists, their sources, and news audiences jointly inhabit. Instead, this book situates unnamed source use within a particular cultural moment marked by the intersection of several journalistic, political, economic, and social trends occurring during the administration of George W. Bush. It is shaped as much by the fervency caused by the September 11, 2001, terrorist attacks as by the rising ambiguity enveloping wars in Afghanistan and Iraq. This volatility bolstered an escalating struggle to shape public opinion concerning both of these wars as well as the larger global "War on Terror." As the wars continued and questions arose concerning their management, public support could not be assumed. This ongoing shift contributed to an increasingly hostile relationship between a White House intent on conveying its message both on and off the record and reporters upset at the press management tactics to which they found themselves subjected. It is not coincidental that, except for the disclosure of Deep Throat, each of the cases involved military-related executive branch actions.

In particular, much attention will be directed at recounting a contentious political climate marked by the ascension of the conservative movement in both government and the larger culture. During this span, conservatives controlled all three branches of the federal government. This was underscored by Republican election victories in 2004 and the installation of two conservative justices to the Supreme Court. With its majority status, the Right was able to exercise power over the news media through multiple official channels. Bureaucratically, this power ranged from efforts to rewrite media ownership rules to prohibitions against pictures of returning coffins of U.S. soldiers killed in Iraq and Afghanistan. An increasing number of government materials were branded classified and kept out of the news. Judicially, journalists faced federal subpoenas for their sources' identities while government employees faced harsh treatment for leaking information to the press. These efforts occurred alongside the regular news access conservatives gained through their capacities as governing officials. Outside of the government, conservative commentators, many of whom consider themselves to be journalists, continually lashed out at what they alleged to be pervasive liberal bias plaguing U.S. newsrooms.

In addition to these political tensions, journalists expressed their own institutional anxieties in what was widely perceived as a moment of crisis. This crisis showed many symptoms, including waning audiences, receding credibility, and challenges from new, competing media forms. Similarly, the economics of news presented difficulties for working journalists facing cuts in resources, ownership consolidation, and an uncertain future for the viability of comprehensive news reporting. Less tangible, but no less important, was the precariousness of journalism's cultural status made visible through the declining public perception of its credibility and authority. Related to this, the battle to shape public opinion toward unnamed sources was increasingly carried out away from traditional news outlets within other media formats. Another defining element of the period was the proliferation of new media channels, including talk radio, cable news, and, perhaps the most revolutionary, online sites. This changing technological environment created new forms of competition that exacerbated the instability of journalism's already porous boundaries and increased the number of sites publicly scrutinizing mainstream media reporting and traditional journalism practices. These intermingling forces produced what journalists often considered to be a moment of crisis.

What does it mean for journalism to be in crisis? It is not important to prove such a moment exists or to present criteria showing the degree to which crisis exists or does not exist. What is more important to our understanding of journalism is the question of what it means for journalists to frame their work as being in a state of crisis. Or, slightly altered, we should ask how journalists construct a notion of crisis. This question illustrates the active way in which crises become reified. Rather than assuming a crisis to be a freestanding entity, it instead "resides in the person as well as in the situation."[54] The labeling of a confluence of events or factors as a crisis is a reference both to the material circumstance of the crisis as well as the interpretive work of practitioners to label such an episode as a crisis and demand an appropriate response.

Throughout the cases, the concept of crisis offers an interpretive lens for understanding unnamed sources. The struggle over anonymity connects to sweeping shifts impacting the economic, cultural, political, and technological conditions of news. These are not background issues, but decisive forces shaping the particular moment in which the incidents occurred. Journalists and others confronted these shifts implicitly and explicitly in their efforts to create meaning around news controversies involving unnamed sources. But first, we gain a better understanding of the particular moment of the cases by looking at three related issues: the continued cultural place of a small band of elite news outlets, changes in media technology, and the growing contestation around news content by external critics.

THE CULTURAL PLACE OF ELITE U.S. NEWS

As the landscape shifts around them, much of the trepidation experienced by journalists flows from a concern over their waning cultural role. Panic arises when the model of democracy put forth by journalists—one that locates news as central—begins to weaken. Journalists argue for their own indispensability through appealing to their function of disseminating information in a useful form (i.e., ideally objective and without hidden interests) to large audiences. The news also creates a shared sense of the world across its audience, helping to foster a feeling of community.[55] The problem of relevancy arises when fragmenting media and changing political processes suggest different models of communication. Assumptions of the centrality of journalism (particularly among the news outlets that have enjoyed a half century or more of dominance) give way to an increasingly nebulous media world. Evidence for this shift can be found in a variety of places, including trends involving public opinion, audience size, and advertising revenues.

A sense of the slipping cultural role of journalism in American life at the time of the incidents can be gleaned from surveys of attitudes toward news. This was not a new phenomenon in 2004 and 2005, but a trend indicated by two decades of survey research into public perceptions of news credibility. In a summary of these trends, the Pew Research Center pointed to an industrywide "erosion of trust" between 1985 and 2005 across audience demographics.[56] Findings indicating a negative shift in public attitudes toward the news during the time of the incidents in this book were not unusual. In a

September 2004 Gallup poll during the controversy at *60 Minutes*, 44 percent expressed a great deal or fair amount of trust in news while 55 percent had not very much or no trust at all.[57] While surveys of media credibility fluctuated, journalists were only occasionally able to amass the trust of a majority of survey respondents. In keeping with this trend, news outlets involved in the cases in this study each experienced substantial declines in credibility over the past two decades.[58] This lack of support is cause for worry in the news industry.

Declining credibility, especially at elite news outlets, exists alongside the migration of news audiences away from traditional news media sources—especially from newspapers and network television. The newspaper industry has witnessed a sea change in the past half century due to consolidation among owners and competition from other media. In 2004, total weekday circulation stood at 54.6 million, down from 62.3 million in 1990.[59] Only forty-one cities supported multiple daily newspapers, including twelve cities with joint operating agreements to share noneditorial functions.[60] Network television news experienced an even more severe decline in audiences. In 1980, the combined audience for the ABC, CBS, and NBC evening newscasts was 52 million. By 2005, total viewership stood at 27 million, a decline of 48 percent.[61] Similarly, the percentage of people watching network television magazine shows (such as *60 Minutes*) on a regular basis dropped from 52 percent in 1993 to 22 percent in 2004.[62] Seeking to reinforce their cultural role, journalists working in traditional media faced a quantitative decline in the amount of the public they attracted.

These news outlets were also hampered by economic instability across traditional media.[63] Following the end of the technology boom in the 1990s, news outlets had a more difficult time attracting advertising revenue as advertisers looked to new venues, including online sites. Meanwhile, fewer viewers and readers meant lower revenue, which was compounded by the undesirability to advertisers of the older average age of remaining news audiences.

Changes in the economics of news coincided with shifts in media ownership. While journalism in the United States has always been predominately conducted as a business, the last few decades have seen a shift from private to corporate media ownership. As part of publicly traded corporations, news organizations have been expected to generate profits—to meet the expectations of shareholders and market analysts above any sense of journalism's public service role.[64] Media consolidation accelerated in the decade following the Telecommunications Act of 1996.[65] The emphasis on intermedia consolidation under the rubric of convergence prevailed during this period. This was visible in the logic behind the Federal Communications Commission's efforts to relax ownership laws in 2003—a move widely criticized by the public.[66]

For working journalists, ownership issues mattered to the degree to which media owners prioritized profits over journalistic quality by reducing resources or averting potentially controversial reporting. Tensions arising from the clash between journalistic and economic priorities were evident in a 2004 Project for Excellence in Journalism survey that found 66 percent of national journalists and 57 percent of local ones agreeing that the "bottom-line pressure on news coverage" was "hurting" journalism.[67] These concerns were up sharply for both groups since 1995. Ownership pressures raised questions of autonomy for journalists both in terms of procuring resources to do reporting and in possessing the requisite independence to pursue stories.

The impact of this context can be seen in the work journalists do, including their use of anonymity to procure information from sources. The economic conditions of news constrain the resources journalists have at their disposal, which, in turn, shapes the resulting news coverage. For example, the scramble to right declining indicators begets a new consciousness of seeking not to alienate already receding audiences. In light of this, news outlets may decline to pursue investigative reporting relying on unnamed sources for fear of sparking controversy that would drive away audiences. Timidity becomes preferential, even if it cuts out difficult-to-attain yet worthwhile stories. This is compounded by economic pressures that make news organizations wary of supporting potentially costly legal battles to preserve source confidentiality. Attorney fees and court fines can escalate quickly when news outlets step in to defend a reporter. Finally, journalists working with reduced resources opt for available sources over the time and expense of seeking out new sources.

NEW TECHNOLOGIES OF JOURNALISM

In the past, a small handful of news organizations dominated the news landscape. These outlets were secure in their status partly due to their control over communication channels. The cost of establishing a comprehensive news organization was prohibitive, and for a time, Ted Turner's CNN and Gannett's *USA Today* were the only new entrants in the field. Yet the explosion of networked digital computer technology has added new complications to the broader question of journalism's continued cultural place by altering the barriers to entry that previously restricted the mass distribution of news.

The rise of Internet-based news forms and the continued expansion of cable television news altered the competitive environment of news at the time of the incidents in this study. While intramedia competition continued, intermedia rivalries increased between print, television, and online outlets. As part of this shift, new media forms have gained substantial audiences.[68] The increase in competition and the concomitant shift in news audiences have complicated efforts by elite news outlets to retain their viewers and readers.

While friction between old and new media is not new,[69] purveyors of online networked technologies promoted a fundamental reimagining of the relationship between producers and consumers. A diverse wave of independent sites under the heading of citizen journalism challenged the primacy of traditional journalism and its orientation toward mass-consumed, unidirectional accounts of the world. Technology writer Dan Gillmor elevated the significance of this development as a watershed moment: "For the first time in history, at least in the developed world, anyone with a computer and Internet connection could own a press. Just about anyone could make the news."[70] Citizen journalists situate their work against norms of traditional journalism, which they portray as inadequate for addressing the needs of the public. Bloggers and others working online accuse traditional news of ignoring audience needs and opinions. Certainly, forms of citizen journalism existed in other media (e.g., cable access television, zines, community newsletters), but online communication networks allow for a new scale of instant distribution of content regardless of geographical and production constraints.

Citizen journalism takes different forms, but the most publicized politically oriented form during the time of the cases was the blog. Created as interlinked sites of opinions, blogs became a much-noted force during the 2004 presidential campaign with the securing of press passes to the party conventions and ample media attention that included a cover article in the *New York Times Magazine*.[71] Bloggers remained a top media story in the 2004 election, earning notoriety for their release of incomplete exit polls predicting an easy victory for John Kerry during Election Day.[72] These sites were especially important for their continued scrutiny of traditional news. Rather than remaining at the margins, this criticism of mainstream news reporting occasionally expanded into major news controversies. For example, criticisms of the *60 Minutes* story of Bush's National Guard service examined in chapter 2 started through blogs and the message boards of conservative Web sites. In addition, audiences for blogs have risen over time: 39 percent of Internet users spent some time reading blogs in 2006, up from 17 percent in 2004.[73]

Whether or not blogs constitute a form of journalism, they do represent an alternative form of cultural production that exists alongside and interacts with traditional news channels.

Novel modes of news distribution proved to be a double-edged sword for long established news outlets. On the positive side, new platforms for content delivery—including the Web, portable music devices such as iPods, and mobile phones—opened up new potential audiences. However, the low barriers for entry facilitated by online media created new competition. Rather than emulation, the creators of these new media forms proclaimed a different set of norms than traditional media, including a refusal to adhere to traditional notions of objectivity.[74] Journalists were forced to defend the value of their practices. This mattered for unnamed sources, since the inherent opacity of withholding a source's identity clashed with the transparency norms underlying developing media forms. Purveyors of new forms expressed a wariness regarding journalists' efforts to restrict access to their procedures and withhold information from audiences. This perspective challenged journalism's penchant for unnamed sources as more self-serving than aiding the public.

CONTESTING ELITE U.S. NEWS

The declining role of elite news outlets and the rise of new media alternatives have received both public and scholarly attention, but the growing prominence of media criticism adds another crucial element to understanding the media situation during the first years of the twenty-first century. While there have long been public voices challenging news practices, journalism has come to endure increased contestation, often at a structural level. Journalists faced charges from across the political spectrum that they systematically violate their claims of objectivity and political detachedness, as liberal and conservative press critics publicly objected to both news content and news practices.[75]

Liberal critiques often adopted a political economy perspective focusing on how economic structures force the news into a consensus position that reaffirms and legitimizes existing power structures. These critics examine how news sourcing practices reproduce the power of particular sources while ignoring or marginalizing other voices. Several established institutions, including Fairness and Accuracy in Reporting, Media Matters for America, Media Channel, and Free Press, regularly berate news reporting from this perspective. Authors such as Eric Alterman, Al Franken, and Michael Moore have challenged the conservative media critique though books and other media. In 2005, Stephen Colbert created a satirical conservative talk show host character on *The Colbert Report* to lampoon conservative media and the *Daily Show with Jon Stewart* continued to satirize journalism. In addition, many blogs and other online sites, such as the Huffington Post, promote a liberal critique of journalism.

On the other end of the political spectrum, the conservative movement aggressively pursued its principles through traditional media channels such as newspapers (e.g., *Washington Times, Wall Street Journal* editorial page, *New York Post,* syndicated columnists), television (e.g., Fox News, conservative Christian programming), and radio (e.g. Rush Limbaugh, Bill O'Reilly), as well as new media channels such as blogs and online sites. In addition, conservative pundits acted as "news shapers" through regularly appearing on television and in print to present conservative views.[76] This environment created an antagonistic relationship between journalism and conservatives. This was not haphazard, as conservative media watch groups such as Accuracy in Media and the Media Research Center conducted organized criticism of the news with a particular focus on certain "elite" news outlets such as CBS News and the *New York Times.* Robert McChesney points to the funding conservative groups directed toward altering the news: "Around half of all the expenditures of the twelve largest conservative foundations have been devoted to moving the news rightward."[77] In its combined forms, the methodical assault on news outlets from the right further complicated journalism by instilling the fear of a critical reprisal for reporting that challenged conservative efforts or individuals

Both liberal and conservative critics found fault with the opacity of unnamed sources and the trust required with their use. While journalists articulated their roles as providing unseen information to the public in order to monitor government actions, an alternative conception espoused by conservatives, especially those in government positions, held that journalists should respect boundaries of secrecy and not undermine government functioning with gratuitous exposure. Meanwhile, liberal critics charged that unnamed sources resulted not in watchdog journalism, but the reproduction of official voices without accountability. In viewing the patterned relationships between journalists and unnamed sources, liberal critics accused reporters of not being antagonistic enough while conservatives portrayed reporters as too antagonistic. Thus, discussions of appropriate unnamed source use became a debate over the normative role of journalism in exposing internal government affairs. At issue was how aggressive or passive journalists should be in covering the state.

Outside of these critics, perceptions of journalistic bias increased among the public as well. An October 2004 Pew Research Center poll found, when asked, "How often do you think members of the news media let their own political preferences influence the way they report the news," 58 percent responded often and 32 percent sometimes.[78] In a 2005 Pew survey, 60 percent of respondents considered journalists to be "politically biased in their reporting" and 50 percent viewed journalists as liberal.[79] In addition to bias, many survey respondents expressed negative opinions of the press as interfering with government processes or damaging the image of the United States. A full third of the public, 33 percent, accused the news of "hurt[ing] democracy."[80] These surveys indicated a broader cultural cleavage over the role of the press. Against journalism's self-conception as working in the public interest, a significant portion of the public viewed journalists as a detrimental force prone to abusing its power through hiding liberal bias behind objective reporting or in failing to aggressively cover officials.

Alongside the economic and audience uncertainties described in the previous sections, these findings portray a moment of instability and uncertainty for journalism in the first decade of the twenty-first century. Any assessment of the use of unnamed sources cannot be extracted from this context. Instead, this environment became the battleground in which journalists, their critics, and the public confronted questions of anonymity.

The Battle to Define Journalism

Five incidents spanning the buildup to the 2003 Iraq War to the 2007 trial of Scooter Libby together comprise an unfolding drama exposing tensions plaguing journalistic authority and autonomy, growing problems attributed to unnamed sourcing practices, and mounting concern over the shifting media and political contexts in which journalists work. Ordinarily, the inner workings of source anonymity prove difficult to examine as sources and journalists jointly protect their confidential arrangements. With the onset of controversy, the doors of this secretive practice get thrown open for all to see. Otherwise hidden mechanics become public in often unsettling ways. It is in these moments of public fixation that journalists and others compete to supply the public with an explanation of what was right and wrong with unnamed sourcing practices and what should be done.[81] A diverse array of commentators promotes not only varying interpretations of the value of source anonymity, but also the appropriate dynamic between journalism, the government, and the public. Journalism itself becomes the object of intense struggle.

Given their notoriety, there is no shortage of reporting delving into the intricacies of the incidents analyzed in the following chapters. Well-researched pieces in a variety of media teem with behind-the-scenes details about the people and organizations involved. With that information out there, the present work does not seek to reconstruct the incidents in journalistic fashion. It steers clear of interviewing individuals to unearth unknown facts or motives. Instead, what this book analyzes is how these incidents gave rise to a public battle to define appropriate journalistic practice and, by extension, the role of journalism in society. Pertinent evidence, then, is not what is hidden, but what is public. It is not the whispers about the cases that matter; it is the shouts.

INTERPRETIVE COMMUNITIES TAKE AIM AT ANONYMITY

Journalists confronting these controversies aim to shore up their cultural authority. Recognizing the discursive means through which journalism is constructed gives us a way of looking at the discourse around unnamed sources as not idle navel-gazing or finger-pointing, but the very process through which journalists and others create public meaning about what a journalist should do. Efforts to pin down definitions of "journalism" and "journalist" encounter obstacles due to the porousness of journalistic boundaries and the lack of uniformity among those laying claim to the title of journalist.[82] Attempts to categorize journalism as a profession encounter problems when closing off journalism in any systematic way. Journalists have never been able to set solid boundaries, establish uniformity, or achieve professional recognition on par with other professions, such as doctors and lawyers.[83] The lack of a fortified professionalism with its built-in mechanisms for self-maintenance makes journalism into what Michael Schudson terms an "uninsulated profession."[84] Journalists must create strategies to confront constant criticism and commentary directed at them from outside of journalism. As Pierre Bourdieu notes, "The *boundary* of the field is a stake of struggles."[85] Journalism works to define itself and, therefore, its cultural place and expected privileges, but it by no means does so exclusively.

Journalists have developed a number of discursive strategies to shore up their authority in the face of external challenges and a lack of internal cohesiveness. Despite lacking the trappings of an exclusive professionalism, journalists come together to form collective notions of their work. While journalists do congregate in newsrooms, press briefings, conferences, award ceremonies, and elsewhere, they also come together through the mediated discussion of news practices occurring in the trade press and in mainstream news media. In these spaces, journalists define incidents of good and bad journalism and further mark out their territory. These are discursive efforts to create, define, and defend shared ideas of what journalism is, including overarching norms, specific practices, and the general context of news production.

Because journalism lacks sturdy professional boundaries, viewing journalists as constituting an interpretive community usefully connects the role of discourse with the establishment of a shared identity.[86] An interpretive community refers to an assemblage of individuals who employ similar culturally derived strategies of interpretation. Thus, understandings of collectivity form based not simply on common experience, but on culturally structured ways of understanding and interpreting these experiences.[87] This involves shared evidentiary strategies as well as beliefs as to what is important and what is not. Through different modes of interaction—education and training, media, interpersonal, and so forth—these communities come to shape members and be shaped by members. Specific to this discussion, journalists confront challenges of an ever-changing economic, political, technological, and cultural context through discourse about their work.[88] This was true of unnamed sources as journalists wrestled openly with tensions accompanying the deployment of anonymity.

The interpretive community of journalists does not operate in isolation from other entities. Rather, it is a response to the conditions in which the news is made and consumed. Members seek cohesiveness against competing internal divergences and external pressures. Peter Dahlgren identifies the process through which journalists react to affronts from critics, politicians, the judiciary, owners, and others as a strategy of "discursive containment." Through addressing challenges to their work, journalists seek to "retain definitional control of the field, its problems and potential solutions."[89] In line with the interpretive communities approach, journalists strive to hold onto their authority not only in delivering the news, but also in dictating, as much as possible, conceptions of its social function. Dahlgren situates the consequences of such discourse at a foundational level: "In these processes, what is at stake, at least in the long run, is definitional and ideological control over what journalism is, can and should be."[90] Journalists seek definitional control over the meaning of their work against external critics who seek to redefine journalism according to differing motivations. This view acknowledges both internal and external competition to dictate what journalism should be.

The notion of interpretive communities is useful for analyzing discourse around unnamed sourcing practices. Instead of being constrained by assessing journalism's suitability as a profession, it recognizes the importance of shared perceptions of journalism's cultural and political role while being appropriately flexible to permit disparity. An interpretive community does not denote static uniformity but rather a dynamic, contested realm continuously shaped by various discursive means. Aside from struggles within the interpretive community, the approach allows for an acknowledgement of outside competition directed at the community. In the case of journalism, many voices outside of the news—politicians, public relations practitioners, media watch groups, concerned news consumers, academics—strive to influence the news and challenge its forms. Taken together, the notion of interpretive communities demonstrates efforts by journalists to maintain their cultural authority and to shore up journalistic boundaries in the face of contestation and uncertainty over news practices. Because it provides a useful framework for thinking about how discourse on unnamed sources affects both journalism and the larger public, it retains a central role in this book.

MAKING MEANING OUT OF CONTROVERSY

That journalists and others talk about the news does not, by itself, tell us much about how discourse works in defining journalism's cultural role. What is important is *how* the news gets discussed.[91] In the chapters that follow, a chief concern is the extent to which incidents are viewed as isolated examples of errant practice or seen as indicative of broader trends afflicting journalism. What level of significance gets assigned to an incident is an interpretive move that then opens up or closes down certain avenues for making sense of it. Analytically, two strategies for confronting a news controversy can be contrasted: isolating the controversy as lacking broader significance or expanding its meaning. The first interpretive course is epitomized in the literature on a paradigm repair while the second can be apprehended through the work on critical incidents. How controversies involving unnamed sources come to be considered across this spectrum matters for the variety of conclusions and solutions that can be offered.

In the face of controversies arising over news practices, the notion of "paradigm repair" provides a discursive model in which journalists strive to individualize controversies as aberrant to protect the whole of journalism.[92] This line of inquiry descends from the sociology of knowledge and Thomas Kuhn's work on scientific paradigms and their relationship to scientific authority.[93] Similarly, journalists rely on the paradigm of objectivity as a guiding strategy, even in the face of criticism.[94] The concept comes specifically from W. Lance Bennett and colleagues, who note the regular disparity between objectivity as a guiding paradigm for news practice and its unattainability in actual practice.[95] With this disconnect threatening the viability of stated ideals, journalists must defend the prevailing news paradigm in an ongoing, active process.[96] Paradigm repair describes strategies employed by journalists to confront a journalistic mishap in a manner that protects the overall structures of journalism. Thus, violations of journalistic norms are cast as deviant rather than as resulting from structural flaws.

Aside from expelling violators, the paradigm repair process strengthens the journalistic community by reasserting core norms, similar to the notion of interpretive communities described above.[97] They both rely on discourse to inform the characteristics of the group and to bolster its authority. The process of paradigm repair displaces the part to preserve the whole by portraying controversies as the result of deviance from journalistic norms. Once this deviance is eliminated and values are reasserted, the process is seen as complete.

With unnamed sources, placing blame at the level of the individual disconnects the actions of a single journalist from generalized questions concerning the appropriate deployment of anonymity. Blame for abusing or misusing anonymity falls to the agency of an individual reporter, which limits the extent of the controversy. Criticisms on this level focus on diagnosing the cause of the controversy without extending its significance to encompass unnamed sourcing practice generally. However, this approach is limited to only controversies contained through individualization. The repetition of unnamed sourcing controversies and efforts to tie them to deeper issues impacting journalistic authority necessitate a different discursive model.

While it may be tempting to blame controversies on individual actions in order to protect journalism, at times journalism is better served by extending culpability to larger tensions. Instead of falling back on charges of isolated deviancy, problem incidents can be used to call attention to deeper structural issues affecting journalism.[98] This move may invite journalists to engage in critical self-reflection aimed at how their practices go awry, or it may encourage a defensive enumeration of external constraints on reporting. Meanwhile, journalism's critics, including those in the academy, are also keen to present individual incidents as symptomatic of larger ailments.

Favoring contextualization over individualization gives rise to the "critical incidents" interpretive framework. In an early use of the term, John C. Flanagan describes critical incidents "as extreme behavior, either outlandishly effective or ineffective with respect to attaining the general aims of the activity."[99] While this definition comes out of psychology and is concerned with individual action over collective processes, it supports as an object of inquiry the relationship between practices, context, and intentions. From a concern with institutional workings, George Gerbner identifies critical incidents as "a clash of powers, when things 'go wrong.'"[100] Such incidents arise from a breakdown of codified conduct that prompts institutional power to react. Through this response, critical incidents bring an entire practice into relief.

This book considers critical incidents as periodic ruptures of established activities and norms that force a public rethinking. Writing about identity, Kobena Mercer notes that it "only becomes an issue when it is in crisis, when something assumed to be fixed, coherent and stable is displaced by the experience of doubt and uncertainty."[101] This same principle applies to crisis moments for journalism. Critical incidents draw public attention to news practices in ways journalism cannot ignore. Yet how this attention manifests itself requires careful consideration.

A String of Controversies

How did a series of incidents involving unnamed sources spark a broader conversation about journalism in the first decade of the twenty-first century? Through thorough analysis of public mediated discourse, the subsequent chapters identify discursive patterns and divergent narratives recurring throughout this era. Each chapter involved a comprehensive search and analysis of the mediated discourse surrounding a case, including newspapers, magazines, radio, television, books, the trade press, and online materials that offer public discussions and interpretations of what happened and its significance for journalism.[102] Out of this cacophony emerges a story about the perils and promises of unnamed sources, precarious relationships between journalists and sources, and questions about the cultural role of journalism.

Chapter 1, "Media Culpas: Prewar Reporting Mistakes at the *New York Times* and *Washington Post*," looks at how the two newspapers used unnamed sources in reports leading up to the invasion of Iraq in March 2003. When Iraq's weapons of mass destruction failed to materialize, critics on the left and from within journalism chastised the *Times* and *Post* for overly credulous, unnamed source-laden investigative reporting appearing on their front pages in the buildup to the war. The newspapers responded by revisiting their unnamed sourcing practices, but not until more than a year after the invasion. These self-assessments generated attention around two problems negatively impacting prewar coverage: the calculated press management strategies of the Bush administration, and the willingness of the competing newspapers to reproduce official statements anonymously—especially the

Times through the work of reporter Judith Miller. The complex problems marking the journalist–unnamed source exchange come to light through these efforts to attach blame both to the sources and the journalists.

Chapter 2, "'Blogs 1, CBS 0': *60 Minutes* and the Killian Memos Controversy," begins with *60 Minutes* alleging that President Bush shirked National Guard duty in the 1970s in a story based on documents provided by an unnamed source. Immediately after it aired, conservative bloggers charged that the piece was a deliberate attempt to discredit Bush with fake documents two months before the 2004 election. CBS News spent two weeks defending its reporting before Dan Rather apologized and retracted the story. The incident hastened Rather's retirement and led to the firing of senior news producers. Discussions of what happened resulted in conservative claims of widespread liberal bias, concern by journalists over competitive constraints on news work, and a consideration of how the growing influence of new media challenged journalists' use of unnamed sources in their prosecution of controversial subjects.

Chapter 3, "Journalists Fight Back: *Newsweek* and the Koran Abuse Story," follows the controversy caused by a small *Newsweek* item in which an unnamed source alleged an upcoming military report would contain charges of Koran desecration by interrogators at Guantanamo Bay. The story gained attention after government officials blamed a number of deadly riots in Afghanistan directly on *Newsweek*. When the magazine's unnamed source rescinded the allegation, *Newsweek* retracted its claims. The magazine was attacked for not properly corroborating the unnamed source's accusations, which produced broader charges of journalists using anonymity to further an antimilitary bias. However, the journalistic community responded to escalating Bush administration criticism of *Newsweek* by chastising the administration for its own poor intelligence record leading up to the Iraq War and by turning attention to the previously underreported treatment of Guantanamo Bay detainees.

Chapter 4, "Deep Throat and the Question of Motives," begins two weeks after *Newsweek*'s retraction when *Vanity Fair* ended over thirty years of speculation by revealing the famous Watergate-era unnamed source Deep Throat to be Mark Felt, an ex-FBI official. In contrast to the other incidents, the journalism community celebrated Deep Throat as a triumph of unnamed source use. Drawing on the collective memory of Watergate, journalists reaffirmed the value of using unnamed sources to expose wrongdoing. The heroic interpretation of Felt encountered resistance from others who questioned Felt's motives and actions. In the larger view, these critics railed against anonymity by promoting an alternative normative argument suggesting government employees should work internally to resolve issues rather than in public through journalists.

Chapter 5, "'Journalism on Trial': Confidentiality and the Plame Leak Case," examines the fallout caused by Robert Novak's July 2003 column revealing Valerie Plame, wife of Bush administration critic Joseph Wilson, to be a CIA operative. The potential illegality of the leak prompted an inquiry that escalated into a grand jury investigation by a special prosecutor to uncover Novak's two unnamed administration sources. When journalists were subpoenaed to testify before the grand jury, Matt Cooper of *Time* and Judith Miller of the *New York Times* resisted vocally and litigiously. After their court battles failed, *Time* turned over Cooper's notes against his will. Miller went to jail for eighty-five days, but ultimately resigned from the *Times* in the face of intense scrutiny of her sourcing practices. Similarly, legendary *Washington Post* reporter Bob Woodward faced criticism for failing to reveal his knowledge of the Plame leak. The Plame leak case culminated in a parade of elite journalists testifying about their relationships with official sources in the trial of vice presidential aide Scooter Libby.

Finally, chapter 6, "Rethinking Anonymity: Problems and Solutions," draws together major themes that persist across the chapters. Journalists responded to the struggle over unnamed sources as victims of structural hindrances they encountered in their work. While contemporary journalism does face complex problems, the conclusion argues we cannot account for controversies over unnamed sources solely through this frame. Such a perspective ignores the relationship between unnamed sources and the status needs of elite journalists and their news outlets. This combination of media structure and individual action complicates efforts to repair journalism. The culture of unnamed sources as it exists benefits sources and journalists—while often ignoring the public interest.

There is no easy solution to the problems arising when a journalist withholds a source's identity. Instead of proposing a mechanical fix or set of universal rules, I advocate for an emphasis on three principles—contingency, transparency, and aggressiveness—as a means for going forward. These ideas help guide the occasional use of unnamed sources as part of journalism's continued vigilance of government actions and other social institutions. They move the originating force behind issuing anonymity away from the source and toward the journalist. Most importantly, they root anonymity in a vision of journalism working as an agent on behalf of audiences, not a servant to its sources.

In the end, to try to supply the dominant interpretation of why a controversy occurred is to seek to attain the privileged position of prescribing the shape of future practices. It is a position fought for among speakers with competing vested interests. Journalists sought to maintain authority through advocating for the autonomy to define their own reporting shortcomings, solutions, and norms. Specifically, the cases involved the subset of elite national news outlets striving to retain their status among the public, sources, and other journalism outlets. Within journalism, factions competed to promote their perspectives. Meanwhile, critics portrayed the controversies as indicative of larger deficiencies in journalistic practice that should be addressed. In many of the cases, the Bush administration endeavored to avoid journalistic scrutiny of its policies by pressuring news outlets. Similarly, conservative critics sought to limit the role of the press, which was viewed as antithetical to their interests. In contrast to this, critics on the left viewed anonymity as often masking overly close journalist-source ties. It is apparent that what was contested was not merely discrete stories or the reputations of individual journalists, but the continued viability of journalism to fulfill its democratic pledge.

1

Media Culpas: Prewar Reporting Mistakes at the *New York Times* and *Washington Post*

How did a country on the leading edge
of the information age get this so wrong and
express so little skepticism and challenge?
—*Washington Post* ombudsman
Michael Getler

In the early months of 2007, a federal courtroom in Washington, D.C., hosted the unusual spectacle of journalists testifying about their behind-the-scenes interactions with executive branch officials. The trial of Lewis "Scooter" Libby, the result of a three-year investigation by U.S. Attorney Patrick Fitzgerald, occasioned a rare glimpse into how the news is made. Legally, the trial resulted in Libby's conviction for lying under oath, which was subsequently nullified when President George W. Bush commuted his sentence. Yet the trial also exposed the close relationships journalists have with their official sources. The resulting parade of journalists spilling details of their encounters with sources was, in the view of the *Washington Post* ombudsman, a "disaster for the media."[1] Understanding this trial requires an appreciation of not only the events leading up to Libby's conviction, but also misgivings over the central role unnamed sources played in reporting on Iraq between the September 11, 2001, terrorist attacks and the start of the war two and a half years later.

It is no understatement to label 9/11 a moment of rupture for many sectors of American life. This was true for journalists who, on that blue-sky autumnal morning, mediated collision and collapse to a watching world. In the immediate aftermath, the quest for answers—explanatory, cultural, spiritual—became the driving news story. The summer news slumber of shark attack stories and the disappearance of Washington intern Chandra

Levy gave way to a primer on foreign relations, global terrorism, and national security. On television, the news diet reverted to a menu reminiscent of an earlier era of hard news.[2] With the aftermath came a newfound improved estimation of both the news and the government; 89 percent of Americans rated the news as excellent or good in the week after the attacks.[3] President George W. Bush saw similar gains in popularity when his approval rating soared from a scant majority before the attacks to 90 percent afterwards.[4] Likewise, Congress saw its rating increase to 80 percent approval.[5] It was a moment of cohesion in the face of tragedy—one that endowed the press and politicians with a widespread trust and dependency.

This was not a purely positive development. The violence of the attacks induced a retributive bellicosity that led to two wars: Afghanistan, beginning in November 2001, and Iraq, beginning seventeen months later in March 2003. During the period, reporters operated within a charged political environment in which patriotism and support for government officials remained a barrier to critical reporting.[6] This environment, coupled with increased scrutiny by nontraditional media forms ranging from talk radio to blogs, compelled journalists to display a particular cautiousness with their reporting. Michael Massing noted how reporters avoided stories that would have conservative critics "branding them liberals or traitors—labels that could permanently damage a career." As a result, "journalists began to muzzle themselves."[7] During this era, journalists faced several obstacles dissuading them from critical work, including a Bush administration determined to promote its policies and squash divergent views.

It was in this environment on the eve of the 2003 invasion of Iraq that much of the journalistic community echoed the certainty espoused publicly by the Bush administration—certainty that the rush to a second war barely a year and a half after the attacks on September 11, 2001, was necessary for confronting the grave threat posed by the dictatorial Iraqi regime. This assuredness sprang from public arguments repeated across the Bush administration by President Bush, Vice President Dick Cheney, Secretary of State Colin Powell, and others. While the case for war put forth by the U.S. government warrants questioning, the broader effort to understand the drive to war must also focus on how journalists, particularly through their use of unnamed sources, endowed intelligence claims with an unearned corroboration—and then had to respond to criticism for doing so. High-level officials speaking under condition of anonymity provided the core material for a layer of reporting seconding public claims of Iraqi malfeasance posed by the Bush administration through press conferences and speeches. Dissenting and divergent perspectives, when present at all, were buried deep in stories or the stories were buried deep in the news. The domination of official perspectives precluded balance from other factions with differing views. This situation persisted across media outlets in the run up to the Iraq War, promulgating a pack mentality among news outlets not wanting to stray from what other outlets were reporting.[8]

Once the war began, the absence of weapons of mass destruction (WMDs), errant predictions of a welcoming reception, mounting U.S. and Iraqi casualties, and escalating costs engendered a wide array of criticism directed not only at U.S. government officials, but also at the journalists who failed to adequately question and correct intelligence claims. While the degree of journalistic culpability may be—and often is—argued,[9] the existence of unnamed-source–laden reporting substantiating administration claims led to its eventual reappraisal as journalists looked inward to account for their part in reproducing arguments favoring the war. This undertaking was not without great reluctance. In particular, this chapter will focus on prewar reporting self-critiques in the *New York Times* and the *Washington Post* well after the commencement of war. Looking back at the prewar reporting, journalists and critics, including those on the left, charged the reporting with inaccurately or inappropriately legitimating official claims through the use of anonymity. Rather then revealing hidden information about prewar intelligence, unnamed sources were construed as echoing—and therefore reinforcing—already publicized claims.

But before turning to these reappraisals, a clarification needs to be made upfront: not all unnamed-source–based reporting missed the story. Reporters Warren Strobel and Jonathan Landay of the Knight Ridder Washington Bureau followed the same stories as other reporters using the same practices of exchanging anonymity for access, but turned up different stories that, as it turned out, more accurately portrayed questions plaguing the case for war against Iraq. Strobel attributed their success to a relative lack of access compared with higher-profile journalists: "We were mostly talking to the lower-level people or dissidents, who didn't necessarily repeat the party line."[10] Before the war, the pair faced skepticism from other reporters and rebukes from the administration. But after the war began, Landay and Strobel became the celebrated exception to the excess of poor reporting. Their work demonstrates that when appropriately utilized, unnamed sources have a use.[11] In other words, unnamed sourcing practices go awry not because of the very existence of anonymity, but because of how it is implemented.

Criticizing the Coverage

Before turning to the unusual reviews issued by the *Times* and the *Post*, we must first acknowledge scrutiny connecting unnamed sources to faulty intelligence claims by the Bush administration before and during the start of the Iraq War. This criticism originated outside of mainstream media outlets in trade press magazines, liberal news outlets, and online sites.[12] Critiques appeared in the trade press through work in *Editor & Publisher, American Journalism Review,* and *Nieman Reports,* with one of the most comprehensive critiques of the prewar intelligence reporting coming from media critic Michael Massing in an article titled "Now They Tell Us" appearing in the February 26, 2004, issue of the *New York Review of Books*.[13] In addition, press critic Jack Shafer regularly weighed in on the oversized role unnamed sources played in the prewar reporting in his Press Box column on the online magazine *Slate*.

The journalism trade press, a collection of print publications whose circulation mainly comprises working journalists, news executives, and educators, was quite active in castigating journalists for their mistakes in the prewar reporting. Charges that journalists improperly legitimized faulty intelligence claims through unnamed sources materialized in the journalism trade press a full year before the *Times* and the *Post* issued self-reviews. On the eve of war, columns chastising the prewar reporting appeared from seasoned investigative reporter Ted Gup in a March 2003 *Columbia Journalism Review* article,[14] and former *New York Times* columnist Tom Wicker in *Editor & Publisher.* In criticizing journalists for failing to execute their watchdog role, Wicker asserted the news coverage "seems sometimes to be playing on the administration team rather than pursuing the necessary search for truth."[15] Such criticisms, while rare before the start of the war, would become more common once the full extent of the prewar intelligence failures became known.

Once the initial news of the 2003 invasion subsided and the promise of WMD caches seemed increasingly suspect, criticism of the journalistic role in propagating the war increased. Just five weeks into the war, *Harper's* publisher John MacArthur ascribed complicity to the news in a *Columbia Journalism Review* article titled "The Lies We Bought." For MacArthur, the overuse of unnamed sources, mainly those originating in the White House, coupled with a secretive administration reduced journalists' ability to challenge administration allegations. While blaming the administration for the war, MacArthur noted "the American media provided free transportation to get the White House from there to here."[16] Similarly, *Editor & Publisher's*

Joe Strupp distributed responsibility to both the press and the government: "The press must take some of the blame, for failing to push the administration hard enough prior to the war about the existence of such weapons."[17] Strupp dismissed cries by newspaper editors that government officials had stymied a helpless press and instead rebuked newspapers for failing to properly investigate government claims.

The problem, critics pointed out, was that the legions of unnamed sources seldom provided insights beyond the official discourse. Looking back at the prewar intelligence coverage, the *New York Observer*, a weekly newspaper that includes stories on New York media, identified a lack of knowledge behind the motivations of sources seeking anonymity to be an inherent problem of unnamed sources. The article specifically criticized the *Times* for its over-reliance on unnamed sources, writing that it takes a "decoding machine" to understand its anonymous attribution techniques: "There are days when the *Times* looks more like a bulletin board for various entities than a paper with articles chased down by enterprising reporters."[18] As an elite newspaper, the *Times* demonstrates its access to the upper echelons of the government through the copious use of unnamed sources. These unnamed sources serve as a marker for the newspaper's authority. The result, however, can be a confusingly coded system of anonymity that prevents non-elite readers from being able to understand sources' motivations or credibility, let alone the accuracy of evidence justifying war. This amounts to an abdication of journalistic skepticism in order to secure access to sources and avoid the scrutiny engendered by more aggressive reporting.

Judith Miller as Symbol

Out of the swirling complexity and ambiguity of the prewar news environment, the *New York Times*'s Judith Miller, above any other individual, came to personify prewar reporting mistakes. As a target of intense scrutiny, critics portrayed Miller's use of unnamed sources not as providing citizens with background information about the case for war, but as echoing official pronouncements without identifying underlying uncertainty. In making her a symbol, Miller's detractors constructed her as the antithesis of a model reporter; she was cast as an antimodel for journalism and the use of unnamed sources. This was not a temporary designation. More than four years after her WMD reporting proved incorrect, a *Salon* columnist invoked Miller's continued legacy: "'Judy Miller' is not just a disgraced journalist, but is also a method of journalism that extends far beyond her."[19]

Miller joined the *New York Times* Washington bureau in 1977 covering domestic politics before establishing her niche in international affairs—including the Middle East. Miller helped the newspaper win the 2002 Pulitzer Prize for Explanatory Reporting by writing or cowriting three of the ten articles on global terrorism that won the award. Aside from her newspaper work, Miller also authored several books, including two on the Middle East and one on germ warfare. While many *Times* reporters contributed stories chronicling the Bush administration's case for invading Iraq, Miller's background led to front page stories detailing Iraq's supposed arsenal of unconventional weapons based on unnamed U.S. intelligence and Iraqi exile sources. This beat took her to Iraq at the start of the war, where she was an embed with Mobile Exploitation Team Alpha, a unit tasked with using prewar intelligence to locate WMDs in Iraq.

Given her visibility, Miller was well known—and maligned—for her close ties with government and military officials as well as a network of refugee Iraqi scientists and politicians. When it became clear that the prewar intelligence was incorrect, the spotlight fell on Miller's reportage in particular to explain how and why the reporting had been inaccurate. Five months after the invasion, the *American Journalism Review* labeled her "the most-criticized journalist of the war" after Fox News Channel's Geraldo Rivera[20]—nearly ten months before the *Times* apology. Similarly, an *Editor & Publisher* story called Miller's faulty reporting worse than Jayson Blair's and recommended that the *Times* conduct an "honest review" of Miller's work to preserve the newspaper's credibility.[21] *Slate*'s Shafer, one of the most vocal and prolific critics of Miller's prewar intelligence reporting,[22] also began calling for the *Times* to launch an investigation in May 2003—a full year before the editor's note would be published.[23] These critics situated Miller as a model of improperly executed journalistic practice for her coverage of the prewar intelligence as well as her actions in the Plame leak case (detailed in chapter 5).

Critics blasted Miller for reporting that appeared, on the surface, to provide insider accounts, but that only reproduced the same set of claims offered through public channels without recognizing the overlap. An often repeated example of Miller's errant sourcing practices involved a story about an Iraq-bound shipment of aluminum tubes that the Bush administration asserted were to be used in making centrifuges to prepare uranium for nuclear weapons.[24] In the September 8, 2002, edition of the *Times,* a front page story by Michael Gordon and Miller quoted a number of unnamed sources, identified as "Bush administration officials," who corroborated this contention despite other U.S. and international analysts who claimed the tubes were to be used for making conventional rockets because they were not the proper size.[25] The article attributed intelligence information to unnamed sources with such vague appellations as "administration officials," "a senior administration official," and a "senior government official." No current administration officials were quoted on the record; a former Clinton administration official was quoted by name in the twenty-seventh paragraph.

In a follow-up story five days later, Miller and Gordon again turned to unnamed sources to convey the assuredness of the U.S. intelligence community in response to doubts about the intended use of the tubes. In a mystifying passage, the article seemed to dismiss challenges to the aluminum tube findings made by one set of unnamed sources through promoting the relative superiority of other unnamed sources: "Specifically, Washington officials said, some experts in the State Department and the Energy Department were said to have raised that question [about noncentrifuge uses of the tubes]. But other, more senior, officials insisted last night that this was a minority view among intelligence experts and that the C.I.A. had wide support, particularly among the government's top technical experts and nuclear scientists. 'This is a footnote, not a split,' a senior administration official said."[26] In the face of a dispute occurring over intelligence claims, the lack of transparent debate eliminated the ability of readers, be they citizens or policy makers, to adequately evaluate the different opinions presented. Instead, the reporters inserted their own evaluation and justified it through citing an indeterminate hierarchy among the ranks of government officials. This appeal to seniority, in the end, elided real concerns among intelligence analysts.

The process did not end with the publishing of the above stories. Instead, senior administration officials recirculated them as corroborating their public statements. Notably, on the day the first story was published, Vice President Cheney appeared on NBC's *Meet the Press* and cited the Gordon and Miller article as supporting administration claims that the tubes were to be used in Iraq's nuclear program. Because the leak originated from within the administration, the story provided the false appearance of verification when it was only an echo of the same voices. In the *Columbia Journalism Review,* John MacArthur revisited Miller's reporting on the aluminum tubes after the failure to locate WMDs and described it as "a disgraceful piece of stenography."[27] MacArthur situated Miller's lack of skepticism and her adherence to the administration message as going against the normative model of news reporting. Ideally, Miller's use of anonymity to secure access to U.S. intelligence agencies provided a valuable check on official messages. However, in this case, Miller failed to recognize dissenting voices within the intelligence community and only reinforced assessments in synch with official claims being made publicly.

In another front-page *Times* story, Miller reported that Iraq sought to purchase a nerve gas antidote from Turkey, "according to senior Bush administration officials."[28] The article repeatedly referred to unnamed officials to offer evidence of Iraq's action without quoting any current administration officials by name. The only named sources in the article included a Turkish ambassador claiming he had no knowledge of Iraq's request or U.S. government efforts to intervene in the sale and two ex-U.S. military officials quoted in the closing paragraphs. The article demonstrated Miller's pattern of citing claims of Iraqi malfeasance through repetitious references to unnamed sources. The article seemed to be further evidence of Iraq's weapons capabilities, which connected it to the ongoing discourse about the need for invasion. However, as in the above stories, the opacity of these claims prevented public assessment. As is the case with unnamed sources, news audiences had no option beyond trusting that they had been accurately reported.

Public criticism of Miller surrounded not only these stories, but also her involvement in the Plame leak scandal. The origins of the case trace back to the period after the invasion of Iraq. With no WMD stockpiles uncovered, attention turned to why the administration had been so sure of what it would find. Amidst this search for answers, former ambassador Joseph Wilson wrote an op-ed for the *New York Times* on July 6, 2003, revealing that while the Bush administration maintained that Iraq was seeking uranium from Africa, his mission to Niger failed to turn up any corroborating evidence. In a harsh critique (see chapter 5), Wilson accused the administration of inflating its case against Iraq. A week later, on July 14, columnist Robert Novak exposed Wilson's wife—Valerie Plame—to be a CIA operative working on weapons of mass destruction. This information, attributed to unnamed sources identified as "two senior administration officials," sparked an investigation into whether the leak of Plame's position at the CIA constituted a crime by the anonymous administration officials. Because the case turned on a leak, the resulting investigation by special prosecutor Patrick Fitzgerald hinged on exposing the exchange of information between journalists and government officials. On August 12, 2004—the day the *Washington Post* issued a front page analysis of its prewar reporting (recounted below)—Fitzgerald subpoenaed several journalists to testify in front of a grand jury about the case. After Fitzgerald procured waivers from possible sources, all but Judith Miller and *Time* magazine reporter Matt Cooper agreed to testify.

Initially, journalists protested efforts to force reporters to testify about their contact with official sources. They labeled Fitzgerald's investigation a threat to journalism's autonomy and warned that it would dampen their ability to function in the public interest. In doing so, the journalistic community called for a federal shield law that would limit the conditions under which a journalist could be asked to testify about unnamed sources. This effort underscored a tension in all of the incidents in this book over what rights journalists should possess above other citizens. The call for a federal shield law was an attempt to further codify journalistic autonomy beyond the ambiguity accorded to the First Amendment after the Supreme Court ruled 5–4 against a constitutional privilege for journalists in the 1972 case of *Branzburg v. Hayes.* In response to Fitzgerald's subpoenas, editorials supporting a federal shield law appeared frequently in newspapers across the nation, including from the *New York Times, Washington Post, Boston Globe, Houston Chronicle,* and many more.[29]

However, while initially a rallying point for journalists, by October 2005 *American Journalism Review* editor Rem Rieder summed up the Plame leak case as "an unmitigated disaster for journalism."[30] As the specifics of the case emerged, what began as a widespread defense of journalistic confidentiality against incursions by the government ended with prominent Washington journalists facing scrutiny over their relationships with unnamed government sources.

External Problems, Internal Changes

Long before the Plame leak scandal revealed less-than-ideal uses of unnamed sources and even before the *New York Times* and the *Washington Post* would publicly acknowledge problems haunting their coverage, the two newspapers did address problems caused by unnamed sources—but only internally. In February 2004, both newspapers separately issued internal staff memos containing alterations to their unnamed sourcing practices and standards. The documents, while meant to be private, were leaked to Jim Romenesko's blog on the Poynter Institute's Web site—a popular site for insider journalism information and gossip.[31]

The *Post's* memo began by stressing the need to avoid unnamed sources in conventional news coverage. Ideally then, unnamed sources were to be used sparingly. However, when they became necessary to procuring a story, the newspaper stressed the need for transparency to the extent possible without violating the promise of anonymity. Reporters were required to provide "a publishable reason for concealing the source's identity" specifically explaining to readers why a source has been granted anonymity.[32] In addition, the guidelines urged that labels identifying unnamed sources should be as detailed as possible, since a bland tag such as "'an administration official' is useless to readers."[33]

Following the memo leak, *Post* editor Leonard Downie publicly confronted the troublesome increase in unnamed sources at the newspaper while explaining its policy changes. Downie reiterated the normative desire for transparency: "Like our readers, we would like all sources of information in this newspaper to be named . . . even if it means objecting to traditional Washington practices such as 'background briefings.'"[34] This response illustrated the tension news outlets face in reconciling the opacity of unnamed sources with a desire to connect all information to named sources. It recognized the protection journalists receive in being able to shunt blame onto named sources in the face of errant or controversial claims.[35] When journalists lose this ability to deflect fault on unnamed sources, they leave themselves exposed to charges of flawed newsgathering practices.

The *New York Times* took a similar tack to the *Post* in dealing with unnamed sources in 2004. This internal confrontation occurred not only in the face of faulty prewar reporting, but also problems in its coverage of Wen Ho Lee in 1999[36] and the rampant fabrications of Jayson Blair in 2003.[37] While Blair may, at some level, be dismissed for the unusualness of his wanton deception, the Lee episode connects all too well to common pitfalls surrounding the use of unnamed sources. It began on March 6, 1999, when investigative reporters James Risen and Jeff Gerth published a front-page story titled "China Stole Nuclear Secrets For Bombs, U.S. Aides Say." The article consisted of numerous unnamed sources, identified only as "officials," alleging the existence of a Chinese spy within the Los Alamos nuclear research laboratory. Two days later, Lee was fired while an FBI investigation ensued. In December, Lee was indicted on fifty-nine counts involving mishandling secret documents and incarcerated in solitary confinement for nine months before being released with a guilty plea on only one minor count. The flimsiness of the government's case caused the judge to apologize to Lee for how he had been treated.

On September 26, 2000, the *Times* issued an editor's note discussing its coverage of Lee. The less-than-contrite note did admit to regrets, but it evaded the larger structural issue underlying its mismanagement of the story: reporters relying on unnamed Washington officials reproduced their cloaked allegations without examining what was actually occurring thousands of miles away in New Mexico. Even after the government's case against Lee disintegrated,

Risen continued to defend much of the reporting as accurate at least with regard to attitudes within the government: "The fact of the matter is, our story is accurate. It accurately reflected what the government was thinking at the time."[38] Judith Miller would later make a similar argument in her own defense that she merely chronicled commonly held beliefs within Washington regarding Iraq's weapons capabilities. Yet other reporters arriving late to the story found contradicting evidence foretelling the eventual collapse of the case against Lee.[39] Postmortem assessments dissected what went wrong in the case, including a review of the reporting in the *American Journalism Review* that concluded: "The Wen Ho Lee saga will be remembered as a case study of what can go wrong when politics infect criminal investigations, when even highly regarded reporters rely on unnamed, inside-the-Beltway sources and leaks about law enforcement investigations, and when cutthroat competition and pressure to match stories encourage news organizations to repeat instead of challenge reporting by others."[40] A confluence of structural factors—close ties to sources, unsubstantiated leaks, pack journalism—contributed to a flashy story that morphed into a misleading one.

Lee sued the government for violating his privacy when it leaked personal information to journalists. The case meant an attempt to force journalists to testify about the identity of their unnamed sources, which led to a protracted legal skirmish. Reporters were slapped with a $500-a-day fine for their refusal to testify as the case wound through the courts. When the U.S. Supreme Court refused to hear an appeal in 2006, a settlement netted Lee $750,000 from the *Times* as well as the *Washington Post, Los Angeles Times,* ABC, and the Associated Press in exchange for their reporters being able to avoid revealing their sources.[41] While many journalists decried legal efforts to compel the disclosure of unnamed sources, the coda further accentuated the initial failure of the story in its overwhelmingly guilty portrayal of Lee.

With the legacy of the Lee case and brewing consternation surrounding its prewar reporting record, the *Times* internally revamped its policy for unnamed sources. Echoing the *Post,* the newspaper emphasized the need to reserve anonymity for rare circumstances where named attribution jeopardized a source. Plus, it was meant only for sources with direct knowledge of a story. The memo stated: "We do not grant anonymity to people who use it as cover for a personal or partisan attack" because it gives an "unfair advantage" to the source.[42] Additionally, the *Times* memo stressed that when multiple unnamed sources were used, "reporter and editor must be satisfied that the sources are genuinely independent of one another, not connected behind the scenes in any kind of 'echo chamber' that negates the value of a cross-check."

While the memos did not specify or confront Lee or the prewar intelligence reporting, they did indicate unease with persistent problems stemming from confidentiality pledges.

Efforts by the *Post* and the *Times* to rewrite their practices signaled an internal attempt to negotiate the problematic—but potentially fruitful—practice of news anonymity through tweaking their policies. Unfortunately, no easy fix exists or can exist. Ultimately these insider efforts by the newspapers proved insufficient to quell the mounting questions about why the reporting had failed to see the problems in the government's case for war. A public acknowledgement was needed.

The *New York Times* Revisits Its Prewar Reporting

While questions began to surface shortly after the start of the Iraq War in 2003, the *Times* steadfastly resisted calls to revisit its record of prewar intelligence reporting for an entire year. Even just two months before he would publicly deplore deficiencies, editor Bill Keller stated he saw no "prima facie case" for an internal review.[43] This stance weakened following the continued disillusionment with Iraqi exile and important *Times* source Ahmad Chalabi. With Chalabi discredited, Keller changed his mind and decided to personally conduct a reexamination of the newspaper's prewar reporting, which he presented in an editor's note titled "The *Times* and Iraq" in the May 26, 2004, issue. It was not without reluctance. The placement of the 1,200-word editor's note in the middle of the newspaper on page A10—away from the front page or the usual corrections space on page A2—suggested a desire to avoid drawing too much attention to the findings of faulty practices. A few days after Keller's note, public editor Daniel Okrent presented his own views on the prewar reporting and the role of unnamed sources in his Sunday column. Both pieces recognized problems within the newspaper—and journalism more broadly—that led to faulty reporting before the war.

Keller began his note by praising "an enormous amount of journalism that we are proud of" before quickly turning to criticism and contrition: "We have found a number of instances of coverage that was not as rigorous as it should have been. In some cases, information that was controversial then, and seems questionable now, was insufficiently qualified or allowed to stand unchallenged. Looking back, we wish we had been more aggressive in reexamining the claims as new evidence emerged—or failed to emerge."[44] This initial explanation of what went wrong highlighted two issues: the failure to adequately characterize the tenuousness of certain information described as fact and the lack of follow-up reporting tracking these claims over time. Keller presented these as journalistic failures, quickly accepting some level of blame in the note.

However, these two troublesome reporting patterns did not explain why information had been incorrect. On this point, Keller placed the brunt of the blame on discredited Iraqi exiles. He reiterated this conclusion in an internal memo directed to the newspaper staff at the time of the public note: "We, like many of our competitors and many officials in Washington, were misled on a number of stories by Iraqi informants dealing in misinformation."[45] Keller presented a chain of misinformation and disinformation flowing from the exiles to U.S. government officials and then trickling down to reporters. By passing blame from government officials to already discredited Iraqi exiles, this explanation admitted to problematic intelligence while eliminating accusations that the Bush administration intentionally misled the *Times* and other news outlets. Essentially exonerating the administration, the newspaper apologized for faulty reporting without implicating—or even confronting the question of—direct efforts by government officials to manipulate the intelligence, as many critics have asserted.[46] In this sleight of hand, by pinning the blame on Iraqi exiles, Keller preserved the newspaper's ongoing relations with the official sources the newspaper depends on to remain an elite news organization. It stopped the discussion short of raising questions about whether the administration abused its access to the news—particularly through anonymity—to spread intelligence claims it was less than certain about.

Keller's note did much more than single out untrustworthy Iraqi exiles for blame. In analyzing the newspaper's reporting practices, he turned his attention inward to focus on structural constraints influencing the erroneous reporting. Keller offered readers a candid look inside the newsroom of a competitive national newspaper when he indicted a pervading newsroom environment that emphasized breaking news stories while marginalizing follow-up stories questioning administration or exile claims. Editors "perhaps too intent on rushing scoops into the paper" failed to challenge reporters on their facts. In an unusually frank tone, Keller connected competitive pressures to reduced skepticism as the staff aspired to reporting that would bring attention to the newspaper.

Keller supported his effort to blame an unhealthy newsroom culture by not isolating or naming individual editors or reporters. Instead, he isolated six problematic articles published between October 26, 2001, and April 23, 2003—all produced under the previous editorship of Howell Raines.[47] Although Keller did not publish the names of the reporters for these six articles, four were written or cowritten by Judith Miller. For example, Keller dissected the September 8, 2002, article cowritten by Miller in which a number of unnamed officials concluded Iraq had purchased aluminum tubes for its resurgent nuclear program. In reevaluating the story nearly two years later, Keller admitted mistakes but downplayed dissenting opinion in the intelligence community. He claimed that the information came from "the best American intelligence sources available at the time."[48] However, other reporters working on the story showed dissenting opinion to be much more significant and prominent.[49]

Even in its contrite mood, the *Times* did not fully acknowledge the faultiness of its reporting. Instead of isolating reporting errors, it returned to framing the period as awash in misinformation for both reporters and officials. Keller's note avoided positioning journalists as lapdogs tricked by officials or at the mercy of sources escaping accountability with demands of anonymity. By taking the tack of mutually incorrect intelligence for officials and journalists, the *Times* presented a limited correction only focusing on some of the issues impacting news coverage at the exclusion of other structural issues, including the press management tactics of the Bush administration, its strategic use of anonymity, and the general disadvantage reporters face in their reliance on officials. Regardless, the note concluded by drawing on normative journalistic language with a plea "to continue aggressive reporting aimed at setting the record straight."[50]

On the whole, the note tapped into a wider anxiety among national news outlets that prewar reporting errors weakened public opinion of news credibility. This legacy made explanation and repair difficult, which meant Keller could not protect the newspaper by individualizing mistakes and attributing them solely to Miller or former editor Raines. Instead, he took the unusual—and laudable—strategy of framing reporting mistakes as a collective error born out of competitive pressures and distributed blame across the newspaper. This attention to the internal dynamics of the newspaper also resulted in discussions of unnamed sources that veered toward structural and contextual issues rather than individual deviance. Yet even with these positive steps Keller was overly dismissive of the impact of Bush administration news strategies. He presented the U.S. government not as a perpetrator of intelligence claims that should have been discredited, but as a fellow victim of being duped by Iraqi refugees. Nor did the note go into much detail about the specific problems of past stories to better understand their underlying mechanics—particularly involving unnamed sources. Rather, the general self-critique mostly confined itself to an incomplete pinpointing of the faulty intelligence of Iraqi exiles and a competitive context privileging breaking news over careful follow-ups.

Keller's note was not the end of the newspaper's efforts to come to terms with its prewar reporting. Four days after Keller's note, public editor Daniel Okrent's column in the Sunday Week in Review section echoed Keller's frame of stressing context over individual mistakes to explain prewar reporting mishaps: "The failure was not individual, but institutional."[51] Like Keller, Okrent blamed an obsession with generating "scoops" and a tendency for reporters to aim for front-page–worthy articles over follow-up pieces. But Okrent went further than Keller, using both the visibility and autonomy of his position as public editor to present a harsh assessment of the pervasive use of unnamed sources in the newspaper. Labeling unnamed sources as "toxic," Okrent also noted their usefulness when carefully investigated. He rebuked reporters and editors who accepted unattributed statements at face value without checking their veracity, a criticism regularly directed toward Miller: "That automatic editor defense, 'We're not confirming what he says, we're just reporting it,' may apply to the statements of people speaking on the record. For anonymous sources, it's worse than no defense. It's a license granted to liars."[52] Notably, this discussion of anonymity went beyond excavating prewar WMD stories from a year earlier to call into question the extensive use of unnamed sources occurring daily in the pages of the *Times*. He chastised the newspaper for allowing sources to make statements without reprisal by trading confidentiality for access.

PRAISE AND CRITIQUE OF THE *TIMES* SELF-REVIEW

Despite the discreet placement of Keller's note in the middle of the A section, it did not go unnoticed. Many other news outlets picked up the note and immediately undermined Keller's effort to distribute blame across the newspaper by filling in the missing details omitted from the note. Specifically, stories about the self-review made clear Miller's authorship of many of the problematic articles identified by Keller. For example, both the Associated Press and Reuters began by summarizing what Keller wrote before singling out Miller and recounting past scrutiny of the newspaper's prewar coverage by such critics as Jack Shafer and Michael Massing.[53] While, originally, much of this criticism took place outside of mainstream news, coverage of the *Times* self-review bought it to more widespread attention. The inclusion of this record of criticism led the note to be recast from a proactive move by the newspaper—which certainly would have been the *Times*'s preference—to being a public relations–driven reaction to mounting public scrutiny.

This contextualization of the editor's note hampered efforts by the *Times* to control the interpretation of why it erred in its unnamed sourcing practices during the buildup to the war.

Regardless of the framing, Keller's note drew reactions of surprise that the newspaper choose to extend culpability to an overall problematic organizational environment rather than blame a few individuals, including ex-editor Raines. By going against the strategy of isolating deviant individuals, Keller's note drew such adjectives as "unusual,"[54] "extraordinary,"[55] "stunning,"[56] "wondrous,"[57] a "stinging self-rebuke,"[58] a "stark self-indictment,"[59] and a "surprising statement of contrition."[60] These stories recounted the note, interpreting the line "we have found a number of instances of coverage that was not as rigorous as it should have been" to be a form of apology by Keller. While, as this book attests, news organizations apologizing for errors in coverage are not uncommon, both the timing of *Times* review and its institutional focus made Keller's note—and Okrent's subsequent column—noteworthy.

Yet despite the unusualness of expanding rather than individualizing blame, Keller's self-investigation faced criticism for being reluctant and for failing to fully address mistakes and the newsgathering context that enabled them. The editor's note did not appear until May 26, 2004—401 days after the most recent problematic article it cited and 943 days after the oldest one.[61] In the interim, the search for unconventional weapons turned unsuccessful, prewar intelligence estimates came under scrutiny, and the Iraqi exiles supplying information proved untrustworthy. Only after growing controversy discredited Ahmad Chalabi, a significant source for Miller and the *Times,* did a self-investigation actually appear. Howard Kurtz called the timing "about a year too late."[62] With its exile sources in disrepute, the *Times* could no longer support its previous reporting, making its review "less a matter of whether and more a matter of when," according to *Chicago Tribune* public editor Don Wycliff.[63] This inevitability undercut the novelty of the self-review by suggesting that the newspaper waited until the last instance before admitting to problems.

Other critics questioned the placement of the note on page A10, in the middle of Wednesday's news section, instead of in a more prominent location. The article was far from the front page where the offending articles that caused the need for a note originally ran. The next day, the *Wall Street Journal, Boston Globe,* and *Chicago Tribune* each gave their stories about the note more prominent locations than the *Times* gave Keller's note. The managing editor of the Cleveland *Plain Dealer* condemned the placement: "If you're going to go to this length to be up front with your readers you'd think they'd put it where you normally put those things."[64] Critics accused the *Times* of burying the note in contrast to the prominence given to the Wen Ho Lee apology and the Jayson Blair investigation. Many felt the *Times* had tried to avoid rushing into another apology so soon after the Blair scandal in May 2003. On CNN, Margaret Carlson chastised the newspaper for not doing more: "Recall Jayson Blair? He didn't contribute to a war in which over 800 Americans have died, yet he got a page 1 mea culpa and the resignation of two editors."[65] Carlson ranked the prewar reporting mistakes as more serious because they corroborated administration claims for the need to invade Iraq. Meanwhile, the Blair episode was dismissed as perhaps embarrassing, but not publicly harmful.

Keller drew additional disapproval for not naming—or disciplining—individual reporters. Keller intentionally attempted to avoid individualizing errors by distributing blame across the paper to both reporters and editors—even though Judith Miller had been a consistent target before the note.[66] Not everyone agreed with this move. *Washington Post* ombudsman Michael Getler asserted that naming Miller "would have given more credibility to the . . . note."[67] Despite Keller's efforts not to single out anyone, all the subsequent reporting on the note pointed to Miller's authorship of a majority of the cited articles. She became the face of prewar reporting mistakes, and it was clear that many felt she should have been at least reproached verbally in the note, if not further reprimanded. *Salon*'s James Moore criticized her being "shielded from full scrutiny" in the *Times* self-review.[68]

Regardless of Keller's intentions, the *Times* could not control the reception of its self-examination. Further discussions cast the use of unnamed sources as fraught with perils at both an individual and organizational level. Just as unnamed sources obscure transparency, Keller's note appeared to omit details about what went wrong even while being contrite. This made it difficult for the newspaper to reinstate its journalistic authority through vowing to be more vigilant in the future.

The *Washington Post*'s Self-Examination

The *Washington Post* demonstrated its own reluctance to look back at its performance leading up to the Iraq War. Following the *Times* self-review in May 2004, *Washington Post* ombudsman Michael Getler alleged that the *Post* had done better than the *Times,* but admitted it had too often buried skeptical reporting in its back pages.[69] No more was written about this era until a 3,000-word investigation into the newspaper's prewar reporting appeared three months later on the front page of the *Washington Post*'s August 12, 2004, issue.[70] Media critic Howard Kurtz assigned himself the review and was granted independence to do so by the newspaper's editors. Through interviews with the *Post* staff and an examination of the newspaper's prewar intelligence coverage in the six months leading up to the Iraq War, Kurtz found a consistent pattern of intelligence doubts being sequestered in the back of the news section while front page stories—140 of them by Kurtz's count—prominently repeated administration claims of Iraq's weapon capacity, often through unnamed sources.

The patterns in the coverage were partly attributed to political assumptions at the time. Veteran reporter Bob Woodward admitted to being part of "groupthink" prevalent among government officials. This groupthink extended to the newsroom. Pentagon correspondent Thomas Ricks connected story placement to a predetermined sense among the newspaper staff that the war was inevitable: "Administration assertions were on the front page. Things that challenged the administration were on A18 on Sunday or A24 on Monday. There was an attitude among editors: Look, we're going to war, why do we even worry about all this contrary stuff?"[71]

Throughout this period, stories in which unnamed sources expressed doubt about the prevailing assumptions of Iraq's weapons capability had a more difficult time gaining entry into the newspaper. *Post* editor Leonard Downie told Kurtz that "the inability of dissenters 'to speak up with their names' was a factor in some of his news judgments" resulting in stories skeptical of Iraq's weapons being shunted to the back or omitted altogether. In the only area in which he admitted erring, Downie concurred that dissenting perspectives were too rarely emphasized: "Not enough of those stories were put on the front page. That was a mistake on my part." In particular, reporting by Walter Pincus challenging administration claims faced skepticism from editors. In contrast, stories supporting the prewar intelligence, even with unnamed sources, made it into print more readily.

While Kurtz's review did strive to understand the newsroom environment that contributed to problems in the prewar coverage, overall it was less apologetic than Keller's note in the *Times*. Aside from avoiding an all-out apology, Downie confronted critics who positioned the *Washington Post* as culpable for the faulty prewar intelligence. At the end of Kurtz's article, Downie downplayed the influence of the *Post* on the decision to invade Iraq: "People who were opposed to the war from the beginning and have been critical of the media's coverage in the period before the war . . . have the mistaken impression that somehow if the media's coverage had been different, there wouldn't have been a war."[72] Downie asserted that even if the coverage had been more skeptical, the administration's push for war would not have been deterred. The following Sunday, the editorial page carried eight letters to the editor critical of Kurtz's story, mostly due to Downie's comments and the lack of responsibility taken by the *Post* in the march toward war.[73] Several of the letters contradicted Downie's assessment, saying, in essence, that it was precisely journalism's role to call attention to the faults in the official reasons for war. Others pointed out how the elite press, including the *Post,* marginalized antiwar efforts, which produced this feeling of inevitability.

Kurtz responded to charges that the *Post* contributed to the invasion in a column titled "Ultimately, Newspapers Can't Move the Earth" that dismissed notions that the newspaper had wanted war—even if the editorial page had promoted invading Iraq.[74] However, Kurtz did blame the unquestioning tone of the prewar coverage on a mixture of news conventions that favored public officials and a general political atmosphere that largely precluded challenging the administration. Kurtz evaded addressing the power the *Post* wields over public opinion or its culpability—and by extension, the culpability of the news generally—in generating support for the war.

Although both newspapers choose to respond to a chorus of critics blaming them, at least partly, for the Iraq War, the self-investigations by the *New York Times* and the *Washington Post* differed in several substantive ways. The *Times* note was less prominent—1,200 words on page A10 compared to the *Post*'s 3,000-word front page story. However, the *Times* critique had the authority of being from the editor in May 2004 while the *Post* waited nearly three months before Kurtz, a media critic who ordinarily covers *other* news outlets, took it upon himself to act independently. Regarding content, the *Times* piece moved away from individuals to examine articles instead. The *Post* piece used quotes from reporters and editors about the stories and their treatment. Finally, several factors led the *Times* to receive more attention for its review than the *Post* did three months later, including its conciliatory tone, earlier publication, and the stature of the newspaper. In addition, the *Post*'s review emerged the same day Patrick Fitzgerald subpoenaed Judith Miller and several other prominent journalists to testify in the Plame leak case—a development no doubt drawing attention away from the newspaper.

Despite these differences, the self-evaluations were significant moments for news outlets concerned that the poor use of unnamed sources in prewar intelligence reporting would weaken journalistic authority and lead to reputational loss. These analyses opened up formerly hidden newsroom practices just slightly to reveal actions taking place within the black box of elite U.S. newspapers. But this perspective was only advanced with accompanying reluctance, which showed the difficulty journalists face in straying from individualizing and isolating strategies for confronting problems. The *Times* and the *Post* only begrudgingly issued public examinations of their practices more than a year after the problematic stories had run. Neither critique thoroughly excoriated the prewar reporting. The *Times* buried the note in the news section and neglected to name—or chastise—any individual staff members. Meanwhile, the *Post* did not actually apologize, and the media critic authored the review rather than the editor. This combination of factors led a *Christian Science Monitor* columnist to question whether the critiques signaled "a mere bout of self-analysis that amounts to navel-gazing, or a break with the newspaper industry's tradition of considering itself above reproach."[75] Even with this reluctance, the fact that each newspaper would return to much earlier reporting and conclude that its newsroom culture contributed to faulty reporting was notable, whether or not it sparked a transformation across journalism. In the end, the reviews signaled a willingness to discuss the conditions of journalistic practice, the failure of unnamed sources, and discontent with a period of languid reporting between the attacks of September 11, 2001, and the start of the Iraq War in March 2003—a sour legacy that runs throughout this book.

Conclusion: What Kind of Reporting Should We Have?

In the wake of prewar reporting reviews at the *Times* and the *Post,* Howard Kurtz mused on the nebulous, negative legacy of how major news outlets fared in their coverage: "It's not a lie. It's not a plagiarism. But it is a journalistic shortfall that I think a lot of people remember in terms of the prewar coverage."[76] Perhaps the emotion may be best described as disappointment—disappointment that the self-described Fourth Estate in all its post 9/11–pre Iraq War vigor failed to reveal cracks—or even chasms—in the intelligence that would become so obvious after the invasion began. Unnamed sources meant to expose otherwise unreportable qualms instead filled up pseudo-enterprise stories corroborating officials' public statements. Readers were left not knowing the identification of sources, their motives and stakes in offering quotes, or their connection to on-the-record sources.

Widespread problems with the prewar coverage raised the question of whether unnamed sources aided or undermined journalism's self-stated norms. The ongoing conversation confronting the problematic opacity and frequent use—or misuse—of anonymity extended to a larger struggle to define journalism's political and cultural roles. It raised the question: What kind of journalism should we have? To use unnamed sources to get behind official pronouncements entails an aggressive journalism that sometimes stakes out an oppositional position. It also means taking a risk, which, when it backfires, envelops the journalist, her news organization, and—on occasion—the whole of journalism in controversy.

The risks for journalists crafting challenging stories relying on unnamed sources were exacerbated by a post-9/11 political mood encouraging support for administration claims while dampening contrasting assessments—a pressure Paul Krugman termed "misplaced patriotism."[77] Those journalists who did stray faced being harangued by a bevy of critical voices. *New York Times* media critic Jacques Steinberg identified this shift following Kurtz's review of prewar reporting in the *Post*: "These journalistic mea culpas are being made in a news media landscape vastly different than it was just a few years ago" in which, aside from already declining public opinion, "news organizations are now subject to more scrutiny, including by Web logs."[78] While the failures in the case for the Iraq War have had some impact on revitalizing the need for critical journalism, this overall environment—along with a flurry of controversies involving unnamed sources—posed challenges for journalism in asserting its social role that need to be acknowledged more thoroughly.

2

"Blogs 1, CBS 0": *60 Minutes* and the Killian Memos Controversy

We are on notice: Every American is a media critic.
—Joanne Ostrow, *Denver Post* media critic

On Wednesday, September 8, 2004, in the midst of the hard-fought 2004 presidential campaign between incumbent George W. Bush and Senator John Kerry, *60 Minutes* aired a segment titled "For the Record" questioning whether President Bush had completed his service requirements for the Texas Air National Guard. The story, narrated by Dan Rather, featured an interview with former Texas Lieutenant Governor Ben Barnes claiming he had used his political influence to place Bush, as well as other young men, in the Air National Guard to shelter them from the Vietnam War. While this was notable, the public attention that was to follow centered on four documents reportedly from the private file of Jerry Killian, Bush's commanding officer in the National Guard, who died in 1984. The documents indicated that Bush had ignored an order to undergo his required physical and had been suspended from flying for failing to meet Guard standards. Killian also recorded pressure from above to preserve Bush's record from being tarnished. These documents, which became known as the Killian memos, came to CBS News via a source granted anonymity.

While CBS News certainly hoped the story would get attention, it did not expect the flood of controversy that began when the *60 Minutes* broadcast ended. With others chasing the story of Bush's military service record, CBS News viewed its report, backed by exclusive documents, to be a coup. However, conservatives seeking to minimize the potential damage to Bush's reelection campaign raised questions about the authenticity of the memos. A battle ensued over the veracity of the documents, with CBS squaring off against a legion of conservative critics who began to build their case through a network of new media sites immediately after the Wednesday *60 Minutes* broadcast. Questions raised on blogs and message boards of conservative Web sites escalated the following day into charges that the memos were obvious forgeries. Skepticism and criticism spread from the message board of freerepublic.com to conservative blogs including Power Line and Little Green Footballs. By Friday, traditional news outlets began reporting bloggers' claims and digging into whether the memos were authentic or forgeries created on a modern-day computer. Both the *Washington Post* and NBC News raised issues regarding a number of formal aspects of the memos.[1] Critics charged that the typeface, use of superscript, and spacing of the letters were not readily available on typewriters in the early 1970s. With no identified source to vouch for the authenticity of the memos, these speculative claims thrived.

Against a growing chorus of criticism voiced in outlets ranging from blogs to major newspapers, CBS News stiffened in its defense of the story. It refused to give any information about the source who provided the documents, describing him instead as "unimpeachable."[2] As for the authenticity of the documents, CBS News continually asserted its thoroughness in fact-checking the memos through document and signature experts. Using airtime on both the *CBS Evening News* and *60 Minutes,* Dan Rather defended the reporting against criticism from both online and mainstream sources.[3] These efforts included an interview in which Jerry Killian's former secretary claimed the memos must be fakes since she did not type them, but said Killian's negative assessment of Bush was accurate.[4]

CBS News could not sustain its defense and withdrew its support of the authenticity of the memos on September 20—twelve days after the initial report. On the *Evening News,* Rather apologized to viewers: "The failure of CBS News . . . to properly, fully scrutinize the documents and their source, led to our airing the documents when we should not have done so. It was a mistake. CBS News deeply regrets it. Also, I want to say personally and directly, I'm sorry. . . . This was an error made in good faith as we tried to carry on the CBS News tradition of asking tough questions and investigating reports. But it was a mistake."[5] In the same broadcast, CBS News revealed the unnamed source who provided the memos to be Bill Burkett, a disgruntled former Texas Air National Guard officer who had publicly attacked Bush's record in February 2004.[6] As part of the CBS News apology, Burkett confessed to lying about the origins of the memos in an on-air interview. He had originally attributed them to another Guard source, but then admitted to acquiring them at a Texas cattle show from an unknown source.[7] Their origin has still not been discovered. In addition to its public apology, CBS News launched an independent investigation into the reporting practices of the Guard story headed by Louis Boccardi, the former CEO of the Associated Press and a member of the independent panel investigating Jayson Blair a year before, and Richard Thornburgh, a Republican who had been attorney general for George H. W. Bush.

The apology from CBS News touched off a scramble to answer the basic question of what happened within CBS News. While all public controversies produce, on some level, attempts to establish accountability, the ambiguity inherent in news stories relying on unnamed sources allows room for many interpretive possibilities to arise. This was true for CBS News as well as the coverage of the run-up to the invasion of Iraq a year earlier—and it would prove true for the upcoming controversy at *Newsweek* in May 2005. The Killian memos controversy also overlapped with the prewar reporting mistakes and the *Newsweek* controversy in their common focus on military actions. What made Bush's Guard record so salient in 2004—and less so during his initial run in 2000—were the ongoing wars in Iraq and Afghanistan and general tenor of the Bush White House as a wartime presidency. By autumn 2004, the dissipation of hopes for a quick close to combat and the stinging scandal at the Abu Ghraib prison made comparisons between the unpopularity of Vietnam and growing dissatisfaction with Iraq and Afghanistan seem less strained. For these reasons, as well as the attention John Kerry received during the campaign for his own service record, the issue of Bush's Guard service did matter.

At the same time, the Killian memos story stands out from the other incidents because of its use of a non-elite unnamed source. The prewar reporting, the *Newsweek* story, and the disclosure of Deep Throat all involved high-ranking government officials using journalists as a conduit to get unattributed information into the news. Bill Burkett, by contrast, was decidedly not an elite source. Instead, he was an outsider who, under mysterious circumstances, attained evidence purported to damage claims by the Bush administration about the president's service record. What this incident demonstrated was the extent to which anonymity could become a vulnerable target for critics seeking to stymie a potentially injurious story from gaining credence. In the end, this episode shunted public attention toward issues of political bias, corporate influences on news content, and the rise of citizen journalism—three topics far removed from what Bush was or wasn't doing in Texas some decades earlier.

The Broadcasters versus the Bloggers

Once the focus shifted away from the content of the *60 Minutes* story to its reporting practices, a narrative emerged pitting the media establishment against a new guard of online amateurs. Symbolically, the CBS News controversy was frequently portrayed as the old journalistic order—represented by *60 Minutes* and CBS News's septuagenarian anchor—succumbing to a new order of bloggers coming together to mount a networked challenge to the Killian memos story. Having accumulated its cultural authority in the era of Edward R. Murrow, Walter Cronkite, and only three television networks, CBS News weathered the arrival of competitive newcomers ranging from local television news to cable news to talk radio to even online news before meeting its match with bloggers in 2004. Tried as it did to defend the Killian memos story and its unnamed source, CBS News folded under the weight of cyber scrutiny. The outcome was clear to conservative columnist James Pinkerton, who scored the conflict: "Blogs 1, CBS 0."[8]

Bloggers attributed their success to a "self-policing" networked structure permitting stories to flow across sites.[9] While one blogger may not possess a specialized knowledge in typography or document analysis, a series of bloggers working together can amass and sort evidence and then publicize it through interlinking. Charles Johnson of the blog Little Green Footballs—one of the initial sites challenging the Killian memos—described blogs' ability to aggregate knowledge: "We've got a huge pool of highly motivated people who go out there and use the tools to find stuff. We've got an army of citizen journalists out there."[10] Bloggers situated their work as an alternative media form with its own particular strengths stemming from its transparent, homegrown structure. This was perceived as threatening to traditional journalism not only for siphoning audiences but also for redefining appropriate news practices.[11]

The Killian memos story as a symbolic victory for bloggers found reinforcement not only within the blogging community but also among journalists. Following the CBS apology, CNN commentator Jeff Greenfield summed it up as a victory for bloggers: "Well, in this one, you know, the guys in the pajamas are the guerrilla warriors and look much better than [what] was at one time the most prestigious [news] organization in the world."[12] On the same night, Keith Olbermann framed CBS News's apology as a victory for blogs regardless of its other meanings: "It's party time in the world of blogs tonight. . . . This is widely being viewed on the Internet as a triumph of new media over old media, as surely as if the bloggers were marching around tonight with Dan Rather's head on top of a pole."[13] Journalists interpreted the case as indicative of the increased influence of blogs and other online sites. *NBC Nightly News* correspondent Tom Costello called blogs "a new voice in setting the national agenda and a new check on the national media."[14] Others took a more revolutionary tone, asserting that the "Blogosphere Revolution" was "destroying the hegemonic power of a small elite, as information power now spreads to the citizenry at large."[15] Such sentiments indicate a view of traditional news outlets as failing to operate in the public interest while positioning blogs as an inherently democratic counter—a perspective perhaps much more idealistic than attained.

Beyond the symbolic victory of bloggers over broadcasters, the ascension of blogs in public discourse—however realized—marked a new field of scrutiny that brought with it practical concerns for journalists engaged in hidden news practices. Howard Kurtz pointed to the growing difficulty of using unnamed sources in light of new sites of media criticism: "You better be awfully careful when you're relying on confidential sources, documents that may not be what they appear to be, about throwing these kind of charges, because everybody in America now is a media critic."[16] To Kurtz, the power of journalists to base their usage of unnamed sources on their authority as professionals began to dissipate in the face of a media environment in which news audiences easily became critics capable of publicizing their disdain for opaque news practices.

Given the authoritative stakes at play, many journalists responded to the bloggers' victorious rhetoric with uneasiness or even animosity. To protect the authoritative underpinnings of their practices, journalists derided blogs for lacking a set system of sourcing routines, editorial oversight, or fact-checking resources to ensure the accuracy of their posts. Jonathan Klein, a former CBS News executive, marked out this distinction in a much-quoted remark made on the *O'Reilly Factor:* "It's an important moment because you couldn't have a starker contrast between the multiple layers of checks and balances and a guy sitting in his living room in his pajamas writing."[17] Critics of blogs set up a contrast between journalism as a responsible enterprise and blogs as a capricious lot of opinion-driven scribes. On a deeper level, the implied distinction contrasted the norms of journalism as an objective observer, and therefore invested in the accurate relay of facts, with norms of blogging stressing subjectivity and transparency. To counter blogs, journalists asserted that their institutionalized system performed remarkably well in catching mistakes given the time constraints on news production.[18] Yet how convincing this argument was deserves reflection. Certainly, this vaunted system has let through mistakes, as the prewar reporting failures demonstrated. It is not a stretch to attribute at least part of the increase in blog audiences to growing disenchantment with the work of traditional news outlets.

Beyond Blogs: Bias as Explanation

It is likely that the *60 Minutes* story, with its reliance on unattributed documents, its involvement of Dan Rather, and its potential damage to President Bush, would have drawn accusations of political bias at any time. But its airing less than two months before the 2004 presidential election resulted in the unequivocal judgment by critics on the right that the piece was a deliberate attempt to undermine Bush's reelection bid. This episode demonstrated the power of bias allegations to short-circuit attempts to verify content by providing an easy explanation of what went wrong.

When sources go unnamed, allegations of political bias find ample support by arranging what little is known into a coherent narrative in which the missing pieces add up to politically motivated malfeasance. With the Killian memos story, from the start skeptical conservatives stymied any alternative explanations by declaring that "the *only explanation* for CBS's gung-ho-ness in airing it despite misgivings is bad bias, not bad judgment."[19] With the "inarguable"[20] explanation that bias "clearly and unmistakably . . . took over at CBS,"[21] partisanship came to be commonly understood as the only possible explanation for the errant reporting. The severity of this implied bias became magnified to the point that the interpretive community of conservative media critics imbued the Killian memos story with historical importance as a critical incident stripping away journalism's proclaimed neutrality to expose a systematic effort to discredit the right. It became what a *New York Post* columnist called "broadcast journalism's Watergate" by providing a "smoking gun" of elite journalism's liberalism.[22]

Charges of bias often linked the timing of the story during the election season with its attachment to Dan Rather—a longtime lightning rod for charges of liberal bias. Critics asserting Rather's liberalism drew from a reservoir of past evidence, including two key moments in his career repeatedly recounted in print and broadcast stories. First, in an exchange with President Richard Nixon at a 1974 news conference during the height of the Watergate scandal, Rather received a vocal response from the crowd when he got up to ask a question. Nixon asked Rather, "Are you running for something?" and Rather responded, "No, sir, Mr. President, are you?" Later, as *CBS Evening News* anchor, Rather entered into a heated on-air debate with Vice President George H. W. Bush in 1988 over his involvement in the Iran-Contra Affair.

These two events were widely hailed by conservatives as evidence of Rather's leftist bias and his desire to help defeat Republican presidents. Rather also gained notoriety from the right as the target of Bernard Goldberg's 2001 best-selling book: *Bias: A CBS Insider Exposes How the Media Distort the News*. Around the same time, the Web site www.ratherbiased.com started to catalogue evidence of Rather's liberalism.[23]

Conservative critics interpreted the Killian memos story as vindicating decades of Rather criticism: "Rather's apparent liberal, Democrat bias has come home to roost," one column read.[24] In particular, Rather's political leanings provided a subject for cable news talk shows. On MSNBC, Pat Buchanan framed the debate in terms of a conservative victory,[25] while guests on CNN's *Crossfire* twice argued over whether Rather favored Democrats over Republicans (November 23, 2004, and March 9, 2005). At times, criticisms of Rather turned vehement. One *New York Post* columnist began, "Dan Rather, the most recognized talking parrot in TV news, single-handedly removed the 'C' for 'credibility' in the CBS logo—and turned the country's venerable broadcast propaganda machine forever into the network of BS."[26] The Killian memos story joined with this running narrative of Rather's politics, despite his minimal involvement in the story. Rather, occupied with the Republican National Convention in New York and a hurricane in Florida, had not been part of the preplanning or editing of the story. Even still, among conservatives, the schema for Rather was already set and the Killian memos story fit squarely with the community's preexisting beliefs.

Aside from Rather, conservative critics took aim at the story's producer, Mary Mapes. Earlier in the 2004, Mapes headed the *60 Minutes* story breaking the Abu Ghraib prison abuse scandal in Iraq—another story damaging to the Bush administration.[27] Critics portrayed her five-year pursuit of Bush's Texas Air National Guard records as driven by political bias rather than legitimate journalistic reasons. With the *60 Minutes* story, the focus fell on her actions in putting Bill Burkett, the unnamed source who gave CBS the memos, in touch with Joe Lockhart of the Kerry campaign.[28] Lockhart did talk to Burkett, but only once in a short telephone call regarding the anti-Kerry Swift Boat Veterans for Truth ads. Mapes admitted to putting Burkett in contact with the campaign, but denied it was part of an exchange. Nonetheless, conservative critics asserted that CBS News colluded with the Kerry campaign to attack Bush. Mapes was chastised—and not just from the right—for speaking with the Kerry campaign. On CNBC, host Lawrence Kudlow asked a Kerry campaign representative, "When Mary Mapes is either forced to resign or voluntarily resigns from CBS, which is coming any second now, are you going to hire her at the DNC?"[29] On Fox News, Sean Hannity ironically channeled Republican Senator Howard Baker's famous questioning of Nixon's involvement in Watergate by asking: "The question is, what did John Kerry, Terry McAuliffe and Joe Lockhart know about forged documents, and when did they know it?"[30] This was an effort to extend the scandal beyond CBS News to infect the Kerry campaign in the months before the election.

Beyond the explanatory labor situating the Killian memos story as an example of political bias in no uncertain terms lay a broader attempt to cast it as indicative of a common liberal bias among mainstream journalists. The case came to signify not an isolated incident, but political bias encroaching on all levels of news. *Washington Post* columnist Charles Krauthammer wrote, "This is not an isolated case. In fact the case is a perfect illustration of an utterly commonplace phenomenon: the mainstream media's obliviousness to its own liberal bias."[31] Mike Barnicle, who had been embroiled in his own journalistic controversy for fabricating sources while at the *Boston Globe*, echoed this sentiment: "The larger issue is the slow, steady progression of isolation, condescension, arrogance, and the cultural divide between big media, especially big Eastern media, and the customers, the people who buy the papers, the people who watch the TV shows."[32] Efforts to add institutional-level meaning elevated the Killian memos story from an isolated event to the status of a critical incident; it became an incident that could not be explained or ignored in an isolated manner. For this reason, the Killian memos controversy created a much-publicized opportunity for conservatives to position unnamed sources as a tactic journalists use to surreptitiously promote a leftist political agenda. The indictment of the *60 Minutes* story became an indictment of unnamed source–driven stories in general, and especially stories questioning the Bush administration.

Promoting New (Conservative) Forms of News

The action of publicly identifying a problem is often followed by declaring a solution. For conservatives chalking up the cause of the errors at CBS News to pervasive bias, the way forward meant circumventing mainstream news with its disingenuous mask of objectivity and political agenda-driven deployment of anonymity. New—and presumably conservative—media forms were heralded for providing alternative perspectives. For example, Sean Hannity asserted that "talk radio has become popular to fill a void of bias and political agendas like" with the *60 Minutes* story.[33] Hannity and others applauded efforts to expand into other media formats as a way to mitigate what was seen as a limited media sphere. Syndicated columnist Cal Thomas illustrated this viewpoint in his praise of new outlets: "The journalistic equivalent of the Berlin Wall has fallen, and millions are enjoying a new birth of informational freedom they had not previously known. This may not be good for the elite press, but it is great for the people, who feel empowered beyond letters to the editor."[34] This perspective equated the shift away from traditional news outlets to the democratizing of news through the infusion of a greater variety of opinions and topics. Commentators such as Thomas viewed such shifts as counterhegemonic and productive. However, it is unclear what ends he and others like him have in mind. Thomas struck a pluralistic tone, but one primarily supporting the growth of conservative media voices. In this way, arguments like those of Thomas and Hannity upheld the self-interest of many of the conservative commentators already operating—and profiting— outside of traditional news channels. Conservative critics worked to both limit mainstream reporting critical of their political interests and to promote their own media as authoritative and trustworthy.

Disapproval of this self-serving discourse encouraging a shift away from traditionally dominant news outlets arose in arguments countering the normative vision of blogs as a "fifth estate" keeping watch over the news. Several critics pointed out that the bloggers responding to the Killian memos story were not objective fact-checkers, but highly partisan individuals driven to discredit any reporting not in alignment with their worldview. Their interests were not in policing the accuracy of news outlets according to the standards of objective journalism but in presenting and protecting a political perspective. In the *Washington Post,* Tina Brown dismissed the idealized blogger: "Cyberspace is populated by a coalition of political obsessives and pundits on speed who get it wrong as much as they get it right."[35] Similarly, *Newsweek*'s Steven Levy questioned bloggers' pledge to "fact-check Big Media's a—" by focusing on the underlying motivations of bloggers in attacking the reporting of mainstream news outlets.[36] The *60 Minutes* controversy could be better understood as a victory for conservative bloggers in creating a crisis of credibility for an elite news outlet. By contrast, liberal bloggers were mainly shut out of mainstream news discourse responding to the Killian memos story. Despite raising serious questions, efforts by these bloggers to discredit the claims of forgery did not circulate through the news.[37] This one-sidedness indicates that attempts to portray this incident as a triumph for new media confuse the medium with the broader conservative attack against journalism.

Journalists also questioned whether the entire frame of conservative blogs defeating mainstream media was simply overstated. Beyond the initial push in the first twenty-four hours, the story gained strength only when traditional news outlets devoted resources to it. "While bloggers uncovered technical holes in the *60 Minutes* story, the reason Rather fell so quickly was that mainstream media nailed this story," wrote columnist Debra Saunders.[38] The story "gained credence in America's newspapers" as the *Washington Post, New York Times,* and *Dallas Morning News* did their own investigative work into the story.[39] Meanwhile, a review of the evidence offered by blogs presented their case as questionable.[40] Through these arguments, journalists worked to transform a story about a crisis at one traditional news outlet into an example of good journalistic work by others digging into the reporting of the story—even if they ignored the story's original claims.

Chastising CBS News: Reactions from Journalists

Political bias was not the only oversimplified frame for understanding what happened at CBS News. The journalistic community countered claims of partisan motives by attributing the flawed unnamed sourcing practices to mistakes made because of competitive pressures. In this narrative, CBS News got caught up in chasing a provocative story sought by other news outlets in the midst of a heated election. In its haste, it wound up committing serious errors involving the basic mechanics of the story by failing to properly confirm the authenticity of the memos or Bill Burkett's claims.[41] As with the prewar reporting mistakes, the poor use of unnamed sources in the face of competitive pressures led to the dissemination of a story that should not have been released.

In striking the position that competitive pressures contributed to sloppy reporting, the journalistic community unfortunately tended to automatically accept the falsity of the overall Killian memos story instead of seeking to further investigate and verify or dispute its merits. Aside from scant efforts to corroborate the reporting, journalistic opinion coalesced around a narrative of the report as both flawed *and* false, which contributed to a shared self-protective reaction across the broader journalism community and a way to combat the conservative charges of bias. While it was the overwhelming response among journalists, this course did irk some, including bloggers on the left, who felt it unduly distracted attention from the underlying issue. As a blogger on the Daily Kos Web site noted after the election, "The only victor was the White House, which still is enjoying the temporary reprieve from increasingly solid evidence that . . . Bush [was] almost certainly absent without leave."[42] The focus on reporting practices at the expense of the story's content effectively silenced any attempt to examine the merit of the serious claims that were levied. It also ignored the larger issue of conservatives using media criticism as a tool to neutralize potentially damaging stories.

The flawed journalism argument gained strength when details about how the Killian memos story was put together began to emerge following Rather's apology. Journalists criticized CBS News for relying on a single unnamed source, Burkett, without proper corroboration. This went against the accepted practice of requiring a second source to independently verify information, a deficiency that would haunt *Newsweek* months later. Coupled with the failure to identify the origins of the memos, the journalists "trapped themselves," as the Poynter Institute's Bob Steele told NPR.[43] *60 Minutes* was never able to definitively establish the authenticity of the documents and exaggerated the claims of its experts.[44]

The disdain directed at CBS News for its unnamed sourcing practices in the Killian memos story occurred through a variety of public means, including editorials in large and small newspapers immediately following the September 20 apology. Speaking in the unauthored, collective voice of the newspaper, these editorials constructed, in specific ways, a perspective of CBS News as "either sloppy or duped" while directly countering partisan motives espoused by conservative critics.[45] The *Palm Beach Post* dismissed bias claims explicitly: "Those who define 'liberal media' as any news organization that doesn't print or broadcast in lockstep with the White House claimed to have convicted CBS on the felony charge of biased journalism. In fact, it seems more like a simple case of failing to do the basics."[46] In criticizing CBS News for its failure to follow proper verification routines, these editorials presented the solution as procedural, not structural. This was made clear in a recurring trope of CBS News failing "Journalism 101"—a view that simplified errors while suggesting that the journalists involved should have recognized their mistakes.[47] The avoidance of a nuanced examination of how unnamed sourcing practices function eerily resembled the certitude underlying claims of bias offered by conservatives. By eschewing complexity, journalists were able to chastise CBS News while offering assurances that their own news organizations' practices and procedures guard against such mistakes.

Efforts to establish distance from CBS News bespoke an anxiety neatly encapsulated by a *Washington Post* editorial: "No news organization can watch the debacle unfolding at CBS without experiencing an institutional shudder."[48] As the last chapter showed, problems with unnamed source–based reporting—now abundantly clear in the autumn of 2004—along with earlier fabrication scandals involving Jayson Blair at the *New York Times* and

Jack Kelley at *USA Today* heightened concerns over credibility within the journalistic community. *Chicago Sun-Times* media writer Phil Rosenthal wrote: "With public trust in traditional media now challenged almost daily, this is the kind of lapse that hurts all legitimate news outlets by widening the credibility gap."[49] Such commentaries brought into relief contradictory elements of news competition. Individually, news outlets compete for stories and sources—a major motive for the decision by *60 Minutes* to speed up the Killian memos story. From this competitive perspective, a damaging controversy at one news outlet would drive audiences to another outlet. At the same time, blemished stories reverberate across journalism. For example, the Killian memos story reinforced accusations that unnamed sources were being used deceitfully—not just within CBS News but at other outlets as well. This dynamic exposes the tension between news outlets battling each other individually for stories, audiences, reputation, and advertisers while depending on a collective notion of journalistic authority in which concerns over public opinion and legal rights intertwine.

With anxiety over credibility running high, the Killian memos story became an entrée into discussions of structural constraints plaguing the use of unnamed sources within contemporary journalism. The daunting demands of competition and emphasis on profits led to "a conspiracy of the marketplace," in the words of Robert Thompson, that made network news reporting more difficult.[50] Changing economic forces prioritizing profits in television news reduced journalistic judgment: "TV news in general has been given over to the bean counters, who believe that whoever gets the story on the air first is the winner in the bottom line department."[51] Journalists struggled with the growing impetus for news outlets located within larger media conglomerates to reap profits. In the *Wall Street Journal*, former network news executive Av Westin lamented how an emphasis on economics and ratings infringed on journalistic autonomy: "The men and women who are now in senior positions at the networks got their training in a period when ratings and profit started to trump editorial decisions"[52]—a claim that Dan Rather would later iterate in a lawsuit aimed at the management of CBS News (discussed below). Several articles reviewing the Killian memos story cited the negative effect of drastic news cuts made by Laurence Tisch when he owned CBS in the 1980s.[53] More generally, Project for Excellence in Journalism director Tom Rosenstiel connected declines in resources to reporting mistakes: "Television news [outlets] . . . pay their anchors more and they've been cutting the salaries of their reporting staff and they've been cutting the size of their reporting staff. And, you know, there are risks to that."[54] Money invested in star anchors rather than producers and other staff members resulted in fewer available personnel to work on verifying stories. While such cuts worked economically, they threatened the news-gathering and fact-checking abilities of news outlets.

60 Minutes, specifically, faced the challenge of competing with entertainment programming in prime time. The September 8, 2004, *60 Minutes* broadcast featuring the Killian memos story finished second in its 8 P.M. Wednesday timeslot to the drama *Hawaii* on NBC.[55] As a network, CBS intended for *60 Minutes* to draw audiences to make money in the same way as a game show or situation comedy. In fact, CBS cancelled the Wednesday edition of *60 Minutes* in May 2005 following declining ratings.[56] Even though the journalistic community promoted refocusing on news as the core of these programs, the networks expected them to create profits and compete against other programming. Bob Zelnick noted the danger arising in this shift: "Given the evolution of . . . these prime-time magazine shows, which rely on blockbusters and are borderline entertainment to begin with, I'm surprised there haven't been more of these incidents."[57]

Faced with a vexing array of conflicting competitive, journalistic, and economic pressures, journalists regularly reduced these complex tensions to the dichotomy between speed and accuracy.[58] In particular, CBS News was accused of having "violated the most basic precept of journalism: Get the story first, but first get it right."[59] On NPR, former CBS News executive Marvin Kalb attributed CBS News's reporting mistakes to a ubiquitous— and destructive—drive for news outlets to break stories: "People are under phenomenal pressure to get a story, to get it fast, to get it first, to get it out on the air, to let it be known to all of the bloggers of the world that CBS was two-tenths of one second faster in getting this story on the air than was NBC. This is silly."[60] Similarly, the Portland *Oregonian* dismissed charges of political bias by explaining the motivation of CBS News as "inter-network competition and the never-ending quest for the Get. The Scoop. The proof that the stodgy old networks can still knock the stuffing out of those pesky 24/7 cable news operations."[61] Journalistic norms dictate that no story should be published or aired until it can be completely verified according to each news outlet's standards. In practice, the speed/accuracy dichotomy cannot be so easily placated by the normative emphasis on accuracy given the continual craving for haste arising from the competitive demands felt by news divisions and the reputational striving of journalists to be first with a story. Thus, while members of the journalistic community so roundly criticized CBS News, there remained a fear, as the *Washington Post* openly admitted, that the next slipup may be theirs.

Flaws Trump Bias: The Independent Panel Report

At the start of 2005, months after George W. Bush won reelection in a race in which John Kerry's military record drew vicious attacks while the president's own record escaped further scrutiny, an unresolved murkiness continued to pervade the reporting around the Killian memos story. On January 10, the independent review panel put in place by CBS News to sift through the practices of the story completed its three-and-half-month investigation. The 224-page report faulted the *60 Minutes* staff for failing to properly verify all its information and especially chided the lack of knowledge on the origins of the Killian memos. In keeping with the judgment of the broader journalistic community, *60 Minutes* was guilty of "ignoring basic tenets of journalism."[62] The independent panel blamed a "myopic zeal" to beat the competition for hampering routine steps to verify the story.[63] On ABC's *Nightline,* report coauthor Richard Thornburgh singled out the emphasis on speed: "The big culprit was haste."[64] He repeated this claim on PBS's *NewsHour.*[65]

Upon the public release of the report, CBS president Leslie Moonves fired producer Mary Mapes and asked for the resignation of three news executives. CBS News president Andrew Heyward and Rather did not face a reprimand. Meanwhile, the report led to further newspaper editorials chastising CBS News while reaffirming reporting standards involving unnamed sources.[66]

Aside from rebuking the practices behind the Killian memos story, the report was notable in two ways. First, the panel refused to judge whether the memos were authentic or fraudulent. Coincidentally, around the time of the independent panel report, a *Columbia Journalism Review* reexamination deemed the early evidence presented on blogs to be inadequate. The article excoriated these initial arguments, stating, "CBS's critics are guilty of many of the very same sins" as CBS News because "much of the bloggers' vaunted fact-checking was seriously warped. Their driving assumptions were often drawn from flawed information or based on faulty logic. Personal attacks passed for analysis."[67] Problematic evidence was made worse by its unquestioned reproduction and amplification by traditional news outlets. While CBS News did err, the article concluded, the resulting coverage had its own serious deficiencies. This criticism refashioned bloggers' notion of verification as merely repetition, which undercut the original lionizing of the role performed by blogs.

With the independent panel passing on the opportunity to judge the authenticity of the Killian memos, their status as real or fake remained uncertain. Many of the initial technical issues raised turned out to be untrue—

partly because of the ambiguity caused by releasing low quality copies of the documents that had been both photocopied and faxed. Subsequent issues were raised regarding the content of the memos, but their authenticity continued to be disputed.

In another area of disagreement, the report explicitly denied the presence of liberal bias as a motive for airing the story. This conclusion met with immediate dismay and denials from conservative critics who, over a four-month span, consistently held political bias to be the lone cause. Most visibly, the *Weekly Standard* magazine responded with a cover story calling the report a "whitewash."[68] The Media Research Center's Brett Bozell disregarded the report findings by reiterating the bias allegation: "This story was a political hatchet job, based on forged documents, and it was broadcast to the American public because of the liberal bias entrenched at CBS."[69] In the *New York Post*, columnist John Podhoretz challenged the report's findings by reinterpreting the information it contained as clear evidence of bias.[70] Pat Buchanan went even further by labeling what *60 Minutes* did a "criminal conspiracy."[71] Because the narrative of CBS News as politically biased remained central to the portrayal of widespread bias among elite news outlets, conservatives were unable to relinquish the motivation for the story as anything else but an obvious product of leftist motivations. Even after the report and its Republican coauthor dismissed partisan intentions, conservative critiques continued to place political bias at the heart of the story.

The Exit—and Return—of Dan Rather

On November 23, 2004, in the interim before the release of the independent investigation's findings and a few weeks after Bush's reelection, Rather announced he would step down as anchor of the *Evening News* while remaining a correspondent for *60 Minutes*. His last broadcast as anchor came on March 9, 2005, the twenty-fourth anniversary of his appointment as CBS anchor replacing Walter Cronkite. In the past, Rather had discussed retiring after twenty-five years; the controversy was widely viewed as hastening his departure.[72] It was also surmised that Rather chose to announce his decision before the report's findings were released to avoid the perception of being forced out. After a short interim, Rather was replaced by NBC *Today Show* anchor Katie Couric, who struggled to increase the program's sliding ratings.[73]

Rather did not fade away after anchoring the *Evening News* for the final time. In September 2007, nearly three years to the day following his on-air apology for the Killian memos story, Rather announced a $70 million lawsuit against CBS News for breach of contract and for damaging his reputa-tion by forcing him to apologize and take the blame for the Killian memos story.[74] Rather's lawyer described his client's "national reputation for excellent, non-partisan, independent journalism" as "intentionally damaged by CBS, Viacom and their senior executives, who sacrificed independent journalism for corporate financial interests."[75] Rather defended his actions by appearing on CNN's *Larry King Live* on September 20, 2007. He dismissed monetary motivations for the suit and instead suggested that the principle underlying his actions was that "democracy cannot survive, much less thrive, with the level of big corporate and big government interference and intimidation in news." He repeated this claim several times during the interview, noting that the management at CBS News "sacrificed support for independent journalism for corporate financial gain." Rather labeled the independent review panel "a fraud" and a "setup," asserted that "the facts of the story were true," and admitted he "didn't want to apologize" on air about the conduct of the report-ing.[76] Rather continued to situate his suit within this normative journalistic framework as the case was battled over in the courts. As the suit progressed, Rather noted: "It puts us on the road to finding out what really happened involving a big corporation and powerful interests in Washington and their intrusion in the newsroom."[77]

Efforts by Rather to establish a symbolic component to the suit met with resistance from many, including belittlement by a CBS News spokesperson who called it "nothing more than an intrusive and expensive fishing expedi-tion."[78] Much of the criticism stemmed from Rather's assertion that he had only occupied a supervisory position. A former *60 Minutes* producer dis-missed Rather's claims: "I think he's gone off the deep end, or should I say deeper end."[79] The *Philadelphia Inquirer* blasted Rather's actions as shirking responsibility for the reporting.[80]

Other critics ascribed motives to Rather beyond his normative claims. His actions were viewed as a "self-inflicted wound,"[81] since the suit was destined to lead to harsh examinations if it made it to open court. Others labeled it "sad," including Tucker Carlson,[82] and all three of Howard Kurtz's panelists in a discussion on *Reliable Sources*.[83] *Newsweek* magazine's Conventional Wisdom Watch summed up the suit as "the whole thing's pathetic."[84] Meanwhile, on Fox News, Bill O'Reilly called the suit a "revenge play,"[85] and wondered, "Is Dan Rather trying to destroy CBS?"[86] while later dismissing network news as "obsolete dinosaurs."[87]

While Rather anticipated publicizing issues around corporate news own-ership, his suit unintentionally exposed doubts concerning the role of star anchors in the actual news-gathering process. Rather, while atypically inclined to working in the field, admitted in the suit to his "scant involvement" in reporting the story.[88] This excuse raised the issue of just what the proper journalistic role of a television anchor should be. NPR's Daniel Schorr referred to the active news anchor as "a myth" and instead relegated his or her chief role as "the public face of a news collection enterprise."[89] *Washington Post* columnist Eugene Robinson noted that "the reality of TV news" is that "high-priced talent is stretched way too thin to get bogged down in the details of every story."[90] The *Houston Chronicle* put it as "the mighty network anchor is revealed for what he or she is, merely a familiar face reading from a teleprompter reports he or she had nothing to do with preparing."[91]

Television news has evolved in a manner in which often the familiar journalistic faces are not responsible for the bulk of the news work that goes on out of sight. Yet journalistic authority rests on an image of the star anchor as knowledgeable and closely tied to the news.[92] The context of this discussion cannot be overlooked. The vaunted evening network newscasts failed to halt a two-decade-long ratings decline that produced anxiety and calls for either thorough reimagining or outright cancellation. With CBS, critics assailed Katie Couric as a lightweight journalist—an argument that presupposes a role for an anchor beyond news reader. In the face of challenges, it was unclear just what television news anchors were supposed to do. Of course, as long as they drew outsized paychecks—as Rather certainly did—fewer resources would be available to other areas of news production.

Rather's suit progressed slowly in 2007 and 2008, surviving initial legal challenges from CBS News before being thrown out in September 2009. While Rather never received his day in court, the discovery process did bring to light the careful selection of the independent panel members to appease conservative critics—including the suggestion to bring on a well-known conservative commentator such as Rush Limbaugh or Ann Coulter.[93] From this glimpse, it is clear that the network feared the loss of credibility and audiences in the wake of the Killian memos story as it worked to restore its image.

Conclusion: An Assault on Unnamed Sources

Three years after its initial airing, the Killian memos story was awarded the legacy of "one of the most significant errors in the history of American TV journalism" by the *Philadelphia Inquirer*.[94] The casual appellation indicates that the story did not dissipate with the reelection of President Bush in November 2004 or even with the end of Dan Rather's role as *Evening News* anchor in March 2005. Instead, it has endured as a symbol: for some, of sloppy new reporting; for others, proof of widespread liberal bias; and for still others, the moment when bloggers beat the broadcasters. This array of competing meanings reveals the difficulties journalists face using unnamed sources within a transformed field of public discourse. No longer are assurances of correctly carried out hidden practices enough to quell critics. At the same time, the incident suggests that the accuracy of criticism may be less important that its volume.

Any effort to understand the Killian memos story requires an acknowledgment that competitive pressures—manifested both reputationally and economically—haunt elite news outlets. In the *Washington Post,* Tina Brown summed up the difficult environment for working journalists exposed by the *60 Minutes* controversy: "Every editor, producer and reporter knows that the warp speed of the news cycle means we are all only one step ahead of some career-ending debacle. But still the panic to beat the competition trumps every other concern."[95] Brown's candid remarks situated the Killian memos story not as an aberrant case, but as symptomatic of a tension often metaphorically articulated as a dance between speed and accuracy. Whether seeking scoops about the government's intelligence findings before the Iraq War, Bush's military records during a close election, or, as discussed in the next chapter, the secretive conduct of the so-called "War on Terror," journalists vied against one another to get the story. This competition encourages a turn to anonymity to secure sources quickly, efficiently, and exclusively.

When controversy does surface, the lack of transparency inherent with unnamed sources allows a limited set of known facts to be woven into multiple interpretations serving different authoritative needs for separate interpretive communities. But not all narratives are equal, prompting questions not only about what interpretations develop, but also what ones are left out. From the outset, agreement seemed to coalesce in framing the Killian memos story as a controversy, with little space for CBS News's defense or further investigation into the considerable questions surrounding Bush's National Guard service record. The issue essentially disappeared from the campaign news radar. The trepidation journalists felt to not fall into the same hole as CBS News extended beyond just Bush's service record to encompass any potentially controversial reporting relying on unnamed sources. Robert Thompson identified the true harm of the incident as deadening critical reporting: "Let's say, for example, CBS, just hypothetically tomorrow, or any of the networks, got a hold of a Watergate-like story that required a number of . . . sources that were not identifiable, it would be very hard to prosecute a story like that now, which is not a good thing."[96] In fact, CBS News *did* postpone a story on the Bush administration's use of forged documents to bolster its claims that Iraq was rebuilding its nuclear weapons program. In an ironic twist, that story was scheduled to air on *60 Minutes* on September 8—in place of the Killian memos story—but was bumped to beat the competition over Bush's National Guard service record. Although the forgery story remained ready to air during the last months of the election, CBS News decided to hold it until after November to stave off charges of liberal bias.

The decision by CBS News to hold its story and the dearth of reporting on Bush's record from other outlets raises serious questions over whether journalists will choose to abandon or curtail the use of unnamed sources out of fear of subjecting their own reporting to criticism when covering certain topics. Certainly, the Killian memos story as well as other incidents in this book should encourage newsrooms to review their verification procedures while addressing the detrimental drive for speed. But what should not happen is the abandonment of critical news reporting out of fear of a stormy reaction. If, ultimately, this is to be the legacy of the Killian memos story, it will be one that only hinders journalism.

3

Journalists Fight Back: *Newsweek* and the Koran Abuse Story

> Anonymous sources are like atomic energy—
> beneficial when handled carefully for proper public
> purposes, such as exposing government wrongdoing,
> but dangerous when used without safeguards.
>
> —Clark Hoyt, Knight Ridder
> Washington editor

In the first decade of the twenty-first century, no political topic consumed the American public more than the constellation of actions and policies dubbed the "War on Terror" by the U.S. government. The Bush administration's aggressive multipronged response to the September 11, 2001, attacks in New York and Washington included such visible measures as wars abroad in Iraq and Afghanistan along with clandestine actions occurring across the globe out of public view. A public stunned in the immediate aftermath of the attacks rallied around the nation's institutions, but soon a whole host of policy debates would arise around such issues as privacy, authoritarianism, torture, illegal rendition, surveillance, and deficit spending. As time went on, solidarity gave way to vicious political disagreements grounded in disputes over the very idea of how to act as a citizen.

In this contentious climate, journalists struggled with a shifting balance of seemingly competing interests. The standard self-definition of journalism keeping watch over governmental actions taking place far out of sight of average citizens provided the normative backing to encourage aggressive reporting, seeking out what was happening in the shadowy spaces where the War on Terror was being conducted. Yet this view, however much it buttressed arguments for journalistic authority, came up against the Bush administration's overt framing of this era as nothing less than wartime. Given the extraordinary circumstances, this argument contended, the true public benefit was not in journalistic disclosure, but in journalistic restraint. What's more, covert operations served the public so long as they remained secret. This argument ensured that journalistic efforts to uncover government actions, no matter the findings, would face accusations of being unpatriotic and harmful. This was not a distant concern; in a 2004 poll, 42 percent of respondents judged that journalists "stand up for America" while a near-even 40 percent deemed them "too critical of America."[1] In an era of uncertain economics and concerns over shrinking audiences, the fear of alienating audiences was never far from the surface of discussions about journalism.

In the initial aftermath of the 2001 terrorist attacks, journalists seemed more willing to support administration claims. However, as time went on, the pendulum began to swing toward a renewed journalistic vigor to uncover government actions. Certainly, the failure to find WMDs in Iraq—and the ensuing criticism not only of the government but also of journalists—signaled a need to be vigilant and distrustful of government aims. As journalists struggled to find their voice, they met with consternation from the administration and its supporters. At the nexus of this debate lies the unnamed source. The sensitivity of the War on Terror coupled with an administration intent on controlling its message made the utilization of unnamed sources an undeniable must to expose hidden governmental actions. But, as we have seen, because unnamed sourcing practices necessarily obscure details, they become a target for critics. Such was the case for *Newsweek* magazine when an all-but-ignored story on the mistreatment of terrorist suspects turned into a melee of recriminations and defenses that furthered the ongoing debate over unnamed sources. But before recounting what happened at the magazine, we must attend to how the journalistic community was already confronting the problems of source anonymity around the time of the *Newsweek* incident.

Unease over Unnamed Sources

The decidedly epigraphic tone of a *Columbia Journalism Review* article captured the shifting opinions toward unnamed sources among journalists: "Poor 'Anon.' Once he was the journalist's trusty sidekick . . . now everywhere you look, civic-minded editors and consultants have the broom out and are swatting at 'anonymice.'"[2] The article signaled an ongoing concern that controversies involving unnamed sources hurt journalism at a time when mounting economic pressures, a hostile legal environment, and growing scrutiny from blogs made it more difficult to grant sources anonymity.

That same month, an *Editor & Publisher* cover story similarly surveying the precarious state of unnamed sources connected the use of anonymity to a growing disdain by news audiences: "On the popularity scale, anonymous sources ranked somewhere between steroid-engorged ballplayers and IRS agents."[3] Faced with this growing distrust, news outlets everywhere began formally reevaluating sourcing standards with an eye toward the reduction of unnamed sources: "Nearly all of the nation's major newspapers and news services have either rewritten their policies on sourcing, or at least reminded journalists of their existence—and those on the beat say the message is clear: Back off!"[4] The *Editor & Publisher* article also specified contemporary media scrutiny as making unnamed sources more difficult to use. At the same time, journalists reported sources to be increasingly insistent on anonymity as a precondition for an interview.

While unnamed sources came under fire amidst broader concerns over news credibility, several journalists defended their indispensability when it came to holding officials accountable. Bob Woodward, who famously relied on Deep Throat in uncovering the Watergate scandal, told the *Wall Street Journal:* "I think there's not enough use of unnamed sources, frankly."[5] These defenders struck a democratic chord with their pleas against abolishing anonymity. As NPR's Frank Stasio put it, "Anonymous sources made Watergate. It broke Dan Rather. And it is a question for all of us in a democracy about how we can get information to the public when it is sensitive and when the lives and the jobs of informants are on the line."[6] By reiterating the need for anonymity in certain situations, the discussion of unnamed sources was not entirely negative. However, the ideal of the whistle-blower, while still deemed necessary, appeared more and more a quaint notion often unfamiliar to real journalist–unnamed source relations—a pattern examined in the next chapter.

Controversy at *Newsweek* over unnamed sources occurred alongside efforts by other news organizations to confront problems with the practice. Most notably, the *New York Times* issued a public report in May 2005 on improving its credibility that suggested lengthy alterations to the newspaper's sourcing practices.[7] The report stressed the need to curb the use of unnamed sources and, when they do appear, to convey, as much as possible, information as to who the sources are and why anonymity was granted. The report carried a markedly defensive tone in its attempts to stave off criticism. *Times* editor Bill Keller admitted that the excessive use of anonymity "cheapens the currency of source protection," making it more difficult to continue to guard sources' identities.[8] The *New York Times* report surfaced at a time when other outlets were also rethinking how they used unnamed sources.[9] Following the Jack

Kelley scandal, *USA Today* reworked its policy toward anonymity and saw a 75 percent decline in the number of unnamed sources.[10] The newspaper presented this reduction in the use of unnamed sources as an unambiguously positive development, which reinforced pervasive judgments of anonymity's overuse across journalism.

At the same time the *New York Times* was publicly confronting its un-named sourcing practices, behind-the-scenes efforts aimed to reduce the use of anonymity among White House sources. The Washington bureau chiefs of seven large news organizations initiated this effort in a meeting with White House press secretary Scott McClellan in April 2005 with the purpose of reducing the use of "backgrounders"—nonattributable meet-ings between journalists and officials—to spread information. This was a collective effort by journalists to alter the entrenched use of nonattributed information. *USA Today* Washington bureau chief Susan Page described the administration as "pretty responsive" and noted some initial progress.[11] In all these ways, the journalistic community struggled to account for why its use of unnamed sources so often proved undesirable or controversial. There was, in many places, a real effort to better protect journalism by reining in the problematic uses of confidentiality. However, despite altered policies and pervasive fretting, journalists and sources continued to exchange anonymity for access in a myriad of hidden deals providing audiences with a spectrum of unattributed information. One such exchange would push *Newsweek* into the limelight of journalistic controversy.

Controversy Comes to *Newsweek*

Only two months after Dan Rather's last broadcast as anchor of the *CBS Eve-ning News,* journalists and the public confronted another news controversy involving an unnamed source. This latest incident developed around a short item in the Periscope section in the front pages of *Newsweek*. Page four of the May 9, 2005,[12] issue of *Newsweek* included a 212-word article written by veteran investigative reporter Michael Isikoff and Pentagon correspondent John Barry alleging that an upcoming government report would confirm reports of Koran abuse by the U.S. military at its Guantanamo Bay, Cuba, de-tention facility. The first part of the article read: "Investigators probing abuses at Guantanamo Bay have confirmed some infractions alleged in internal FBI e-mails that surfaced late last year. Among the previously unreported cases, sources tell *NEWSWEEK:* interrogators, in an attempt to rattle suspects, placed Qur'ans on toilets and, in at least one case, flushed a holy book down the toilet."[13] The short article by Isikoff and Barry originally appeared alongside other small news items in the Periscope section of the magazine. It did not spur any further reporting on the conditions at Guantanamo Bay, nor did it instigate any official reaction from the Pentagon or the White House, according to Isikoff.[14] The story remained invisible in the U.S. press. However, it did invoke condemnation from Pakistani politician and former cricket star Imran Khan in a press conference on May 6.[15]

A few days later, the first reported Afghan demonstration occurred on May 10 when a small peaceful protest responding to the Koran abuse allegations took place in Jalalabad, a restive city in the eastern part of Afghanistan near the Pakistani border.[16] The next night, violent protests in Jalalabad resulted in four deaths, according to Agence France Presse (AFP).[17] That same day, the U.S. State Department disavowed any systematic Koran abuse by the U.S. military. Separately, General Richard Myers, chairman of the Joint Chiefs of Staff, publicly negated charges that the *Newsweek* story caused the riots by instead connecting them to internal Afghan politics[18]—an assessment echoed by Afghan president Hamid Karzai.[19] On the next day, May 12, peaceful protests were held in Kabul while violent protests around the country included attacks on United Nations and foreign aid offices. AFP quoted one protestor who blamed the U.S. military presence in Afghanistan: "We're against permanent US bases in Afghanistan. They're invaders, they've done nothing good for Islam."[20] Nonviolent protests occurred in other places including Pakistan, Indonesia, and the Gaza Strip.

Despite the early disavowal of the link between the riots and the story by sources who would normally be considered authoritative, the Afghan violence came to be connected to the *Newsweek* piece in the U.S. press. *Newsweek* was most commonly described as "sparking" the riots. The *Boston Globe* characterized it as "a report that sparked anti-American protests throughout the Muslim world,"[21] while the *CBS Evening News* said that the piece "sparked widespread outrage in the Muslim world."[22] Other outlets used more equivocal language. The *San Francisco Chronicle* described *Newsweek*'s article as having "inspired riots."[23] In addition, a great deal of imprecision permeated the reportage, including the number of deaths and even the nations in which fatalities occurred. In its May 17 edition, *USA Today* listed the number killed in the riots as seventeen in Afghanistan and Pakistan in one article[24] and fifteen in another.[25] The actual mechanics of the riots, and *Newsweek*'s role, rarely received detailed discussion. This lack of information opened up the interpretive space around the riots, making it possible to equate them with poor news practices at *Newsweek*—creating a direct correlation between *Newsweek*'s one source and the death of seventeen people.

The continual suggestion that the Isikoff and Barry article was directly responsible for the riots contributed to pressure on the magazine to respond. *Newsweek* issued an apology on May 15 after its unnamed source withdrew his claim that an upcoming report would include charges of U.S. military personnel flushing a Koran down a toilet. The next day, May 16, *Newsweek* extended its apology into a retraction. The magazine's statement read: "Based on what we know now, we are retracting our original story that an internal military investigation had uncovered Koran abuse at Guantanamo Bay."[26] While imprecise in its wording, the retraction only included the reporting of the upcoming military report. It was *not* extended to dismiss all allegations of Koran abuse or other misconduct at Guantanamo Bay. However, many critics misconstrued the retraction as a full dismissal of abuse charges.

The consistent imprecision concerning both the riots in Afghanistan and the degree of the *Newsweek* retraction mattered because the struggle to define the meaning of the controversy was closely connected to the riots. A thorough assessment of the riots would have required a degree of geographical contextualization largely lacking in news reports. As a result, the ambiguity that resulted from omitting details about the riots allowed critics to unequivocally tie *Newsweek* to the violence, which ratcheted up the consequences of *Newsweek*'s errant reporting. Directly attributing deaths to *Newsweek* raised the severity of the story and increased the visibility of the controversy and the discourse around it. Reporting on *Newsweek* proliferated on the front pages and opinion sections of newspapers, cable news talk shows, and the network evening news. The resulting discussion extended to larger questions of how to report on a government so prone to secrecy in an environment in which journalists were so often criticized.

Blaming an Antimilitary News Bias

On the surface, the onslaught of conservative media critics railing against *Newsweek* appeared to be quite similar to the Killian memos controversy detailed in the previous chapter. In this shared explanatory narrative, when experienced mainstream journalists deviated from accepted unnamed sourcing practices to do a story critical of the Bush administration, it must, in no uncertain terms, be the result of bias by liberal-minded journalists. However, the circumstances of the *Newsweek* incident diverged in key ways from what occurred at *60 Minutes*. While in the previous chapter bias was connected to individuals involved with the story (mostly Dan Rather and producer Mary Mapes), here the focus moved from the individual reporters to broader critiques of political bias against the War on Terror. With the *Newsweek* story, few charges of political bias were directed at the level of the reporters or the news organization. Instead, the bulk of attention focused on journalism more broadly.

The chief obstacle preventing the linking of *Newsweek* with CBS News had to do with the article's reporters: veteran investigative reporter Michael Isikoff and Pentagon correspondent John Barry. Certainly, experience did not insulate reporters from scrutiny over their reporting practices, as criticism received by Judith Miller, Dan Rather, and Bob Woodward in other chapters attests. However, attempts to attribute an individual antimilitary or anti-administration bias came up against Isikoff's reputation for critical reporting on President Bill Clinton during the Monica Lewinsky scandal,[27] including his book: *Uncovering Clinton: A Reporter's Story.*[28] When the Koran abuse controversy emerged, the editor of *Salon* referred to Isikoff's Clinton reporting as protecting him from charges of a leftist bias: "It's absurd for rightist blowhards to try to paint Clinton-critic Isikoff and his editors as part of a vast left-wing conspiracy determined to undermine our troops in Iraq. And they need to be called on their intimidation campaign."[29] Isikoff's record inoculated his reporting from claims of bias regularly dogging Washington reporters while also supplying a basis to counter blanket charges of bias aimed at the news media.

Newsweek also differed from CBS News by more swiftly acknowledging mistakes and by a refusal to reprimand anyone within the organization. Editors quickly confirmed that Isikoff and Barry adhered to the magazine's standards in reporting the story. Editor Mark Whitaker told PBS's *NewsHour* that "everyone behaved professionally."[30] Rather than identify any motivations of deception or bias, *Newsweek* exonerated its staff and declined to further investigate the matter. This went against the internal strife plaguing CBS News and the *New York Times*.

Instead of meticulously dissecting the *Newsweek* story, as they did with CBS News, conservative critics instead accused journalists of possessing an institutionalized antimilitary bias in place since the Vietnam War. This bias permitted relaxed reporting standards for stories disparaging the military. In assailing journalists for gratuitously damaging the image of the U.S. military, these critics promoted norms of citizenry requiring a more supportive journalistic mode. The Koran abuse story, in this way, provoked a larger discussion of appropriate reporting norms during wartime.

One of the loudest critics to connect the *Newsweek* story to widespread bias was Fox News Channel host Bill O'Reilly. In keeping with his broader repertoire of accusing mainstream news organizations of political bias,[31] O'Reilly was quick to explain the *Newsweek* case through a specifically antimilitary bias among journalists. On the day of *Newsweek*'s retraction, he related this bias to the riots in Afghanistan: "The truth is that some news agencies can't wait to get dirt on the military so they can embarrass the Bush administration. Ideological reporting is rampant in this country and it is getting people killed."[32] The following night, O'Reilly dismissed efforts to diffuse blame for the riots, focusing again on the subject of bias: "So let's place the blame where it belongs, on news agencies that are blinded by ideology, and who make mistakes because of that blindness."[33] In making this argument, O'Reilly connected the *Newsweek* story with the earlier *60 Minutes* story on Bush's National Guard service (discussed in the previous chapter). He repeated this claim in his syndicated newspaper column.[34]

In the following days, O'Reilly switched his focus from the *Newsweek* story and the ensuing riots to targeting newspaper editorials branding the administration's harsh reaction to *Newsweek* as hypocritical: "Reading these editorials is like walking through a liberal theme park."[35] O'Reilly charged that a "liberal media cabal" was responsible for this reaction by newspapers. The following night, O'Reilly chastised newspapers for their "group think" while further bemoaning biased newspaper editorial pages.[36] Four days later, O'Reilly labeled the Bush administration a victim of aggressively biased journalism: "Even if you don't like the Bush administration, you have to admit they're really up against it. Many in the American press don't like them, obviously."[37]

Over several days, O'Reilly worked to define the *Newsweek* story as an example of an institutional political bias among journalists. Rather than addressing the individual facts of the Koran abuse story, he and his guests attacked it through broad allegations of political bias among elite news outlets. Thus, leftist ideology—rather than any reporting gaffe—was to blame for the *Newsweek* controversy, and, in an explicit connection, Afghan deaths. This was not an effort to isolate the magazine. Rather, the particularities of the *Newsweek* story along with an interest in what actually occurred in Afghanistan vanished as O'Reilly sought to institutionalize a problematic political bias underpinning a large swath of contemporary journalism. This diagnosis prompted a call for administration-friendly news favoring the interests of the interpretive community of conservative media critics.

O'Reilly was not the lone voice among cable television talk shows trying to bend the *Newsweek* story into an indictment of journalists for possessing an antimilitary bias. The medium provided ample space to such accusations. Elsewhere on the Fox News Channel, Media Research Center president Brent Bozell compared the *Newsweek* story to CBS News's National Guard story and asserted that the press "is so fiercely against the American presence in Iraq and Afghanistan" that it would publish "stories about which they have no confirmation."[38] Bozell offered this argument the same evening on MSNBC's *Scarborough Country,* noting that journalists were "blinded by their hostility to the United States' position in Iraq."[39] On *Fox News Watch,* columnist Cal Thomas said the story "fed into the anti-Bush, anti-military template" that audiences increasingly see in the news.[40] This theme continued the next day on *Fox News Sunday* when *Wall Street Journal* editorial page editor Paul Gigot asserted journalists "just don't trust anything the military does." The *Weekly Standard*'s William Kristol immediately concurred, stating: "There is a liberal, anti-military bias in the media."[41]

Cable news channels provided conservative critics with a national venue to develop shared accusations of bias. As with CBS News, bias served as a frame to guide interpretations of how to treat *Newsweek* while letting the particulars of the incident fall away. The same themes espoused by conservative pundits on television also appeared in a variety of right-leaning print sources, including the *Wall Street Journal* editorial page,[42] the *Washington Times,*[43] the *Boston Herald,*[44] the *New York Post,*[45] and the columns of Rich Lowry[46] and Michelle Malkin.[47]

Criticisms of journalists as biased against the military promoted a normative model of wartime journalism as supportive of military and government action. Journalism was expected to surrender its adversarial stance to support the state's military efforts by subsuming norms of holding power accountable or remaining objective under a patriotic function of supporting the government during war—a stance that seemed to occlude any use of unnamed sources to uncover governmental actions. While this stance was not without its limits, it did place patriotic norms above objectivity norms to suggest that supporting military efforts was an acceptable bias. This argument also connected the left with being antimilitary and, therefore, unpatriotic; it was a double critique of the left and of journalists—with the latter purported to be an offshoot of the former. All of this occurred with little attention to the actual reporting of the *Newsweek* story or Isikoff's previous critical Clinton reporting. Rather, the controversy provided an entry to arguing for less-adversarial wartime journalism and the restriction of acceptable news topics.

At the extreme end of this position, some commentators advocating for patriotic norms of journalistic practice during war held that, even if entirely true, the *Newsweek* story should not have run because of its potential to damage the war effort. This interpretation relied partly on the direct link between the riots and the *Newsweek* article and a belief that the magazine's retraction meant charges of Koran abuse had no merit—both untrue assertions. An editorial in the *New York Post* opposed the negative story on the grounds that it would provide ammunition for anti-U.S. sentiment: "Let's face it: America is at war. Even if the story were true, printing it would give aid and comfort to the enemy, stiffening the resolve of fanatical Islamist jihadists to kill Americans in the field."[48] The *Post* and other critics ignored the individual incident at *Newsweek* to present a broader normative argument judging less-adversarial journalism to be in the public interest during war. A similar argument emerged in response to the breaking of the Abu Ghraib prison scandal a year earlier by *60 Minutes* and the *New Yorker*.[49] The expectation that journalists would restrict their reporting efforts contradicted journalism's self-proclaimed norms of holding power accountable—however uneven in its application. In the end, the battle came down to competing notions of the public interest with the provision of information outside of official government disclosures pitted against support for official policies in an act of unity.

Uncommon Mistakes and Common Pressures

Like with the Killian memos story, the clamoring of conservative media critics to link reporting mistakes to a pervasive liberal media bias clashed with a journalistic community focused on what were judged to be misguided unnamed sourcing practices. This perspective emphasized the reporting mechanics to explain why "*Newsweek* fell on its face," as the *Buffalo News* put it.[50] In many ways, criticisms of *Newsweek*'s reporting practices mapped onto the paradigm repair process proposed by Lance Bennett and colleagues described in the introduction to this book.[51] In this perspective, journalists confront controversies around news practice through constructing the controversy as an isolated deviation from accepted news practices. Individualizing the controversy allows journalists to affix fallibility to individual actors to protect institutional norms and practices from criticism. This occurs through what Stephen Reese describes as a "normalization process" in which journalists both define the characteristics of deviant practice and "reassert journalistic routines."[52] The incident in question is removed from the framework of proper journalism, which comes to be reaffirmed through discourse about the incident.

Journalistic criticisms echoed this model through their excoriation of *Newsweek* for its reliance on a single unnamed source and in interpreting the absence of a Pentagon denial as confirmation. Project for Excellence in Journalism director Tom Rosenstiel chastised *Newsweek* for taking silence from the Pentagon to be tacit approval: "Inferring that if someone doesn't knock your story down that that by implication proves what you're claiming, you know, it's unprofessional. It's sloppy."[53] *Newsweek* was accused of misleading its news audiences into inferring an unwarranted corroboration. Aside from relying on only one source, *Slate*'s Jack Shafer attributed *Newsweek*'s visit to "journalistic purgatory" as the result of allowing an unnamed source to predict the future in the form of an upcoming report.[54] In isolating the controversy, critics focused on the significance of the *Newsweek* story both as an example of the poor use of unnamed sources and for damaging the credibility of journalism. As a result, the controversy was made to stand as a "cautionary tale for all news organizations."[55] Newspapers frequently addressed the *Newsweek* controversy in either an editorial or a column from the editor.[56] Through the forum of the editorial page, newspaper journalists lambasted the sourcing practices involved in the Koran abuse story, calling *Newsweek*'s reporting "careless,"[57] "poor journalism,"[58] "shoddy journalism," and "unprofessional."[59]

Paradigm repair cannot fully account for journalists' discursive practices in the wake of the Koran abuse story. *Newsweek* could be—and was—blamed for flawed reporting practices, but the broader result was a reconsideration of the successes and perils of unnamed sources. This occurred in large part through an interpretive frame stressing the continuity of news controversies as a way of understanding the *Newsweek* incident. Assessments of *Newsweek* frequently situated the Koran abuse story alongside other journalism controversies, such as the CBS News–Killian memos story and *New York Times*–Jayson Blair controversy. In a front page *Washington Post* article, Howard Kurtz remarked on how swiftly the *Newsweek* incident came to be compared to other scandals: "Critics are already pouncing on the story as the latest in a high-profile series of media blunders."[60]

Comparisons to the CBS News–Killian memos story appeared often. The *Newsweek* controversy occurred only a few months after Dan Rather's final broadcast as *CBS Evening News* anchor. On cable news, *Newsweek*-CBS comparisons frequently emerged, especially on the Fox News Channel,[61] but also on CNN[62] and MSNBC.[63] A *Hartford Courant* editorial connected *Newsweek* to CBS: "Were there no lessons learned from the Dan Rather–CBS debacle, in which the source of a *60 Minutes* story about President Bush's service record later proved unreliable?"[64] This parallelism ascribed to the two incidents developed out of their sharing of a paramount obsession with the unreliability of their respective unnamed sources. Whether or not such parallels extended beyond the surface, the use of the *60 Minutes* controversy to apprehend the *Newsweek* one signaled the wide mistrust of unnamed sources brewing within the journalistic community.

Comparisons to CBS News forced *Newsweek* to actively disassociate itself from the practices behind the *60 Minutes* incident. *Newsweek* editor Mark Whitaker made this explicitly clear: "Unlike CBS, we felt we were being extremely forthcoming by publishing all the details and publishing the Pentagon's denials and saying we committed an error."[65] Whitaker lauded his magazine's reaction as more transparent and immediately conciliatory—although the pattern of apology first, retraction second, was widely criticized for not immediately acknowledging the severity of the mishap. *Newsweek* presented its error not as the result of bad journalistic practice, but as an unfortunate circumstance stemming from an incorrect source. In the *Washington Post,* media critic Howard Kurtz contrasted *Newsweek* with CBS News, pointing out that it took the latter twelve days to retract its story while it only took *Newsweek* a little more than a day.[66]

Placing the *Newsweek* story in a succession of controversies enabled the journalistic community to confront broader declines in news credibility that hindered their work. In coupling the *Newsweek* controversy to these past incidents, a *Seattle Post-Intelligencer* columnist wrote, "Witness journalism's latest inductees to the Hall of Shame."[67] Rather than an independent incident, *Newsweek* came to be assessed through a generalized frame identifying negative trends threatening journalism. The parade of scandals was viewed as hampering news reporting efforts: "The media is on trial. The jury is already thinking guilty."[68] By placing unnamed sourcing practices under scrutiny, these discussions elevated the *Newsweek* controversy as a critical incident representing the general problems of unnamed sources in an unfriendly context for journalism.

As with the prewar reporting and CBS News, the journalistic community pinned the overuse and misuse of unnamed sources on unending competitive pressures. Columbia Journalism School Dean Nicholas Lemann identified "scoopmania"—the driving desire to continuously break news—as a culprit in the *Newsweek* controversy as well as others.[69] As with the Killian memos story in the previous chapter, journalists attributed poorly sourced stories to the strain of having to constantly generate news. Journalism's normative emphasis on accuracy faced challenges from the competitive need to produce news texts quickly. *Newsweek,* in particular, exists in a complex competitive nexus consisting of other weekly news magazines, especially *Time* and *US News & World Report,* as well as network and cable television news, the wire services, and several of the larger newspapers. All these outlets vie to generate fresh national and international affairs reporting to supplement the flow of carefully packaged press releases government officials manufacture for the news daily. In contrast to its daily counterparts, *Newsweek* faced the added disadvantage of being a weekly publication. While the magazine is able to report more quickly through its Web site, its print presence remains temporally bound. These reasons compel the magazine, with its weekly circulation of 3.1 million copies in 2005, to differentiate itself with its reporting.[70]

The View from Outside the Beltway

Of course, not all news outlets face the same competitive conditions as *Newsweek,* CBS News, or the *New York Times.* Washington reporting, arguably the most competitive and, in many ways, the most prestigious sector of U.S. journalism, differs from the news-gathering environment of the vast majority of journalists throughout the country. The field of journalism varies not only by medium—perhaps the most obvious division—but also by audience, size, language, region, voice, stature, and so on. The discussion around *Newsweek* demonstrated the diversity of practices amalgamated in any concept of journalism. But more so than the other incidents in this book, the Koran abuse story led many subnational news outlets to vocally question the practices of Washington journalists while differentiating their own. Why this was more salient for the *Newsweek* controversy than the others probably is due to the apparent simplicity of the incident—*Newsweek* did, after all, admit its mistakes—compared to the widespread mistakes of the prewar reporting. The Killian memos story, by contrast, took place in the extremely busy period before the election when journalists and media critics were occupied with many other stories. Also, the framing of the Koran abuse story as the *latest* unnamed source controversy signals a breaking point in which many journalists around the country expressed their dismay that such high-profile incidents continued to happen.

Whatever sparked it, the reaction to the *Newsweek* controversy exposed a rift between Washington and non-Washington news outlets over acceptable unnamed source use. Smaller newspapers articulated their discontent with the practices of journalists at more elite outlets. For example, a *Des Moines Register* editorial situated unnamed sources as a problem for Washington reporting, away from its own experience: "If any good comes of *Newsweek's* embarrassing retraction of an item that sparked anti-American riots in the Muslim world, it will be a new resolve among the Washington press corps to stop using so many unidentified sources."[71] The editor of the *St. Petersburg Times* referred to Washington reporting as the "culture of anonymous quotation."[72] The disdain regional newspapers directed toward the practices of Washington correspondents indicated a schism in accepted news practices.

The divide over unnamed sources at small newspapers and elite news outlets corresponded to the diversity of strategies for pursuing journalistic authority. Smaller newspapers portrayed their limited or nonuse of unnamed sources as a marker of both transparency and their connection to readers instead of sources. By contrast, Washington reporting received criticism for its entrenched reliance on anonymity and worshipping of access. A news editor at the *Lancaster* (Pennsylvania) *Sunday News* explicitly indicated this contrast: "Relatively little of this goes on at hometown papers like this one; in Washington, though, it's de rigueur."[73] Similarly the managing editor of the *Marshfield* (Wisconsin) *News-Herald*—with a daily circulation of 11,588[74]—pointed to the "clear divide between the big media and thousands of working journalists around the globe."[75] This comment positioned elite journalism as atypical in the broader context of what may be considered news. The editor of the *Decatur* (Illinois) *Herald & Review* contrasted his newspaper's reporting practices with those of Washington journalists where "off-the-record briefings are part of the daily routine."[76]

For these newspapers, authority did not rest on producing insider accounts of national stories but in connecting their reporting to the communities in which the newspapers were embedded. In serving this end, these journalists viewed unnamed sources as a disservice to readers for inhibiting transparency. By distancing their practices from Washington reporting, local news outlets highlighted discrepancies of acceptable unnamed sourcing practice across news outlets even in the same medium. The lesson is not to treat all journalists as operating within a homogenous interpretive community, but to recognize a community possessing a mix of views concerning appropriate news practices.

The gulf between the sourcing practices of small and large news outlets is not so neat as editorials so often described it. Attempts at creating stark divisions are complicated by the intermeshing of local news, created under its own rubrics, with content from other news outlets produced under other rules. Specifically, small papers restricting anonymity in original reporting faced difficulty when having to rely on news from other sources—both wire services and other newspapers—using unnamed sources in ways that conflicted with local sourcing rules. An editorial in the *Lancaster* (Ohio) *Eagle-Gazette,* a newspaper with a daily circulation of 13,166,[77] noted that despite a local no–unnamed source rule, it carried wire reporting rife with unnamed sources: "These stories are most always based out of Washington, where granting anonymity almost is a tradition."[78] Because they lacked the resources to conduct their own Washington reporting, smaller newspapers relied on news stories that employed practices that went against their reporting standards. Despite external origins, these stories still appeared under the banner of the newspapers in which they were printed, implicating their culpability when stories became contested. Yet these newspapers were compelled to participate to meet the competitive needs of supplying a mixture of local and nonlocal content. In this way, the differences between outlets collapsed under the constant intermeshing that occurred. Problems at one outlet easily spread to infect a much larger swathe of news, sparking resentment and concern.

Fighting Back Against the Administration

While the *Newsweek* Koran abuse story occupied the journalistic community with another controversy to confront and control, discussions of what happened spilled over from the confines of the story to a public clash with the Bush administration over its heavy-handed press tactics. This reaction came about as a rejoinder to members of the administration who continued to blame the Afghan violence on *Newsweek* despite the early dismissal of *Newsweek*'s culpability by General Myers.[79] In particular, White House Press Secretary Scott McClellan and Pentagon spokesperson Larry DiRita consistently admonished *Newsweek*. Betraying the standard calm demeanor endemic to spokespersons, DiRita blasted *Newsweek*'s unnamed government source: "People are dead because of what this son of a bitch said."[80] McClellan repeatedly criticized *Newsweek,* stating in a press conference: "One of the concerns is that some media organizations have used anonymous sources that are hiding behind that anonymity in order to generate negative attacks."[81]

Ironically ignoring the regular insistence of off-the-record interviews by members of the Bush White House, McClellan critiqued the lack of transparency of unnamed sources and insinuated the culpability of news organizations for allowing them. The assault on *Newsweek,* according to an anonymous Bush adviser quoted in the *New York Times,* was a strategic move intended to gain favorable future coverage: "No White House is ever going to love the way it's covered—you have to highlight those places where there is a screw-up."[82] This quote indicated a desire by the White House to use the *Newsweek* story to stymie reporting on Guantanamo Bay as well as future critical reporting uncovering unseen governmental practices. As with other critics, these spokespersons attributed reporting mistakes to an antimilitary bias by journalists while simultaneously advancing a normative argument that promoted placing patriotic duties above a watchdog role during wartime.

Faced with administration rancor over unnamed sources, the journalistic community responded with a level of indignation absent in the previous two chapters. Journalists at both large news outlets and smaller newspapers signaled their frustration with governmental press management tactics. While not dismissing *Newsweek* from shoddy journalism, this anger expanded the significance of the *Newsweek* story to include scrutiny of how the Bush administration regularly manipulated journalists. As Chris Hanson noted in the *Washington Post:* "Journalists must deal with an administration whose penchant for secrecy has grown only stronger since 9/11."[83] While it may be the nature of officials to protect their interests, Jane Kirtley indicated that the Bush administration increased the need for anonymity in order to gain access: "This is one of the most secretive administrations in U.S. history, which really gives journalists no choice other than to rely on anonymous sources if they want to report anything other than government handouts."[84]

This dynamic placed journalists at a disadvantage. They were forced to trade anonymity for access, which had the effect of reducing journalists to "hapless conduits" through which official statements passed.[85] In addition, the blame for the overuse of unnamed sources often fell to the news outlet rather than to the source. *Washington Post* reporter Dana Priest expressed her aggravation: "We get bashed for all the anonymous sources but the administration is the one that insists on it."[86] This anger arose, in part, because journalists felt forced to participate in a sourcing dynamic that worked to their disadvantage in order to generate stories in a competitive news environment. The Koran abuse story created an opening for journalists to publicly discuss and address this frustration.

Journalists explicitly rebuked the administration for using the *Newsweek* controversy to obstruct investigative reporting on the treatment of Guantanamo Bay detainees. An editorial in the *Washington Post* accused the administration of waging "a cynical campaign to capitalize politically while deflecting attention from serious issues."[87] This theme of distraction was echoed elsewhere, including by *Editor & Publisher* Editor Greg Mitchell: "So it seems to me that the White House, in taking the offensive here in trying to put *Newsweek* on the ultradefensive, may be trying to forestall future work by *Newsweek* in this area."[88] In the *New Yorker,* Hendrik Hertzberg wrote: "Is it really necessary at this late date to point out that the problem is torture and abuse, not dubiously sourced reports of torture and abuse?"[89] Unlike the CBS News case, the administration tactic of focusing on the reporting practices to distract from the content of the reporting became a topic of scrutiny all its own. These critics brought to light administration efforts to chastise journalists in the face of undesirable reporting.

The stark divergence from the *60 Minutes*–Killian memos story eight months earlier raises the question of why journalists treated these two controversies in such distinctly different ways. In one view, the *Newsweek* incident was the inversion of what occurred with the Killian memos story. In September 2004, with less than two months before the election, George W. Bush's military record was an ongoing news story until criticisms of *60 Minutes* by the administration and other conservatives impeded further investigative work on Bush's Texas Air National Guard service record. After controversy overtook CBS News, the story vanished. By contrast, Michael Isikoff admitted that the *Newsweek* story had generated absolutely no attention to the treatment of prisoners at Guantanamo Bay following its publication.[90] However, following the magazine's apology and retraction, the *Newsweek* case provoked *more* attention toward Guantanamo. The controversy propelled other news outlets and the U.S. government to examine what was happening in Cuba. The *New York Times*[91] and *Washington Post*[92] ran stories recounting other Koran desecration charges as did a *Chicago Tribune* editorial.[93] The *NBC Nightly News* aired a segment on charges of prisoner torture in Afghanistan.[94] That same day, the *New York Daily News* broke a story about a U.S. soldier in Guantanamo Bay who had been reprimanded for Koran abuse—although the abuse was not specified.[95] This attention demonstrated how criticism of *Newsweek*'s reporting practices backfired. Thrusting the unnoticed story into public view provoked reconsiderations of the Iraq War, prewar intelligence, prisoner detainment, torture, and government-press relations—all subjects the administration would have preferred be left silent.

While the administration deflected intelligence failures onto untrustworthy Iraqi exiles (as discussed in chapter 1) and ended reporting on Bush's Guard service by attacking CBS News (discussed in chapter 2), its assault on *News-*

week was roundly condemned. As one columnist put it, "What this White House is good at—all it's really good at—is deflecting blame for its own catastrophic blunders by diverting attention."[96] This deflection occurred through a strategy Josh Marshall of the blog Talking Points Memo summarized as the administration "trying to decapitate another news organization."[97] Elsewhere, *Salon* extended this critique to accuse the administration of being fundamentally opposed to journalism: "With increasing forcefulness, Bush has tried to undermine the legitimacy of the media, or at least that subculture within it that shows any tendency to challenge him."[98] In its showdown with a disapproving White House, the interpretive community of journalists fell back on the watchdog norm as under siege and, therefore, a rallying point. Of course, by taking this tack, journalists accomplished their own deflection from the problems of unnamed sources by switching the focus to the Bush administration's press management tactics. As such, the particulars of what *Newsweek* did—along with the willingness of reporters to issue anonymity— melted away in favor of a moment of revolt against the White House.

Journalistic counterattacks commonly accused the Bush administration of hypocrisy for ignoring its own poorly sourced prewar intelligence claims two years earlier. For the administration to then chastise *Newsweek* was, in the words of *Washington Post* columnist Richard Cohen, the "height of hypocrisy."[99] Syndicated columnist Leonard Pitts Jr., in a mock letter to Bush, wrote: "I'm pleased by your concern for *Newsweek*'s accuracy. And I'm wondering if this means you will soon evince similar concern for your own."[100] In particular, newspaper editorials taking umbrage against the Bush administration's criticisms of *Newsweek* often showed their anger by recalling the administration's abhorrent record of faulty prewar intelligence based on dissembling Iraqi exiles as detailed in chapter 1. The *San Francisco Chronicle* bought up the issue of weapons of mass destruction specifically in casting the administration as hypocritical: "It's also more than a bit curious for an administration that was led astray on weapons of mass destruction to be lecturing anyone on the consequences of flawed sourcing."[101]

While *Newsweek* was not exonerated and many editorials pointed to the faults of the Koran abuse story, charges of hypocrisy shifted attention to the motives of the administration for vehemently attacking the magazine. The severity of the administration criticism was presented as out of synch with the transgressions of the magazine. A *New York Times* editorial acknowledged that *Newsweek* must address its internal issues, but then criticized the administration for hypocritically attacking *Newsweek,* calling it "ludicrous for spokesmen for this White House and Defense Department to offer pious declarations about accountability, openness and concern for America's image abroad."[102] In the same tone, the *Los Angeles Times* wrote, "For all the administration's huffing and puffing about *Newsweek* getting the story wrong, it has produced such a catalog of misdeeds at Abu Ghraib and Guantanamo that almost any allegation is instantly credited abroad."[103] In connecting the Koran abuse story with other offenses by the Bush administration, these criticisms undermined the credibility of the administration's assault by turning the administration's criticism against itself.[104]

Conclusion: The Defense of *Newsweek* as Journalistic Atonement

How was it that a problem with a small *Newsweek* item resulted in such an outpouring of journalistic anger and frustration aimed at the Bush administration? Certainly, the magazine did err in basing its claim of an upcoming military report detailing Koran abuse at Guantanamo Bay on only one source while using the absence of denial from another source as corroboration. Left without the identity of the source, audiences could not know the reason why the source had erred or his motives for the leak in the first place. At first, the story disappeared in the crush of news until it became connected to exaggerated accounts of overseas hysteria. While the backpedaling of *Newsweek* received attention, so did serious accusations of abuse and misconduct at Guantanamo Bay. As it turned out, the magazine may have been off on the specifics, but not wrong in stoking the need for direct attention to what was happening out of sight of the public in the War on Terror.

How this turned to anger at the Bush administration owes to two strategies officials used to shape news reports about their actions. As shown in chapters 1 and 5, the administration understood how to dangle desired information to reporters under the condition of anonymity. Such information, when released into the stream of news without attribution, served to reinforce its public claims. This was coupled with a second strategy, shown here and in chapter 2, in which unnamed source-backed reporting conflicting with administration aims received voluminous criticism from both officials and commentators siding with the administration. With the Killian memos case, this move effectively silenced questions about Bush's military service record. But it did not work the same way with *Newsweek*. Instead, the anger journalists expressed over administration attacks on *Newsweek* invoked lingering resentment between the two parties.

The backlash against the administration was more than simply journalists rallying around one of their own or their displeasure at the heavy-handedness of the administration. Instead, the journalistic response needs to be understood within the broader context of press-government relations in the era after the September 11 attacks. After an initial uptick in public approval, journalists had to publicly account for credulous, unnamed source-laden prewar intelligence that reinforced administration claims of the pressing need to invade Iraq in 2003. By spring 2005, the original arguments for war had been invalidated, causing problems not only for the Bush administration and the Republican Party, but also for journalists unable to dodge their role in spreading evidence supporting a war that later turned out to be seriously flawed.

More than two years later, journalists found a second chance to reassert their core norms of independence and holding the government accountable through criticism of the administration and renewed interest in the conditions at Guantanamo Bay—as well as other covert ventures. While far less than the radical wave of adversarial reporting many on the left had hoped for, it was part of an effort to reinvigorate critical journalism in the face of earlier failures of startling severity. This entailed a cautious reaffirmation of the centrality of anonymity as a journalistic tool while warning against the perils of its misapplication. This perspective would soon gain strength with the outing of FBI insider Mark Felt as Deep Throat, discussed in the next chapter.

Although journalistic criticism of the administration signaled a healthy attempt to confront the pressures elite news outlets faced from the officials they cover, it did not go far enough in addressing the imbalance between the norms underlying their work and contradictory necessities of sourcing practices. That is, it provided a telling portrait of how the administration pressured the news without taking into account the agency of reporters as part of these same problems. The role of journalists in this arrangement was what irked so many smaller newspapers that exempted themselves from such practices. But for elite news outlets, this discussion would soon arise when the normative defenses behind Plamegate began to unravel.

4

Deep Throat and
the Question of Motives

We already know what Deep Throat did.
Do we know what it means?

—*Pittsburgh Post-Gazette* columnist
Daniel Roddy

The public struggle to define news controversies involving unnamed sources regularly centers on questions of motive. Why has the source come forward, but only partly? Why be veiled at all? What is being left out? The subject of motive is particularly thorny when journalists defend their use of unnamed sources through invoking watchdog norms. In an ideal scenario, a potential source possesses information of value to the public but faces risks over being connected to any disclosure. When the whistle-blowing source reaches out to a journalist (or vice versa), the willingness of the journalist to publicize this information while holding her identity secret creates an arrangement seemingly beneficial to all. The question of motive dissolves into the assumption that the public gains from knowing the hidden information.

However, the rarity of this idealized arrangement means that the problem of unknowable motives constantly plagues the ordinary use of unnamed sources in news discourse. This results in distrust of unnamed sources that often boils down to a belief that what is being concealed is not simply the source's identity, but also underlying motivations essential to judging how to interpret the source's claims. Journalists are implicated for abetting the source either out of bias or an unceasing appetite for access. In sum, journalists face a quandary over the question of motives that is not easily avoided. Pledges of careful fact-checking only alleviate some of the suspicion while leaving open the question of why the source demanded anonymity in the first place.

Throughout the incidents in this book, the problem of motives has been evinced through the plethora of interpretations cropping up in the vacuum left open by opaque unnamed sourcing practices. Various speakers are free to impute a variety of motives that often contradict the normative model put forth by the journalistic community. For example, the *New York Times* largely accounted for its prewar reporting errors, summarized in chapter 1, by pinning blame on competitive pressures that allowed into the paper unnamed sources possessing questionable motives relating to the administration's flimsy intelligence claims. Allegations in chapter 2 flowed in the politically opposite direction when, after his identity emerged, conservatives discounted Bill Burkett, the unnamed supplier of the Killian memos to CBS News, as bent on harming the president's reputation. This explanation also arose in the more abstracted accusations of an antimilitary bias among journalists described in chapter 3. In all three cases, postmortem assessments dismissed the unnamed sources as advocates—for and against the Bush administration respectively—who could not be trusted. Journalists, it followed, failed out of ingrained bias, the fetishizing of access, or plain sloppiness in pursuing these stories.

While questions of motives simmered within larger discussions of unnamed sources taking place in 2004 and 2005, they boiled over on the last day of May 2005 when journalism's biggest secret came to an end. During the morning hours of May 31, 2005, word quickly spread that W. Mark Felt, the former associate director of the FBI under President Richard Nixon, was Deep Throat—the unnamed source made famous by Bob Woodward and Carl Bernstein in their *Washington Post* reporting on the Watergate scandal. Woodward and Bernstein initially refused to confirm Felt's claims, stating instead that they would honor their pledge to keep Deep Throat's identity confidential until after their source's death. Hours later, the duo officially ended the search for Deep Throat through a statement corroborating Felt's claims on the *Washington Post*'s Web site. Deep Throat now had a name.

Watergate Once More

Even for journalists who were not involved or who entered into news work after Nixon's resignation, journalistic retellings of Watergate have been foundational to journalism's self-identity. Woodward and Bernstein have become deeply embedded in the mythology of journalism as a pair of intrepid reporters bringing down a corrupt presidential administration. Yet, from the start, the connection between the facts of the Watergate reporting and its mythologizing appeared somewhat tenuous. Writing amidst the initial aggrandizing of Woodward and Bernstein in the mid-1970s, Edward Jay Epstein declared that "the actual role that journalists played remains ill understood."[1] By detailing the complex investigative activities taking place at different levels within the government, he cast doubt on the efficacy of Woodward and Bernstein's work. Epstein even foreshadowed the eventual revelation of Felt by suggesting that many of the leaks the reporters received were simply part of internal strife across the Nixon administration—including in the FBI—fought publicly through the strategic use of unnamed sources. That is, the motives behind Watergate leaks were more opportunistic than altruistic.

So, how did Woodward and Bernstein's reporting come to occupy a starring role in a narrative of the scandal's unfolding "that often bore little resemblance to the event as it unfolded"?[2] Both Michael Schudson and Barbie Zelizer have examined how, over time, Watergate became less about the actual news practices involved and more an event signifying quality journalistic practice and promoting investigative reporting as journalism's defining mode. By privileging the reportage of Woodward and Bernstein above judicial and congressional actions, the story of Watergate increasingly omitted how different institutions functioned together in complex ways over the course of two years to result in Nixon's resignation and dozens of indictments. Instead, journalists have long represented Watergate in a manner that has reinforced journalism's cultural role. For journalism, "the Watergate myth is sustaining. It survives to a large extent impervious to critique. It offers journalism a charter, an inspiration, a reason for being large enough to justify the constitutional protections that journalism enjoys."[3]

Within the Watergate story, the existence of Deep Throat remained unknown until he appeared in Woodward and Bernstein's bestselling book *All the President's Men* as an unnamed source providing insider information on a not-for-attribution arrangement deemed "deep background."[4] The mystery of Deep Throat was further solidified through Hal Holbrook's shadowy portrayal in the popular film adaptation in 1976. Deep Throat became an iconic anonymous source not only through his presence in journalistic retellings of Watergate but also through his place in popular culture. Speculation as to Deep Throat's identity remained fashionable for decades among political, journalistic, and academic circles. Throughout this era, Woodward and Bernstein dictated the terms in which Deep Throat could be comprehended by maintaining their promise of anonymity for over thirty years. The persistence of Deep Throat's anonymity allowed others to construct a narrative around him as an ideal without being hampered by the complexity of human motivations accompanying any specific individual—until what had been secret became public knowledge.

The focus quickly fell on figuring out who Mark Felt is. Journalists had long ascribed a praiseworthy status to Deep Throat while preserving his phantasmal aura. With the question of Deep Throat's identity answered, new questions took its place. The merging of Felt, a real person, with Deep Throat, an iconic symbol, meant the Watergate narrative now had to incorporate, in the corporal sense of the term, Felt into the narrative. While journalists were free to portray the previously unembodied Deep Throat as they pleased, Felt introduced problematic and contradictory elements to the narrative. Simply put, for journalism Felt was far from the ideal candidate to assume the identity of Deep Throat. His record and the circumstances of his disclosure provided ample ammunition for critics to question Felt's character and motivations for surreptitiously working with journalists. Journalists responded by heralding Felt in a bid to retain the usefulness of Watergate as a collective marker of journalistic success. They rallied around the memory of Watergate to defend the viability of unnamed sources in the face of sourcing controversies, a strained relationship with the secretive Bush administration, and the broader context of a changed news landscape post-Watergate.

More than the conclusion of an irrelevant journalistic mystery, Felt's outing came only two weeks after *Newsweek*'s May 16, 2005, retraction (described in chapter 3), and at the same time the *New York Times*'s Judith Miller and *Time*'s Matt Cooper waged a public battle to avoid testifying before a grand jury in the Plame leak case (recounted in chapter 5). In this swirl of unnamed source–centered stories, Felt's actions added a new layer to the ongoing discussion through the promotion of Deep Throat as a symbolic counter to the other cases while, at the same time, raising further questions as to the motives of unnamed sources. He became a key figure in the broader contest to define appropriate modes of journalistic practice in covering powerful institutions and individuals.

Making Mark Felt Deep Throat

The unveiling of Mark Felt as Deep Throat took place through a *Vanity Fair* article written by John O'Connor, a San Francisco lawyer who learned of Felt's secret identity through Felt's family and acted as a liaison between the family and the magazine.[5] Shortly after the story became public on May 31, 2005, the linking of Felt and Deep Throat meant the source's actions could be debated, contested, and criticized anew. The situation was made even more complex by Felt's decreased ability to communicate. Felt, at ninety-one, had suffered a stroke several years earlier and was living in Santa Rosa, California, with his daughter and grandson. Beyond a few words to reporters outside his home, Felt lacked the capacity to speak for himself or to provide answers to questions regarding his motivations. This inability to provide direct answers ensured that ambiguity would surround the reasons for his actions. Felt emerged as "a blank canvas on which to paint its thoughts about a man whose existence in the flesh raised issues of the most metaphysical."[6] Felt continued on with limited lucidity until his death on December 18, 2008, at age ninety-five.

With Felt effectively silenced, others competed to define his motives, interpret his actions, and judge his merit. How Felt was positioned mattered for his entrance into the Watergate narrative, which contributed to contestation around his role. From the outset of the story, critics emerged to question Felt's character, his motivations for surreptitiously working with journalists, and—most problematically for journalism—the degree to which the press actually uncovered the Watergate scandal. In response, journalists and others supported the continued usefulness of Deep Throat/Felt—and by extension, Woodward and Bernstein—as praiseworthy symbols for journalism.

Within this discourse, journalists and commentators regularly reduced the contest to define Felt's actions to the dichotomy of "hero or villain." This division was a particularly salient frame for cable television news discussions of Felt. It was posed on all three major cable networks.[7] On *Scarborough Country,* host Joe Scarborough posed the question as, "Is Felt a hero or a rat?" (June 1). On *Fox News Sunday* (June 5), the question was asked whether he should be "praised or condemned." The hero question also occurred on each of the three network evening news broadcasts. The *CBS Evening News* asked if Felt was "a hero or FBI turncoat," (June 1) while the *NBC Nightly News* (June 1) and *ABC World News Tonight* (June 1) each offered similar frames.

Print publications also framed their discussions of Felt around the question of motives and his heroic status—or lack thereof. For example, *Time* magazine asked: "Was Deep Throat a villain or a hero, driven by base motives or noble ones?"[8] Newspapers assessing Felt's heroic status used a number of different formulations. For example, the *Boston Globe* inquired of Felt: "Was the most famous leaker of recent times a selfless good guy looking out for his country or a craven self-promoter?"[9] An *Arkansas Democrat Gazette* editorial phrased it as "Secret patriot, or a self-serving stoolie?" and sided with the former.[10] An editorial in the Raleigh *News & Observer* posed it as "a snitch or a patriot."[11]

Journalists reporting on Felt removed themselves from the story and instead let sources signify the meaning of the Watergate narrative—even if other journalists often served as sources. Anderson Cooper made this structure clear at the beginning of a segment on Felt, stating "We don't take sides on 360" before proceeding to present opposing views of Felt's character.[12] This recurring configuration infused evaluations of Felt with the facade of balanced debate. It epitomized so-called "he-said, she-said" journalism, which relieved journalists from presenting their own evaluations.[13] Without entering into a larger critique of the assumptions of this journalistic style, in this case attempts at balance appeared particularly suspect given the interests behind journalists praising Felt's actions as heroic—or at least admirable—and a small set of mostly former Nixon administration officials challenging this label. Regardless, this dichotomization structured the debate around Felt by inviting and privileging certain perspectives. By directing attention to arguments of why he deserved the label of hero or villain, Felt's motives became the chief criterion of his worth.

ALL OF NIXON'S MEN

With Deep Throat now connected to the person of Felt, critics seized on both known biographical details and imagined motives of Felt as impacting—or even negating—the mythic image of Deep Throat. This opposition between personal motivations and heroic value developed around both Felt's action of providing information to Woodward in 1972 and for revealing his identity publicly in 2005. According to this argument, the more muddled the motivations, the less applicable a meritorious reception. These criticisms challenged the role accorded Felt in uncovering Watergate as inaccurately portrayed and, therefore, unable to support the symbolic weight assigned to him by journalists.

The most vocal negative interpreters of Felt's actions were former Nixon administration officials. These men—all of them were male—had an immediate stake in downplaying the heroism of Felt's actions in order to preserve their own reputation as well as Nixon's. Particular vehemence toward Felt came from Pat Buchanan, Charles Colson, and G. Gordon Liddy through television and print outlets during the initial days of the story. Lesser disapproval or skepticism emerged from John Dean, Henry Kissinger, and David Gergen. These former Nixon officials quickly became prominent sources on network and cable news during the first and second day of the story.

Buchanan was particularly vocal at an early stage. On May 31, only a few hours after Woodward and Bernstein confirmed Felt's identity as Deep Throat, Buchanan sharply rebuked Felt on the *NBC Nightly News:* "I think

Deep Throat is a snake." On the following day, Buchanan appeared on NBC's *Today* (with Colson), the *NBC Nightly News,* the *CBS Evening News,* and MSNBC's *Scarborough Country.* Colson, who connected Felt's revelation to "a sad legacy,"[14] appeared on the June 1 broadcasts of CNN's *Anderson Cooper 360,* Fox News Channel's the *O'Reilly Factor* and NPR's *All Things Considered.* Having their quotes reproduced in newspaper stories the next day further magnified their presence. The amplification of Nixon loyalists through frequent appearances served at the outset to focus debate around Felt's specific motives for seeking anonymity. This frame elided questions of the value of the disclosed information by emphasizing the unnamed source's intentions in providing information. This view also took into account the status of the leaker in judgments of the leak's suitability.

Adhering to this frame, much of the Felt criticism dissected his motives, both in acting as a source for the *Washington Post* and for coming forward with his identity thirty years later. Critics emphasized the ambiguity of Felt's motives, which conservative columnist Robert Novak identified as "reasons that were not necessarily noble or patriotic."[15] In particular, Felt was passed over for FBI director after the death of J. Edgar Hoover some six weeks before the Watergate break-in. The appointment instead went to a non-FBI Nixon loyalist, L. Patrick Gray. Felt was accused of being upset at not getting the post and retaliating through providing anonymous information to the *Washington Post. Chicago Sun-Times* columnist Mary Laney countered heroic classifications of Felt: "That's not whistle-blowing heroism. That's a man who wants revenge, but wants to make certain he saves his own job while he gets his pound of flesh from another."[16] These critics presented two claims: that Felt's actions were attributable to revenge and that a motive of revenge discounted the ability for an individual to be considered heroic. Both of these conditions had to be accepted for the argument against lauding Felt to be valid.

Another area of criticism focused on Felt's motives for revealing his identity as Deep Throat in 2005, thirty-three years after the break-in and thirty-two years after his retirement from the FBI. Felt drew accusations of acting purely out of financial interest. An editorial in the conservative *New York Post* raised this issue and labeled Felt as "disloyal."[17] On the *O'Reilly Factor,* legal analyst Andrew Napolitano warned that Felt could be indicted on bribery charges if he received any money from Woodward.[18] The previous night, Fox News Channel's John Gibson also questioned Felt's monetary incentive,[19] as did syndicated conservative columnist William F. Buckley.[20] With Felt unable to speak, others were able to suggest monetary reasons as the determining factor in his disclosure.

Conservatives were not the only ones targeting Felt. He also received specific criticism, often from the left, for his role in conducting illegal searches of homes belonging to acquaintances of the Weather Underground in the early 1970s. These activities—referred to as "black bag operations"—resulted in Felt's indictment and trial for violating the Fourth Amendment. An unapologetic Felt was convicted in 1981, but avoided prison through a pardon from President Ronald Reagan. The involvement of Felt in illegal search activities around the same time as the Watergate burglary complicated heroic assessments of his character. Felt came up through the FBI under Hoover, a notorious autocrat and ruthless protector of the bureau. In assessing Felt, critics dismissed lavishing praise due to this questionable record. *Slate's* Jack Shafer wrote, "He wasn't an idealist or a whistle-blower or a patriot. He was just another vigilant protector of Washington turf, a player who didn't want his side to lose."[21] Similarly, *Boston Globe* columnist Eileen McNamara dismissed Felt as "self-serving."[22] The *Washington Post's* Colbert King also tied Felt to a legacy of corruption, rather than that of a crusader for justice.[23] This criticism presented a nonidealized view of Felt, including his ironic involvement in unauthorized break-ins.

Portrayals of Felt as territorial, spurned, or a systematic violator of the U.S. Constitution made it difficult for journalists to connect Felt to the mythic image of Deep Throat promulgated since the 1970s. Discussions of Felt were often politicized, as many of the critics possessed strong conservative ties, as did the cadre of former Nixon administration officials repeatedly called upon as sources. Attacks also occurred through conservative news outlets, including the *New York Post* and the Fox News Channel. Taken as a whole, these critiques of Felt's motives coalesced into an effort to discredit him, and, in many ways, an effort to redefine Watergate and resuscitate Nixon's reputation. This perspective did not go unchallenged.

RECONCILING THE MAN AND THE MYTH

For Watergate to retain its mythic utility for journalism, the existing Watergate narrative needed to withstand attacks on Felt's actions and motivations. Situating Felt as a hero was crucial to maintaining the symbolic power of Deep Throat and the overall account of Watergate as a key moment of journalistic success and a reminder of the value of unnamed sources. To this end, those with stakes in preserving positive perceptions of Felt often explicitly presented him as a hero who performed honorably by becoming an unnamed source. The chief advocates alleging Felt's heroism were his lawyer John O'Connor (who authored the *Vanity Fair* article) and Felt's daughter and grandson. In addition, Bob Woodward and Carl Bernstein, along with the *Washington Post,* worked against stigmatizing Felt to protect their reputation and their role in Watergate. Outside the immediate stakeholders, Watergate's enduring symbolic importance impelled journalists to buttress the cultural standing of Deep Throat and, by extension, the journalistic role in the story.

The Felt family, along with O'Connor, actively and explicitly situated Felt as a hero both to maintain his reputation and also out of financial interest. O'Connor frequently invoked the word "hero" in discussions of Felt. On the day the story broke, O'Connor called Felt "a great hero" on the *NBC Nightly News* and told *ABC World News Tonight* that "he was protecting our system of justice." O'Connor also labeled Felt a "hero" on ABC's *Nightline* (May 31). The same day on PBS's *NewsHour,* O'Connor described Felt as "a true American Hero." Felt's daughter was quoted as calling the revelation of Felt "a great moment in . . . American history."[24] In a *New York Times* story dichotomously titled "Felt Is Praised as a Hero and Condemned as a Traitor," Felt's grandson Nick Jones saluted his actions: "What he did was the right thing to do. Heroic. He's an honorable guy."[25] In *Time,* Jones was quoted as saying, "He is a great American hero who went well above and beyond the call of duty at much risk to himself to save his country from horrible injustice."[26] The explicit invocation of hero status by the Felt family worked in opposition to the above efforts to weaken or discredit Felt.

Aside from O'Connor and the Felt family, Woodward and Bernstein were quick to laud Felt. On *Larry King Live,* Bernstein highlighted Felt's contribution: "The country was served because here was a man who told the truth."[27] Woodward, withholding the "hero" term, referred to Felt as "a man of immense courage" in an interview with Tom Brokaw in the parking garage where he and Felt would secretly meet.[28] Woodward and Bernstein remained closely linked to Deep Throat, despite their copious use of other sources. Former *Washington Post* editor Ben Bradlee was also quoted often and appeared on network and cable news programs, including the *NBC Nightly News* and ABC's *Nightline* on June 1 and MSNBC's *Hardball* on June 3.

In addition to Woodward and Bernstein's assessments, the *Washington Post* devoted a great deal of space to covering the Felt revelation. Having housed Woodward and Bernstein throughout their Watergate coverage, the image and credibility of the *Post* was closely intertwined with the image of Watergate. Its authority as an elite newspaper was bound up in its Watergate reporting legacy. This was reflected in the space it allotted to covering Felt. In the week following Felt's revelation—Wednesday, June 1, to Tuesday, June 7—the *Post* ran thirty-one articles on Felt and Watergate. This included nine articles on the first day (June 1) and eight on the second (June 2). Many of the articles revisited the *Post*'s Watergate reporting, including a 5,000-word front page story by Bob Woodward recounting his relationship with Felt.[29] That piece was carried by other newspapers and formed the core of Woodward's bestselling book *The Secret Man* released in July 2005.[30] Several of the *Post* columnists weighed in on Felt, including David Broder, Art Buchwald, Jim Hoagland, Colbert King, and ombudsman Michael Getler. By comparison, the *New York Times* ran sixteen stories during the first week. Having been scooped on the story by *Vanity Fair,* the *Post* reacted with a barrage of coverage, much of it retelling the Watergate story, and therefore reasserting the authority of the *Post* as an essential element in the century's top political story.

Felt was actively and explicitly protected as a heroic figure against competing assessments from Nixon loyalists and others. Often journalists turned to less restricted forms of opinion writing to make the case for Felt rather than work through non-opinion news pieces. Beyond direct stakeholders, numerous newspaper editorials and columns conferred hero status on Felt. A Cleveland *Plain Dealer* editorial called Felt, "the best of American heroes,"[31] and the *Seattle Times* said he "served the greater good of his country."[32] To be clear, the *Arizona Republic* labeled Felt "hero, not villain,"[33] while the *Kansas City Star* vouched that Felt made the "right decision" to go through Woodward.[34] The *Rochester Democrat and Courier* lauded Felt as "a genuine hero, worthy of a place in the whistle-blower's hall of fame."[35] The *San Antonio Express-News* dismissed ulterior motivations of Felt: "Felt was a patriot, placing the nation ahead of its government when their interests conflicted."[36]

Other journalists turned the charges around on critics of Felt by casting their statements as self-serving. On NBC's *Today,* former NBC anchor Tom Brokaw dismissed Buchanan's criticism of Felt: "I think Pat said yesterday that Mark Felt was a traitor. A traitor to what, the truth? Here's a man who didn't make this stuff up."[37] Also on *Today,* Woodward rejected Buchanan's claims: "Pat is a propagandist."[38] On the *NBC Nightly News,* Bradlee chastised G. Gordon Liddy for disparaging Felt: "It makes me sick to hear Gordon Liddy talk about morality in government. I mean, he hasn't been out of jail all that long."[39] A *Chicago Sun-Times* columnist referred to the Nixon loyalists as "Richard Nixon's old gang of felons, villains and assorted scum."[40] Another columnist at the *Arkansas Democrat Gazette* noted that Felt "has to suffer the denunciations of unrepentant jailbirds who would still put loyalty to an individual above loyalty to the country's greater good."[41] Remarks by former Nixon officials did not go uncontested. Rather, they were confronted and dismissed either through attacking the actual claims of speakers or their motives and stakes in diminishing Felt. Of course, journalists possessed their own stake in keeping Deep Throat the centerpiece of a narrative positioning Watergate as a model for the continued use of unnamed sources. In this view, the explicit protection the journalistic community gave to Felt stemmed from the extent that his flaws made such a defense necessary.

Ultimately, the frame of "hero or villain" pertaining to Felt's motives led to blind spots on both sides. While Felt's detractors held that ulterior motives for supplying background information to Woodward negated his heroic value, journalists and others rightly countered by weighing the question of motivations against the outcome of the deserved resignation of Nixon—however directly or indirectly this ending could be attributed to Deep Throat. At the same time, the general question of motives cannot be so easily dismissed as irrelevant when considering ongoing problems surrounding the use of unnamed sources.

The journalistic portrayal of Deep Throat as a whistle-blower limited the scope of unnamed sources to only a subset comprising altruistic actors resisting unethical organizational behavior. This reduction ignored the more common variety of unnamed sources as insiders providing information on topics far less vital than executive-level conspiracy. In many instances of blind sourcing, motives *do* matter when the veil of anonymity hides a source from public scrutiny. Audiences understandably and appropriately want to know why a source reveals information or makes a particular judgment (along with the quality of these disclosures). In turn, journalists should provide this information to the extent it is possible to retain confidentiality—if it is even warranted in the first place. Nonetheless, it is the dexterity of collective memory that allows journalists to construct one situation—the connection of Deep Throat qua whistle-blower to the deserved resignation of Nixon—as synecdochic of other situations that are less clear fits, therefore pushing aside the tricky question of motives underlying source anonymity.

The Resilience of Deep Throat

A central contention of collective memory is that the past is made useful to the present. Journalists have long used Deep Throat, journalism's enduring unnamed source, as evidence for a larger argument connecting unnamed sources to journalism's ability to fulfill its normative democratic role. With Felt's disclosure, a resurgent Deep Throat entered into an era marked by the contentious relationship between journalism and the Bush administration, recent controversies involving unnamed sources (especially at *Newsweek* and

60 Minutes), and a general rethinking of unnamed sourcing practices at many news outlets. The Felt revelation and the revival of the Deep Throat narrative complicated this larger discussion of unnamed sources by adding what was largely portrayed—outside of ex-Nixon officials and some conservative commentators—as a positive example of journalists holding power accountable.

With Felt entering the fray only two weeks after the *Newsweek* retraction and only a few months after Dan Rather's last broadcast as the *CBS Evening News* anchor following the Killian memos story controversy, journalists repeatedly situated him as a reminder of the value of unnamed sources. This frame developed quickly; only hours after the Felt disclosure, former NBC News anchor Tom Brokaw called the story "a reminder of the importance of anonymous sources for the American public."[42] NPR's Daniel Schorr viewed the impact of the story as "reignit[ing] the controversy over the role of the confidential source."[43]

The larger context of unnamed sources shaped discussions of Felt from the outset. Connections between Deep Throat and the preservation of unnamed sources were quite visible in newspaper editorials and columns. This movement of Felt from news sections to the editorial pages indicated the active process through which journalists situated Felt as a model for journalism through nonobjective news forms.[44] In these spaces, journalists directly argued that Felt confirmed the viability of unnamed sources against the spate of recent controversies. The *Boston Globe* called the revelation "timely," as did the *Chicago Sun-Times, San Diego Union Tribune,* and the Memphis *Commercial Appeal,* while the *Seattle Post-Intelligencer* labeled it "a nostalgic and welcome reminder."[45] The *Austin American-Statesman* labeled it an "object lesson in the importance of the judicious use of anonymous sources."[46] The prevailing trend was to reopen the debate on unnamed sources with its successful functioning held against problematic incidents. Mark Felt/Deep Throat provided a frame through which to reevaluate unnamed sources during a troubled time when their viability remained under fire.

The discussion of unnamed sources following Felt's disclosure included juxtapositions between Felt and specific controversies involving unnamed sources. The still-fresh *Newsweek* Koran abuse story received the most attention from journalists who portrayed the magazine as having made mistakes that the *Washington Post* avoided with Deep Throat: "Deep Throat is the plus side of using anonymous sources—fleshing out and pinning down one of the 20th century's most important stories. The downside was what happened to *Newsweek* magazine."[47] An editorial in the *Indianapolis Star* was more explicit in dividing the two cases according to steps taken to verify information from an unnamed source: "[Woodward and Bernstein] relied on many other sources (named and unnamed) in pursuing his leads, sparing themselves and their readers the sort of debacle *Newsweek* precipitated with its recent single-source story of Quran desecration."[48] In assessing the meaning of the two cases for journalistic practice, *Newsweek* became the negative case, solidified as a low point for journalism against the mythical importance of Watergate personified by Deep Throat. In this symbolic spacing, journalists situated the cases as opposing poles of good and bad journalistic practice.

Aside from *Newsweek*, journalists also cited the *60 Minutes* story on Bush's Air National Guard service. A columnist for the *St. Louis Post-Dispatch* contrasted Watergate as a pinnacle of journalism with the CBS controversy: "More than 30 years later, the sloppiness of Dan Rather and CBS News revealed the atrophy of that powerful muscle in the function of democracy."[49] Similarly, a columnist for the *St. Petersburg Times* simplified the two incidents: "Compare Felt's credibility with the source used by Dan Rather when he tossed accusations at President Bush."[50] In the same way as *Newsweek*, the *60 Minutes* story became a negative example. However, the timing of the story and the involvement of an official government source heightened *Newsweek*'s relevance.

In addition to the failures of unnamed sourcing practices, journalists also connected the Mark Felt revelation to the *New York Time*'s Judith Miller and *Time*'s Matt Cooper. Both reporters were waging a legal battle to avoid testifying about their unnamed sources before a grand jury in the Plame leak investigation. The Deep Throat narrative was made to demonstrate the importance of protecting journalists' confidentiality with their sources. This comparison later grew to be problematic when "Plamegate" became a journalistic embarrassment (described in the next chapter). However, connections were made. In the *New York Times*, Carl Bernstein explained the importance of the Deep Throat revelation and his commitment to confidentiality: "Reporters may be going to jail today for upholding that principle, and we don't and won't belittle it now."[51] *Washington Post* columnist Richard Cohen offered a similar argument.[52] Also, the Deep Throat model was used to buttress the defense of Miller and Cooper. These journalists called on the Deep Throat case as a way to reenergize support for Miller and Cooper by moving their justification away from the particular details of the case, which were murky from the start, and toward the normative conception of unnamed sources supported by the Deep Throat narrative.

Beyond Watergate: The Battle over Whistle-Blowers

The outing of Deep Throat, while very much a struggle over how we should remember the journalistic role in uncovering the Watergate scandal, was also an opportunity to examine, at a broad level, how journalism should cover the government. Beyond protecting individual reputations, competing interpretations of Felt's actions three decades earlier came to bear on the present through the promotion of conflicting normative visions of the appropriate relationship between government officials and journalists. Out of the discourse around Felt, two broad positions emerged. By lionizing Felt and reemphasizing the work of Woodward and Bernstein, journalists endorsed a particular formation of their work and its relationship to the government that incorporated unnamed sources as a vital component. Meanwhile, critics denigrating Felt and his actions advocated for an alternative normative organizational perspective that stressed internal policing while disdaining external oversight in the shape of unnamed sources surreptitiously informing journalists. These conflicting positions supporting and undermining the use of unnamed sources in uncovering organizational malfeasance connected to concurrent debates over unnamed sources taking place among journalists. In this environment, Felt's disclosure became a relevant addition to ongoing discussions of how unnamed sources should be used—if at all.

INTERNAL PROCESSES OVER EXTERNAL PUBLICITY

Critics questioning Felt's motives expanded their individualized appraisals into a generalized endorsement of loyalty and internal procedural fidelity on the part of government officials as a way of preserving governmental functioning. This argument made loyalty a salient issue while casting unnamed sources as disloyal. For example, in the initial coverage of Felt's revelation, former Nixon counsel Leonard Garment situated Felt's actions in a debate over the appropriateness of officials becoming whistle-blowers by asking: "When [are] government persons, having private, secret, confidential information, . . . justified to become the whistle-blower and defy or ignore their sworn obligation to maintain security and go to the press with it[?]"[53] Garment portrayed the dilemma of the whistle-blower as a mutually exclusive choice between loyalty and making wrongdoing public. This either/or frame cut into journalism's self-presentation as an indispensable watchdog by disregarding journalism as a legitimate avenue for redressing internal governmental problems. In promoting internal over external organizational oversight, these critics situated journalism as a self-concerned nuisance rather than a public-minded service. Thus, critiques of Felt's actions in the past doubled as critiques of journalism in the present by dismissing its ability to confront institutional problems.

Following from this, the narrative moved beyond individual judgments of Felt to condemn, on a general level, high-ranking government officials acting as unnamed sources without the knowledge or approval of colleagues. This perspective juxtaposed loyalty as an established norm dictating proper actions with an interpretation of Felt's actions as profoundly disloyal. Again, it was largely Nixon administration officials who framed Felt's turning to the press in the larger normative conception of the duty of government officials. On NBC's *Today*, Pat Buchanan enumerated Felt's transgressions: "There's nothing heroic about breaking faith with your people, breaking the law, sneaking around in garages, putting stuff from an investigation out to a Nixon-hating *Washington Post*."[54] Similarly, Chuck Colson told the *CBS Evening News:* "You don't go sneaking around in dark alleys at night, passing tips to reporters."[55] For Buchanan and Colson, circumventing official channels by informing journalists was nothing less than an act of betrayal.

Other Nixon staffers admitted that a government official should address malfeasance, but only by working through preestablished channels in order to prevent a larger breakdown. Former Nixon chief of staff Alexander Haig was quoted on the Fox News Channel: "You have an obligation to resign and take necessary steps within your power to deal with the problem."[56] On CNN's *NewsNight with Aaron Brown,* David Gergen suggested that an insider approach would have been better: "I think you need to use your powers within government to see if you can solve it."[57] These speakers promoted a particular model of behavior for officials that excluded working externally with journalists. In chastising Felt's actions, they treated journalism as superfluous or even counterproductive rather than as an acceptable venue for displaying grievances.

Elsewhere, non-Nixon stakeholders also raised questions regarding the appropriateness of Felt's decision to give information secretly to the press rather than work through other channels. On *Fox News Sunday,* conservative commentator William Kristol dismissed any hero rhetoric due to Felt's ranking in the government: "You really don't want to set the precedent that this guy is a hero, a senior person at the FBI."[58] Kristol implied that Felt's position warranted a respect for process. Without this process, Felt's actions were viewed as damaging to the FBI, as in the view of a *Washington Times* columnist: "He not only destroys his reputation, but he takes a chunk out of the reputation of the agency that supported him and his family in a comfortable lifestyle for so many years."[59] In weighing Felt's actions, *USA Today* found mixed reactions from current and former FBI agents, many of whom were "uneasy" with Felt's role as an unnamed source.[60] Similar FBI reactions appeared in the *Washington Post* and *San Francisco Chronicle*.[61] While journalists promoted Felt as a model of an unnamed source, government officials expressed disapproval or ambivalence about government employees serving as a secret source.

Ironically, this did not preclude officials from seeking anonymity as a tool for spreading nonattributed information as a press management tactic. In other words, this argument shunned unauthorized revelatory unnamed sourcing practices while sustaining the utilization of strategic leaks to journalists. Journalists were useful for spreading messages, but useless in correcting internal problems. This perspective undermined journalism's authoritative basis of providing a watchdog function by representing journalism as dominated by its sources. It situated anonymity as a tool for the government to present information to the public, which went against journalism's normative formation of using anonymity to disclose hidden information.

THE WHISTLE-BLOWER AND THE JOURNALIST UNITED

Journalists and others interpreting Felt's actions regularly condensed the domain of unnamed sources to only the idealized subset of whistle-blowers acting in the public interest. This reduction, coupled with a democratic normative articulation of journalism's function as holding power accountable, situated the whistle-blower as an indispensable element of news work. The emergent formation aligned journalists with their unnamed sources in the common pursuit of bringing organizational malfeasance to public attention. This perspective marked the expansion of the watchdog norm supporting journalism's cultural authority to include a reliance on insiders coming forth with disclosures. By using the memory of Watergate reportage in a manner that disregarded other common types of unnamed source–journalist relationships, journalists repositioned unnamed sources as central to the appropriate functioning of journalism in society.

The centrality of the whistle-blower in conceptions of a watchdog-based journalism was made apparent in a commentary by Daniel Schorr: "[Government institutions] have all kinds of ways of hiding things, and the only way that you can penetrate that is if somebody, as a kind of a whistle-blower, is willing to leak. And I think that's very valuable for our republic."[62] This retelling of the past emphasized how whistle-blowers served the public through exposing the inner actions of the government. Closed news practices worked to open up secretive governmental practices to scrutiny.

For institutions simultaneously prone to secrecy but central to governmental policy, unnamed sources provided access for the public. The indispensability of unnamed sources for holding officials accountable was also invoked by *New York Times* Washington bureau chief Philip Taubman: "The day we outlaw the use of anonymous sources in the coverage of the CIA, the Pentagon, the White House, the State Department and other national security agencies is the day we cease to cover them effectively."[63] Similarly, Bob Woodward called anonymous sources, "a vital lifeline to the underbelly of government."[64] Explicitly tying unnamed sources to democracy, a Cleveland *Plain Dealer* columnist wrote that they "are one means by which a democracy remains of the people, by the people and for the people."[65] Anonymity, having been criticized so stridently in past controversies at the *New York Times, Newsweek,* and CBS News, was revitalized as an enabling mechanism for journalists to provide audiences—inclusively construed as the "public"—with internal information beneficial to self-governance. By drawing on the collective memory of Watergate, journalists simultaneously presented arguments supporting anonymity as well as their own cultural and political relevancy.

Beyond providing a counterexample to contemporaneous news controversies involving anonymity, appeals to the Watergate narrative in the face of the Felt revelation led to praise for the general use of unnamed sources while discounting controversial applications of anonymity as isolated and deviant. For example, David Halberstam acknowledged the frequent misuse of anonymity at the same time as he advocated for its necessity: "Sure, anonymous sources can be abused. But every once in a while they are simply mandatory . . . for a democracy to work."[66] Halberstam's argument prioritized the need for unnamed sources over examples of their misapplication. In drawing on the collective memory of Watergate as the ultimate proof of anonymity's virtue, news controversies involving unnamed sources were not judged to negate the practice.

By embracing Felt as a whistle-blower, journalistic discussions of unnamed sources moved away from problems incumbent in their actual use to a defensive position reiterating journalism's self-described principles. Journalists argued that their ability to hold the government accountable relied on officials coming forward with information out of view of journalists and the public. This discourse marked an effort at utilizing the authoritative potential of collective memory once the revelation of Felt stirred up attention to Watergate. Rather than confining these remembrances to the 1970s, the past was used to tout journalism's continued significance while putting aside controversies taking place in the present. While this view furthered the construction of

Felt as a model for journalistic practice, it ignored the common practice of using non–whistle-blowers as unnamed sources. In embracing Felt, these discussions of unnamed sources moved away from the problems incumbent in actual practice to a normative defense positioned around journalism's self-described principles.

Watergate's Mixed Legacy

Journalists' concerted effort to protect the image of Felt, their continued ex-ultation of Woodward and Bernstein, and their nostalgic veneration of the Watergate era raises an often omitted question: How has the Watergate myth led to negative consequences for journalism? Despite the adulation accom-panying the journalistic retelling of Watergate, its legacy remains much more complicated. The emphasis on the journalistic role has meant disregarding internal government investigations and obscuring the interagency infighting driving many leaks.[67] Meanwhile, the question of motives fell away.

In becoming the high water marker of journalistic success, the idealized version of Watergate simultaneously became the point from which to measure journalistic decline. Woodward and Bernstein, having grown to be the goal contemporary journalists fall short of, have negatively influenced journalism to the extent that the nuances of Watergate have faded.[68] Some critics directly traced the devolution of unnamed sources and investigative journalism to the popularity of Watergate. In this argument, the spectacle of Woodward and Bernstein becoming celebrities and bestselling authors led journalists to shift their energy to pursuing the next career-making investigative break. Howard Kurtz described a shift in which "too many journalists wanting to be the next Woodward . . . and turning every two-bit scandal into a 'gate' that would be a Watergate-like intensity, I think, helped turn the public against the news media."[69] Privileging Watergate as *the* model, while authoritatively useful, actually harms journalism when used to justify the excessive use of unnamed sources. Journalists became aggressive for the sake of being ag-gressive rather than out of a commitment to the public.

Post-Watergate reporting that "turned journalism into a crusade" turned audiences against the news.[70] Pew Research Center director Andrew Kohut tied declining media credibility to dissatisfaction with this style of journal-ism as news audiences "came to see the press as a watchdog that barked too much, and sometimes was out of control."[71] This shift in public opinion sig-naled a threat to the cultural authority journalists draw on to prosecute their work. Perceptions of journalists as self-interested, combined with increased external scrutiny from an array of critics and a series of news controversies, lessened their ability to conduct investigative reporting. This uneasiness with investigative forms of news also emphasized the difficulty journalists face in synching objectivity norms with a prosecutorial reporting style.

As they have in the past, journalists looked to Watergate as evidence for the need of an aggressive journalism to help confront problems in the present. To the interpretive community of journalists, Watergate remains an aspiration for working reporters and a model to be emulated. But this remembering has not all been positive. It has also led to excesses by status-starved reporters and expectations of anonymity for sources no matter the issue. The roles of other institutions have faded away. For these reasons, recalling Watergate can only help journalists to a certain degree since, in many ways, its received history offers less of a panacea and more a mirage of a past era.

Conclusion: Deep Throat Redux

To end, we need to return to the question of "hero or villain" that so often framed efforts to understand the two entirely separate questions of why Mark Felt did what he did and what it meant. This imposed dichotomy may be defeated by proposing a third option of "neither." To answer "villain" is to cast aside sins of the Nixon administration that should not be forgotten or excused. Conversely, the answer of "hero" pushes away the real questions of motives that accompany an unnamed source. It also provides further unchecked support for the vision journalists put forth of a pair of gallant reporters single-handedly exposing scandal in the White House. To avoid rehabilitating Nixon or over-praising Felt, the "neither" option allows us to view Felt as embodying the contractions that come with unnamed sources.

In particular, a separation needs to be made between the individual interests bound up with disclosures from unnamed sources and the public interest value of this information. Individualized motives do not necessarily negate the public benefit just as Felt's motives, whatever they may be, did not render his tips to Woodward unimportant. But by no means does this extend to all unnamed sources. Often, individualized motives serve the source more than the public. This all-too-common outcome continued to come to light with the prewar intelligence reporting, culminating with the trial of vice presidential aide Scooter Libby (recounted at the end of chapter 5). Journalists end up having to adjudicate motives of unnamed sources in a process mostly taking place outside the vision of news audiences. For this reason, it is a disservice to ignore issues of motive by reducing the field of unnamed sources to only that of the idealized, motive-free whistle-blower. Wrestling with motives is at the core of unnamed sourcing practices and it cannot be ignored. As a way of broaching the topic, Felt's flaws should be acknowledged instead of ignored, followed by serious discussion of the conditions in which motives disqualify a potential unnamed source. Perhaps, in this light, Felt should be seen as a "heroic villain"—a figure of moral complexity caught up in a larger web of malfeasance whose leaks were simultaneously self-serving and illuminating of hidden government actions.

Apart from efforts to figure out Felt, it is important not to lose sight of how these discussions grew beyond reputational sniping to become a competition to imagine journalism and its relation to power in particular ways. The struggle over how to remember Felt, and, more broadly, the press role in uncovering Watergate, took place largely between journalists and government officials as each side interpreted Felt's actions with an eye toward shaping conceptions of appropriate behavior. Interpretations of Felt extended beyond considerations of past actions to differing normative formations pitting the responsibilities of public officials with insider information of wrongdoing against the utility of journalism in ameliorating such wrongdoing through turning to unnamed sources. Critics of Felt expressed a general mistrust of journalists to the point of denying their ability to improve government functioning with reporting on internal problems. Journalists responded by reducing the realm of unnamed sources to only that of the whistle-blower. This was a defensive move protective of a normative construct of journalism in an era of diminishing public opinion, a Bush administration resistant to press entreaties, and a series of controversies involving unnamed sources. Rather than inspiring a reexamination of why so many unnamed sources proved problematic or prompting calls to reform news practices, support for Felt closed off any such discussions to instead reassert Watergate as a touchstone upholding the cultural authority of journalism. While understandable, this move did limit the discussions of unnamed sources that were possible given the dynamics of Felt/Deep Throat. What could have been an opportunity to revise how unnamed sources are used ended up a moment of defense via nostalgia.

5

"Journalism on Trial": Confidentiality and the Plame Leak Case

How did what seemed a minor inside-the-Beltway matter just a couple of years ago—the public naming of a CIA agent—become a wildly swinging double-edged sword that threatens to wound a lot of people and perhaps put a big dent in the protective shield reporters thought they had?

—Rudi Bakhtiar on CNN

Dan Rather's hasty retirement, the failings of *Newsweek,* and remembrances of Watergate and Deep Throat were all still fresh in the public mind when, on June 27, 2005, the latest scuffle over unnamed sources grabbed the limelight after the U.S. Supreme Court refused to hear the case of the *New York Times*'s Judith Miller and *Time*'s Matt Cooper. Months earlier, on February 15, an appeals court ruling upheld independent prosecutor Patrick Fitzgerald's subpoena of the two reporters as part of his investigation into who leaked Valerie Plame's status as a covert CIA employee. The two journalists had sought an intervention from the high court as a final legal option to avoid jail for their refusal to testify.

A week later on July 6, with jail eminent, Cooper's and Miller's fates diverged when a last-minute waiver from White House advisor Karl Rove freed Cooper to testify and avoid incarceration. Miller received no such waiver and, after a short hearing, was taken to jail in Alexandria, Virginia, until she chose to relent and testify. On the same day, Bob Woodward released his soon-to-be bestseller on Mark Felt, *The Secret Man.* Woodward used his media appearances for the book to defend Miller, even offering to serve her jail time for her.[1] Months later, when his own involvement in the Plame leak scandal came to light, he would find himself compared to Miller in a far less positive light than would have been imagined in early July.

How did the plight of Judith Miller—and, to a lesser extent, Matt Cooper and Bob Woodward—shift from martyr to outcast? Once the abstracted advocacy for reportorial confidentiality subsided, the Plame leak case brought to public attention the inner workings of newsrooms, the Bush administration, and their interaction in sometimes quite unsettling ways. The interpretive struggles that developed within the journalistic community bespoke a tension between protecting journalism no matter what and recognizing that, in practice, unnamed sources were shot through with a messiness that proved difficult to untangle. All the while, the looming specter of the journalistic role in driving forward a faulty case for the 2003 invasion of Iraq, a sore subject running throughout these chapters, continued to fester with the costs of war still mounting. In many ways, Plamegate marked the culmination of the struggle over unnamed sources recounted here in how it raised questions about what kind of journalism we have, what kind we want, and the distance between these choices.

Stumping for a Reporter's Privilege

With the combination of judicial pressure to compel Miller and Cooper to testify, growing antipathy toward the Bush administration's media management tactics, and journalists still thinking about Deep Throat, it is no surprise that in the summer of 2005 the threat and realization of an imprisoned journalist sparked broad outrage within the journalistic community. The response was not simply a call to free Miller, but a movement to introduce new legal privileges protecting reporters at the federal level. These efforts to extend the plight of Miller and Cooper required a broad normative argument holding that journalistic autonomy could only be protected by stopping the government from interfering with journalistic practice in the form of forcing journalists to testify in federal cases. Many in the journalistic community vocally heralded the two reporters through an appeal to ideals without considering what actually transpired between the journalists and their sources to bring about the case—an omission recounted below.

To advocate for legal privileges, journalists had to associate their autonomy with a social value beyond only solidifying the status of journalism for its own individualized purpose. Any rhetorical argument backing journalists' claiming of rights above those of other citizens needed to position journalists as surrogates working for their audiences. Being a conduit for information about the operations of various institutions meant reserving the option of using unnamed sources to bring out otherwise hidden information. The key to this argument lay in presenting threats to journalism as, transitively, threats to the public. The suggestion of a public threat quickly became an abstract claim that drifted away from the specific case of Miller and Cooper to more platitudinous discourse, such as when CNN's Lou Dobbs made the connection between confidentiality and the public good overt: "The ability for journalists to protect their confidential sources is critical for the public's right to know."[2] While this may hold some truth, it also obscures incidents in which the public comes to know less because of anonymity.

This argument also contained another foundational assertion underlying journalism's self-presentation of its social role: information about institutions offered through conventional public channels cannot be trusted. A back-channel flow of information—conceived as a check on front-channel messages—offers a more complete picture of an institution's workings. In this view of itself, journalism presents its role not merely in the relay of authorized messages but in culling unauthorized information. It follows that the diminished use of confidentiality necessarily worsened journalism by leading to an overreliance on official messages—a claim offered by *New York Times* publisher Arthur Sulzberger: "If we're not allowed to have those confidential sources, the amount of information coming out of Washington will be about press releases and news conferences, not about the things that really matter."[3] What really mattered, in this frame, was the service journalism provided by unveiling hidden information relevant to the public.

The normative scale of this argument meant that it could avoid—or attempt to avoid—thorny issues arising in the actual use of unnamed sources. In particular, journalists who publicly advocated for confidentiality rights sidestepped the often undesirable ways in which anonymity led to the reproduction of official views. By ignoring such instances, journalists reduced the range of unnamed sources to include only the whistle-blower, construed as a brave individual going against her organization to bring attention to wrongdoing that would not otherwise be exposed.[4] Such reductions were common. Even in his own defense against testifying, Matt Cooper turned to a whistle-blower centric perspective of unnamed sources: "You know one of the things journalists really rely on to be able to report stories is to be able to have people come forward with information, whistle-blowing about government malfeasance, government waste, maybe some kind of other problems, and they'll only do it under conditions of anonymity. They're afraid of losing their jobs and we have to be able to promise confidentiality to these people."[5] Likewise, the *New York Times* defended Miller by drawing on the collective memory of whistle-blowers: "American history is full of examples of whistle-blowers who were able to inform the public of malfeasance only through reporters who were able to guarantee them confidentiality."[6] These arguments portrayed journalism as an indispensable public safety valve for confronting malfeasance.

Unnamed sources—qua whistle-blowers—became central to journalism's ability to fulfill its democratic role, and, as such, remained closely linked with arguments for its cultural authority. This allowed journalists to declare themselves victims during what was seen as "open season on journalists."[7]

Journalists concretized the threat they perceived through connecting the impact of the subpoenas to a diminished source-base. This claim, commonly expressed using the term "chill" or "chilling," frequently appeared in reactions to Fitzgerald's subpoena. For example, *New York Times* editor Bill Keller used a derivation of "chill" three times in a short statement on the incarceration of Miller.[8] Keller also labeled the subpoenas "chilling" on the *CBS Evening News* and the *NBC Nightly News* after Miller was incarcerated on July 6. "Chilling" was often how journalists thought through the effects of the subpoena in order to demonstrate what was at stake. It attributed an ambiguously negative impact to government constraints placed on news practices involving journalistic confidentiality. The proliferation of "chilling" as the proper metaphor for describing the detrimental impact of the Plame leak case investigation occurred in both print and broadcast news outlets.[9] The allegation that the investigation was "chilling" journalism became an often-used argument across the news to explain the threat to journalistic practice raised by Fitzgerald's subpoenas and their support in the courts.

To cure this chill, the journalistic community, along with some lawmakers, called on Congress to pass a shield law protecting confidentiality at the federal level. Pleas for a shield law highlighted its public good while downplaying the special privilege it would grant journalists. For example, former Republican Senator Bob Dole, not the usual vocal supporter of increased journalistic rights, wrote in a *New York Times* op-ed, "The purpose of a reporter's privilege is not to somehow elevate journalists above other segments of society. Instead, it is designed to help guarantee that the public continues to be well informed."[10] By drawing on these social benefits, journalistic confidentiality was presented not as a protection for a reporter or a source, but for the public explicitly. Testifying before Congress on behalf of a shield law, *New York Times* columnist William Safire told the committee, "By protecting the reporter who is protecting a source, the shield achieves its ultimate goal: to protect the people's access to what's really going on."[11] The *Columbus Dispatch* viewed the transitive power of a shield law as common sense: "The ultimate and most important beneficiaries of shield laws, of course, are not reporters and their sources but the public."[12] The editorial supported a shield law as a tool for ensuring journalistic autonomy, which, in turn, benefited the public and democracy as a whole. These arguments continued to align journalistic and public interests against the government's pursuit of journalists' testimony.

Cooper and the Corporation

While Miller and Cooper fought their subpoenas in unison, a crucial difference separated their cases. Even through she faced a subpoena regarding Plame, Miller had never written about her. Cooper, by contrast, had written an online article about Plame for the *Time* magazine Web site in which he referred to conversations with unnamed administration sources.[13] For this reason, Time Inc. was also named in the suit along with Cooper. When Cooper refused to testify, the court took the coercive measure of slapping *Time* with a $1,000-a-day fine for protecting Cooper's notes—a fine that the court threatened to elevate. Conversely, because Miller had not published a story, the *New York Times* escaped being named in the case or having fines levied against it.

The magazine and its parent company, Time Inc., had backed Cooper's resistance to the grand jury subpoena as the case wound through the courts. In a sudden—and unexpected—reversal on June 30, three days after the Supreme Court's refusal to hear the case, *Time* magazine surrendered Cooper's notes on Valerie Plame to the grand jury. The decision, made by Time Inc. executive Norman Pearlstine, drew contempt from Cooper, who said: "I'm obviously disappointed by what they chose."[14] The move released Time Inc. from the suit, but Cooper continued to face incarceration regardless of the notes until he secured an eleventh-hour waiver from Karl Rove.

In a tense week for journalism between the Supreme Court's decision not to take up Miller and Cooper's case and the hearing to decide on jail, the Time Inc. decision came as a surprise. In response, many in the journalistic community extended their criticism to include not only governmental encroachment through subpoenas but also the placement of corporate values above journalistic ones. Condemnations of Pearlstine soon followed, with charges he had reneged on his previous promises of preserving journalistic confidentiality.[15] In February 2005, the *Wall Street Journal* quoted Pearlstine arguing that a reporter's privilege benefited the public: "Without that right, important information that should be available to the public would never see the light of day."[16]

After the Supreme Court decided not to hear Miller and Cooper's case, Pearlstine justified his decision to turn over documents out of respect for the law. He charged that journalists should not hold themselves above the duties of all citizens: "I think it is detrimental to our journalistic principles to think of ourselves as above the law."[17] Pearlstine attempted to counter allegations that he was motivated by corporate interests, adding, "My decisions were based on journalistic principles, not on financial principles or on anything other than a journalistic belief that the responsible thing for this news organization to do under the circumstances was to obey the law."[18] After stepping down as head of Time Inc., Pearlstine reiterated this point in his book *Off the Record*. Taking the opportunity to provide an inside view of the incident, Pearlstine defended the role of anonymity in certain cases while declining to strike an absolutist stance. At one point, he wondered, "How . . . could we, as journalists, criticize others who ignored the courts if we did so ourselves?"[19] This was an important question raised by others as well during the Plame controversy, but overshadowed by the calls for a shield law.

Pearlstine's attempt to disconnect his decision from corporate interests and spark a more nuanced conversation about anonymity faced harsh skepticism from other journalists. *New York Times* columnist Frank Rich dismissed Pearlstine's claims and instead noted the subtle coercion of corporate values: "A corporate mentality needn't be imposed by direct fiat; it's a virus that metastasizes in the bureaucratic bloodstream."[20] Corporate influence permeated news organizations, posing a threat to journalistic decisions and the effectiveness of the news to challenge society's institutions. Through discussions of Time Inc.'s actions, an opposition arose in which journalistic and corporate values were presented as not only mutually exclusive, but fundamentally opposed.

Echoing this divide, media scholar and former journalist Ben Bagdikian posited a decision for media companies: "Every publication who employs journalists has to decide whether they're going to give priority to their journalism or to their corporate ease of life."[21] The two sides were cast as antagonistic and even irreconcilable. This gave rise to fears that when the two interests diverged, the profit-driven model of journalism meant that news work would be constrained by nonjournalistic interests. The *Columbia Journalism Review* agreed in an editorial that the Time Inc. decision "made economic sense," but did not "make . . . journalistic sense, and thus it raises a fundamental question in this age of media conglomerates: Who has journalism's back?"[22] Likewise, the Portland *Oregonian* warned of dire consequences for the public "if media giants feel more loyalty to their corporate shareholders than to their journalistic ideals."[23]

In the context of the public battle over source confidentiality being waged between Fitzgerald and both Miller and Cooper, Time Inc.'s decision prompted a concern that corporate interests weakened the viability of unnamed sources mainly through a refusal to fight government efforts to compel journalists to reveal their unnamed sources through expensive legal battles. *USA Today* answered its own question: "If the richest, most powerful media companies won't stand behind their reporters' promises, will any source trust a promise of confidentiality? Not likely."[24] Critics held that Time Inc.'s decision damaged the larger battle for increased reporter privileges being waged in the Plame leak case.

Others upset at the Time Inc. decision argued that it was not only journalists who faced injury, but also the unnamed sources themselves. As a *Salt Lake Tribune* editorial put it: "So, because Time Warner Inc. wants to protect the stock market value of the world's largest communications company, reporters, whistle-blowers and the American people face a future where it is harder to know the truth and easier to punish those who would tell it."[25] The editorial linked journalism with the public interest while holding corporate self-interest to be detrimental to the public. The *Salt Lake Tribune* was not speaking as an independently owned news outlet in making these claims. Like most large newspapers, it is owned by a publicly traded media company—in this case, the MediaNews Group.

The visibility of the Plame leak case provided a venue for journalists to work out anxieties concerning their autonomy during a time of reduced resources, shrinking staffs, and an uncertain economic future. While Time Inc. bore the brunt of criticism, a general worry hung in the air that the rules of journalism were being forever transformed by the search for increasingly scant profits.

A Less Than Ideal Case

The combination of the Supreme Court's refusal to hear Miller and Cooper's case, the actions of Time Inc., and the jailing of Miller no doubt led many in the journalistic community to vocally defend the rights of reporters to maintain source confidentiality. Coming only a month after Deep Throat dominated the news about the news, the arguments above supporting Miller and Cooper found their base in linking journalistic confidentiality—reduced to only cases of whistle-blowing—with the public good. Yet at the same time, a steady crescendo of criticism from other journalists emerged to question whether the actual events of the Plame leak case warranted the rhetoric it inspired. "The press has planted its flag on the least favorable ground to fight the larger battle for confidentiality," *Washington Post* columnist David Ignatius wrote following Miller's jailing.[26] In fact, a close look at the mechanics of the Plame leak case even suggested the whole episode may have actually been the inversion of whistle-blowing.

Critical takes on Miller and Cooper's actions and the normative battle for confidentiality waged in their names began by reexamining the string of events that led to the jailing of a journalist. Looking back, it became clear that if an unnamed whistle-blower was to be found, it was former ambassador Joseph Wilson. He first emerged as an unnamed source for Nicholas Kristof in his *New York Times* column on May 6, 2003. In questioning why, after seven weeks of war, no WMDs had been found, Kristof wrote: "I'm told by a person involved in the Niger caper that more than a year ago the vice president's office asked for an investigation of the uranium deal, so a former U.S. ambassador to Africa was dispatched to Niger. In February 2002, according to someone present at the meetings, that envoy reported to the C.I.A. and State Department that the information was unequivocally wrong and that the documents had been forged."[27] Here, Wilson—under the cloak of anonymity—provided insider information to Kristof about firsthand knowledge he had that called into question public prewar intelligence claims made by the Bush administration. In this scenario, Wilson acted as a whistle-blower working through Kristof and the *Times*.

Nonetheless, Kristof's column did not draw significant attention to the false Niger uranium claims. In response, Wilson gave up his anonymity to go on the record as a whistle-blower. In a *New York Times* op-ed titled "What I Didn't Find in Africa," Wilson stated unequivocally, "Based on my experience with the administration in the months leading up to the war, I have little choice but to conclude that some of the intelligence related to Iraq's nuclear weapons program was twisted to exaggerate the Iraqi threat."[28] It was published on July 6, 2003—two years to the day before Miller would be sent to jail for refusing to respond to a subpoena.

In the two months between Kristof's column and Wilson's op-ed, scrutiny continued to mount over the lack of WMDs that had been the driving force for the need to invade Iraq. Wilson's account was particularly threatening to the Bush administration because it suggested that purposeful manipulation—

rather than incorrect information—explained the bad intelligence that led to war. In response, unnamed administration sources seeking to dampen Wilson's criticism revealed to journalists that Wilson's wife was a covert CIA agent. By introducing a link between Wilson and the CIA, these officials attempted to marginalize Wilson's role in the intelligence-gathering process. Simply put, these leaks to reporters about Wilson and Plame were part of a response *against* a whistle-blower who had challenged administration claims both as an unnamed and on-the-record source.

With the case presented as the inversion of whistle-blowing, the connection between calls for increasing journalistic privileges and the public interest became strained. Instead, the leaks signaled the opposite of what they were used to argue, as the general counsel of the *Wall Street Journal* called attention to in an op-ed: "Shielding sources is supposed to enable journalists to report valuable information that the public otherwise couldn't get; here, deals with sources deprived the public of perhaps the most relevant information: the identity not of Mr. Wilson's wife, but of the sources."[29] In the *New Yorker,* Columbia Journalism School Dean Nicholas Lemann also noted this inversion: "The anonymous sources were not whistle-blowers taking on an Administration but an Administration taking on whistle-blowers."[30] Following this frame, the Plame leak case became an example where journalists performed a disservice to the public's understanding of government workings.

A key difference separates the treatment of the Plame leak case from the revelation of Mark Felt as Deep Throat (discussed in chapter 4). In the former situation, the majority of the journalistic community dismissed the question of Felt's motives as irrelevant given the outcome of Nixon's resignation. Yet, for the Plame leak case, many journalists turned to source motives as the key to understanding what happened. For example, shortly after the subpoenas were issued in August 2004, Howard Kurtz raised suspicions regarding motives on his CNN program *Reliable Sources:* "In this particular case, this source or sources were trying to blacken somebody's reputation."[31] More succinctly, *Time* columnist Margaret Carlson said of journalists defending anonymity in this situation, "You're protecting a creep."[32] For these commentators, the intentions of the unnamed sources mattered because they were described as attempting to silence a critic of the Bush administration. Of course, even as the speakers raised questions, the journalistic community was, on balance, more supportive of the efforts of Miller and Cooper to quash their subpoenas—until new questions and doubts arose following Miller's release from jail.

Judith Miller: "From Journalistic Hero to Goat"

After eighty-five days in jail, Miller secured her freedom through a waiver agreement with her unnamed source, Vice Presidential Chief-of-Staff, I. Lewis "Scooter" Libby on September 29, 2005. Miller testified before Fitzgerald's grand jury and returned to civilian life. Yet her release was marked not by a united journalistic community lionizing her heroic stand against the federal government, but a mixture of ambivalence and disapproval over her actions. As *Editor & Publisher* summed up her post-jail fall: "Once out of jail, Miller quickly went from journalistic hero to goat."[33] Her transformation from a paragon of journalistic principle during her battle against the subpoena to a symbol of flawed practices after her incarceration occurred alongside a larger interpretive shift caused by the growing attention to the circumstances of the case.

This shift was encapsulated in two columns by Margaret Sullivan, the editor of the *Buffalo News*. Like many others in the journalistic community, Sullivan lauded Miller when she first went to jail in a July 10 column that connected Miller's resistance to the public benefit derived from a reporter's confidentiality privilege.[34] Months later, following the release of Miller and the surfacing of details concerning her source relationships, Sullivan again wrote about Miller. This time, she retracted her earlier column, noting that Miller was "not protecting a brave whistle-blower," but instead was "acting as a conduit for a high-ranking White House aide with a political ax to grind."[35] The original article praised Miller and the sanctity of whistle-blowers, but the editor felt obligated to revisit these claims when specifics of the case emerged. As some critics had initially warned, the details of the case did not sustain the normative claims that Miller was made to represent.

Like many others, Sullivan's about-face stemmed from a perspectival shift from treating all unnamed sources as praiseworthy whistle-blowers who must be protected to recognizing unnamed source–journalist relations as uneven or even harmful at times for impeding the flow of information they are meant to make possible. Within the sweep of the Plame leak case, support for Miller during her battle against testifying to the grand jury turned to scrutiny of her relationships with her unnamed sources. Miller's critics recast her as an example of a journalist who, out of desire for access or advocacy, granted her sources undue anonymity without adjudicating their statements. These charges extended beyond her dealings with Libby in the Plame leak case to her earlier coverage of WMDs in the *New York Times* (as recounted in chapter 1).

The reversal of opinion toward Miller within the journalistic community began soon after Miller's release from jail after she struck a deal with Libby that allowed her to testify. NPR's *On the Media* host Brook Gladstone characterized the ensuing reaction as "skepticism that she was as steadfast as her paper claims, and concern that the affair sends the message not that the paragons of journalism will not be moved, but rather that reporters may well crumble after a few months in the big house."[36] Gladstone's assessment summed up the initial critique Miller faced. While she had been so lauded during her stand against Fitzgerald, her early release from jail led to questions about her original motives. Critics argued that Miller's deal negated her sacrifice by, ironically, emboldening other prosecutors to use jail to coerce testimony. *Vanity Fair*'s Seth Mnookin identified the ultimate legacy of Miller's jailing as the knowledge that "jail does work as a way to break reporters' wills."[37] In other words, by relenting in her refusal to testify, Miller actually reduced journalists' ability to maintain confidentiality.

THE *NEW YORK TIMES* TURNS ON MILLER

Calls for the *New York Times* to investigate the reporting practices of Miller came as early as the summer of 2003 when the lack of Iraqi WMDs sparked efforts to figure out why the public had been so misled. As chapter 1 detailed, the newspaper shied away from self-examination for over a year until editor Bill Keller undertook a limited review. While Keller did admit mistakes, he also distributed blame evenly across the paper and, in doing so, declined to mention any staff member by name—including the already-much maligned Miller. But Miller did not escape scrutiny indefinitely. On October 18, 2005, the *Times* ran a 6,000-word front-page story delving into her reporting of not only the Plame case, but her body of reporting on WMDs before the start of the war as well.[38] Miller wrote an accompanying first-person article that ran alongside the larger review.[39] Days later, harsh assessments appeared in the paper from columnist Maureen Dowd and public editor Byron Calame.[40] Ultimately, Keller's 2004 attempt to locate fault at an organizational level failed when, seventeen months later, Miller became an individualized target.

Within the October 18 review of Miller, a small item occasioned much criticism of both Miller's behavior and the newspaper's management. According to the article, Miller earned the newsroom nickname of "Miss Run Amok" after it was reported she had once said "I can do whatever I want."[41] The *Times* piece painted a portrait of Miller as operating without supervision during the distraction of the Jayson Blair scandal and the eventual resignation of the newspaper's editor and managing editor. Even when Keller was installed as editor and ordered Miller off the WMD beat, she kept returning to intelligence stories. The sovereignty the *Times* granted to Miller drew harsh assessments from other newspapers. She was cast as a "rogue reporter" in an unmanaged newsroom,[42] which triggered *Washington Post* columnist Tina Brown to ask: "Is the *Times* after Blair some sort of trackless sea, with lone castaways afloat on rafts? To whom do reporters report? IS THERE ANYBODY HOME?"[43] Brown depicted a breakdown of the hierarchical editing structure employed by news outlets to check the power of individual reporters.

Further criticisms developed after Miller's adjoining first-person account of her involvement in the Plame leak case suggested the placing of sources' interests over those of the audience. Miller documented several meetings with Libby in which the subject of Plame arose. During one meeting, Miller agreed to identify Libby as a "former Hill staffer," even though he worked in the vice president's office. "I agreed to the new ground rules because I knew that Mr. Libby had once worked on Capitol Hill," Miller wrote.[44]

This item raised consternation from journalists who construed it as misleading readers for the sake of getting an interview. As former *Times* journalist Steve Roberts put it: "You never, ever, ever agree to any kind of deception of any kind, period."[45] The deception of news audiences was held to be a grave subversion of journalistic principles, especially when anonymity already constrained the audience's ability to appraise quoted statements. A *Denver Post* editorial contrasted Miller's obfuscation with "the goal . . . [of] provid[ing] readers with enough honest detail about an anonymous source so they can discern the credibility of the information and the motive of the source.[46] The *Post* insisted a newspaper is responsible to readers more so than sources and held that Miller—and others like her—moved too far toward being source-centered rather than audience-centered. Normatively, the authority of journalists to do their work—and consequently the basis for any special rights they enjoy, including confidentiality privileges—stem from being an agent of the readers. However, in practice, journalists work to procure access to sources they need to do their job in a reliable and consistent way. Thus, assertions that journalists were improperly close to their sources raised questions regarding the configuration of allegiances between journalists, sources, and audiences.

Two days after the *New York Times* published its account of Miller's reporting, an editorial in the *Los Angeles Times,* in one of the most direct condemnations of Miller, wrote that Miller was "not so much a reporter defending a principle as a reporter using a principle to defend herself," adding, "It's becoming increasingly clear that she and her employer have abused the public's trust by manufacturing a showdown with the government."[47] The *Los Angeles Times* delivered a harsh assessment of the Miller situation, accusing both her and the newspaper of misleading the public through their vocal defense casting Miller as a symbol of the need for journalistic confidentiality. Miller, who had been so lauded initially for her stand against Fitzgerald's subpoenas, faced censure within the journalistic community. This coincided with the steady transformation of viewing unnamed sources as whistle-blowers—no doubt inspired by the recent exposure of Deep Throat's identity—to a broader view of anonymity as damaging public knowledge. Even if she never wrote an article about Valerie Plame, Miller's willingness to let sources use anonymity to attack others was seen as the nadir for unnamed sourcing practices.

Out of jail, facing a hostile *Times* newsroom, and having lost much of the sympathy and support from other journalists she once enjoyed, Miller struck a deal to retire from the newspaper on November 10—two weeks after Libby's October 28 indictment on five counts of perjury, obstruction of justice, and making false statements under oath.

DISSECTING MILLER'S REPORTING

The transformation of Miller into a symbol of journalistic malpractice sheds light on how the journalistic community confronted the contradictions underlying anonymity. Beyond the anger directed at Miller for her prewar reporting lies an uneasy recognition that the high-minded rhetoric employed to protect source anonymity so often falls short of describing actual journalist–unnamed source relations. While journalists sought to further codify their independence legally, in practice the issue was much murkier. This was evidenced by a recurring simple spatial metaphor directed at Miller: "She had gotten too close to her sources."[48]

Critics employed a vocabulary of proximity—for example, "close," "cozy"—to explain Miller's transgressions. Here, her "coziness" made impossible the normative antagonism at the heart of journalism's claims of independence.[49] Good journalism meant being distant, detached, and separate—the vocabulary of autonomy. Bad journalism consisted of journalists and sources sharing the same space—of being interdependent or, worse, journalists being subservient or even supportive.[50] The complaints leveled at Miller suggested nervousness that such stark distinctions may not be realizable in practice. When radio host Amy Goodman wondered aloud, "Is there a separation between the press and the state?"[51] the question dangled in front of more than just Miller.

The coziness factor closely relates to another common complaint that

Miller acted merely as a stenographer instead of as an investigative reporter. On this point, Miller defended herself: "My job isn't to assess the government's information and be an independent intelligence analyst myself. My job is to tell readers of *The New York Times* what the government thought about Iraq's arsenal."[52] *Slate* columnist Jack Shafer, a leading critic of Miller, referred to this as the "It's the sources talking, not me!" defense,[53] and responded by emphasizing verification: "A good reporter is supposed to dig for the truth, no matter what 'people inside the governments' with 'very high security clearances' might say."[54] Rightly so, Shafer, channeling Michael Massing,[55] criticized Miller as confusing attribution with facticity. Negative comparisons of Miller's reporting as stenography buttressed a concept of reporting as an activity beyond mere exact relay. The model of a reporter's obligation—especially when unnamed sources are present—is to investigate claims and verify information on behalf of audiences lacking the ability to do so on their own.

Accusations of undue closeness and unchecked replication fell under an explanation of Miller as "seduced by access."[56] These methods ensured ties with the White House and the intelligence community while earning her an unusual level of autonomy within the *Times*. That is, for elite journalists, access to sources—and especially proprietary confidential sources—has become a requirement for success. The cost of the connection between access and success was well illustrated by an episode recounted by Shafer during the opening of the Iraq War in 2003. By agreeing to a number of restrictions, including a three-day waiting period on all stories and prior submission to the military, Miller landed a spot as an embed with a military unit tasked with locating WMDs. Shafer questioned whether this arrangement involved surrendering too much journalistic independence: "Give Miller kudos for her scoop, but it's worth asking if she and the *Times* secured it at a price too dear."[57] Shafer raised the concern that Miller's arrangement jeopardized other embeds not willing to make such deals. Two days later, he reiterated his criticisms based on the resemblance of Miller's reporting to official announcements: "[Miller's] copy reads more like a government press release than a news story."[58] Shafer criticized Miller for willingly surrendering independence at a time when it was most needed.

No individual journalist reporting on the build-up to the Iraq War in 2002 and 2003 was more loathed than Judith Miller. Yet condemnations of this period of news reporting, particularly within journalism, too often cast her as a scapegoat or exception. Instead, she should more suitably be considered a marker of what went wrong with journalists' use of unnamed sources in this period. Her close ties to sources and emphasis on access were far from unique within the cadre of elite reporters working on the national stage. In the battle over journalism emerging around unnamed sources, the battering of Miller provided one angle for thinking through wider transgressions. And while Miller, an individual, could be banished from the news, the conditions of her problematic work could not be so easily eradicated—a point taken up in chapter 6.

From Watergate Icon to "Judy Woodward"

Days after Miller's retirement from the *Times,* the Plame leak case produced another black eye for journalism when it emerged that Bob Woodward, too, had been snagged by Plamegate. While working on a book, Woodward had learned of Valerie Plame's identity from the State Department's Richard Armitage in June 2003, but withheld the disclosure from *Washington Post* editor Leonard Downie for two years. The details accompanying Libby's indictment made it clear that Woodward was the first journalist to know, prompting a call to Armitage who then informed Fitzgerald. Woodward's testimony to the grand jury on November 14, 2005, became public through a front page *Washington Post* article two days later.[59] In turn, he drew condemnation for failing to tell his editors what he knew about the case even as he vocally defended Miller in her fight to avoid testifying. Woodward's mythic status within journalism and history of bestselling nonfiction books did not immunize him from accusations of being too close to sources, too distant from editors, and too concerned with individual status above the public interest.

While the *Washington Post* actively resisted efforts to draw parallels between Miller and Woodward—Downie called it "not an analogous case at all"[60]—Woodward's ensnarement in the Plame leak case quickly impelled comparisons. Already critical of Miller, bloggers took to calling Woodward "Mr. Run Amok" and "Judy Woodward."[61] Noting the timing, *On the Media*'s Brooke Gladstone placed the two in sequence: "Just as Miss Run Amok exits the stage, having given up her anonymous source, enter Mr. Run Amok."[62] *Boston Globe* columnist James Carroll also made the connection, calling Woodward Miller's "secret co-captain."[63] Miller, who had been a chief object of journalistic attention, provided an interpretive lens through which to view Woodward's actions. As elite Washington reporters, their transgressions were often imbricated. For example, the trade magazine *Editor & Publisher* tied Miller and Woodward together for "withholding information not just from readers, but their own editors."[64]

Woodward's great fault was in not expressing to his editors what he knew about the Plame leak case, an omission that *Post* ombudsman Deborah Howell called "a deeply serious sin."[65] The editor of the *Tallahassee Democrat* was harsher, calling for Woodward's resignation over his lack of notifying editors: "And if journalism icon Bob Woodward of the *Washington Post* worked as a reporter for our newspaper today, he would be fired for his latest act of journalistic hubris. I'd bet that won't happen at the *Post*. But it should."[66]

Woodward's circumventing of expectations placed on other reporters was deemed unacceptable and, more than this, detrimental to journalistic practice. In the face of organizational norms presenting the newspaper as a hierarchical, rule-bound environment in which the staff collaborated to produce the news,[67] Woodward's actions appeared deviant. As Joe Scarborough put it: "He really doesn't work for a newspaper, he works for Woodward."[68] Woodward's "unusual autonomy"[69] and "Lone Ranger-like freedoms"[70] were available only to Woodward because of his mythic status within journalism. Downie defended the arrangement, noting the exclusives delivered by Woodward's use of the paper to promote his books.[71] Yet others bristled at this exceptionalism, including Howell, who wrote, "He has to operate under the rules that govern the rest of the staff—even if he's rich and famous"[72]—a sentiment echoed by her predecessor Michael Getler.[73] Uneasy about what scoops Woodward denied the newspaper, *American Journalism Review* editor Rem Rieder wrote, "It makes you wonder where his loyalty lies."[74]

As with Miller, the culprit was identified as the seductive lure of access. Jay Rosen chastised Woodward for having "gone wholly into access journalism."[75] In this formation, according to *New York Times* columnist Frank Rich, "Mr. Woodward's passive notion of journalistic neutrality is easily manipulated by his sources. He flatters those who give him the most access by upholding their version of events."[76]

This critique of Woodward, powerfully articulated nearly a decade earlier by Joan Didion in the *New York Review of Books*,[77] was taken up in assessments of Woodward during the Bush administration. Arianna Huffington went as far as to separate his actions from what would rightly constitute a journalist: "If you basically become the stenographer to power, if you basically simply reflect, as Woodward has said, the point of view of your sources, you stop being an investigative journalist."[78] Woodward was accused of merely recording and replaying material from unnamed sources, without, as his detractors asserted, the vital step of criticism. *On the Media*'s Gladstone cast the shift of Woodward from an outsider to the ultimate insider as an ironic inversion: "Watergate Bob used disgruntled mid-level bureaucrats to tunnel his way into the bowels of a White House scandal. White House Bob moves easily through closed doors and crafts meticulous narratives seen through the eyes of the powerful."[79]

Critics blamed Woodward for inaugurating an investigative reporting style that, while initially a boon for journalistic authority, had come to damage journalism's credibility by routinizing opaque news practices involving unnamed sources. This could clearly be seen in the movement from the contribution of Deep Throat in reporting uncovering the Watergate scandal to the unsavory revelations surfacing from the trial of Scooter Libby.

The Other Side of Unnamed Sources

At the close of 2005, with Judith Miller's reputation in tatters and Bob Woodward stuck answering questions about his close ties with elite sources, two other unnamed source–based news stories emerged to both shift the political conversation around national security as well as the journalistic conversation about anonymity. In the face of a parade of perilous incidents, these stories restored some hope in the usefulness of source anonymity in producing exceptional journalism.

First, on November 2, *Washington Post* reporter Dana Priest broke the story of secret CIA-run prisons—"black sites"—and the practice of prisoner rendition by the U.S. government.[80] The front-page article included no named sources and only minimal attribution. Six weeks later, a front-page *New York Times* story by James Risen and Eric Lichtblau exposed the government's domestic warrantless wiretapping operation.[81] After the attacks of September 11, 2001, the National Security Agency expanded its surveillance activities to include citizens and others within the United States. While highly secretive, the program did spark disagreements within the government over the legality of these practices. The *Times* acceded to a request by the government to delay reporting the story for a year and omitted some procedural details. In the body of the story, Risen and Lichtblau explained their use of unnamed sources while also confronting their underlying motives for participating in the story: "Nearly a dozen current and former officials, who were granted anonymity because of the classified nature of the program, discussed it with reporters for the *New York Times* because of their concerns about the operation's legality and oversight."

Given the sensitivity of the stories, it seems likely public awareness—and accompanying scrutiny—could have been made possible only through the use of anonymity to protect sources' identities. By relying heavily on unnamed sources, the reporters were able to bring to light secret government operations of questionable legality for public debate. The importance of the revelations contained in these stories was underscored when the reporters all received Pulitzer Prizes in 2006—Priest for Beat Reporting and Risen and Lichtblau for National Reporting. When the awards were announced, the continuing notoriety of anonymity could be read in the Pulitzer committee's commendation of Risen and Lichtblau for "*carefully sourced stories* on secret domestic eavesdropping that stirred a national debate on the boundary line between fighting terrorism and protecting civil liberty."[82] By explicitly invoking the quality of the reporter's unnamed sourcing practices, the committee reaffirmed anonymity as a tool for crafting award-winning journalism.

The two stories were largely lauded within the journalism community. On CNN, Steve Roberts called Priest's story "exactly why we use anonymous sources . . . It's the kind of story that voters really need to know in order to hold their government accountable."[83] Yet the two stories did not receive universal acclaim. The exposure of secret practices related to national security, regardless of questions as to their legality, rankled conservative critics. On powerlineblog.com, Scott Johnson asserted that the Pulitzer Prize was given to Risen and Lichtblau "for their treasonous contribution to the undermining of the highly classified National Security Agency surveillance program of al Qaeda-related terrorists."[84] Meanwhile, a report by Accuracy in Media judged Priest's Pulitzer-winning reporting to have "damaged the security of the United States and endangered the safety of American citizens."[85] The gulf between these views indicates the lack of agreement surrounding revelatory reporting made possible by using unnamed sources to suss out nonpublic information. Even if broad agreement gels around normative ideals of journalists holding the government accountable, deep disparities exist as to how this should look in practice.

Considered in light of the controversies recounted throughout this book, these two stories further confirm the complicated organizational and political cultures that give rise to the best and worst of unnamed source–based reporting. It is notable that Priest's work ran in the *Washington Post*—Woodward's paper—while Risen and Lichtblau's stories appeared in the *New York Times*—Miller's paper. Newsrooms experiencing turmoil also produced award-winning work. Even at the level of individual reporters, Risen was much maligned for his use of unnamed sources in reporting on Wen Ho Lee,[86] while so celebrated for his work on wiretapping. All of this underscores the erratic nature of unnamed source–based reporting. Yet whether comprising the best of journalism or showing its worst side, the impediment of not knowing how stories get put together remained. In 2007, the Scooter Libby trial would showcase some of these practices in unsettling ways.

The Scooter Libby Trial

When Scooter Libby entered federal court as a defendant in early 2007, it was not for the original crime being pursued—the unlawful disclosure of a covert agent. Special Prosecutor Patrick Fitzgerald concluded no one disclosing Valarie Plame's undercover status violated the high threshold set by the Intelligence Identities Protection Act of 1982. Instead of breaking the law for his leak to reporters, Libby stood accused of lying under oath to investigators in an attempt to cover his tracks—even if, as it turned out, what he was covering up was not illegal. Libby claimed he first learned of Plame's identity from Vice President Dick Cheney in June 2003, but subsequently forgot this nugget until he was reminded of it by reporters—including Tim Russert, host of NBC's *Meet the Press,* and Judith Miller. To prove perjury, journalists would have to come forth to testify about their interactions with unnamed sources—normally an extremely rare feat for a prosecutor.

Ultimately, Fitzgerald prevailed in his struggle to subpoena journalists, leading to the indictment of Scooter Libby in late 2005 for perjury and obstruction of justice. The trial came down to competing memories of what happened nearly four years earlier in the summer of 2003. Fitzgerald's case rested on journalists taking the stand in open court to testify about their relationships with Bush administration officials—a scenario Lucy Dalglish of the Reporters Committee for Freedom of the Press described as "unprecedented" and "horrifying."[87] What was noteworthy was not the sight of renowned journalists casting aside previous agreements of confidentiality, but the many questionable details about these source relationships that emerged through testimony. Even through Libby occupied the defendant's chair, the public view offered of journalist-official relations resulted in a symbolic case of "journalism on trial."[88] Or, perhaps more to the point, the array of practices comprising journalistic anonymity found themselves on trial, charged with failing to serve the public in a way that matched the high-minded rhetoric espoused by a journalistic community rabid in its defense of unnamed sources.

The trial drew much political and public interest when, at the outset, Libby's defense team intimated that both Libby and Vice President Cheney would testify at the trial. This was not mere spectacle; if Cheney, the sitting vice president, would take the stand, he would certainly be interrogated on both intelligence failures leading to the Iraq War and how the White House lured journalists looking for scoops with inside information corroborating specious public claims. In the end, neither Cheney nor Libby testified. Instead, the jury, faced with conflicting accounts between Libby's grand jury testimony and the journalists who testified during the trial, returned a verdict of guilty on four of five counts of perjury and obstruction of justice. Libby avoided prison time when President Bush commuted his sentence in July 2007, leaving Libby liable for over $250,000 in fines. Libby was not pardoned by Bush before he left office.

The trial confirmed claims above that, for journalism, Plamegate was far from an ideal case for journalists to mount a public battle for special confidentiality privileges. Instead, journalists became entangled in a complicated finger-pointing contest in which the Office of the Vice President (and the White House, by extension), the State Department, and the CIA all attempted to shirk the blame for faulty prewar intelligence claims in the months following the Iraq invasion. When Joseph Wilson publicly debunked prewar claims that Iraq had sought uranium from Niger for its nuclear program, the White House responded by suggesting that Wilson's wife, Valerie Plame, in her capacity as a CIA employee, engineered Wilson's mission to Niger. High-ranking White House officials sought to lessen the damage of these charges by pushing blame onto the CIA. Meanwhile, Richard Armitage, probably the first to leak Plame's identity in conversations with Woodward and Robert Novak, meant to deflect criticism away from the State Department. Reporters became caught in the middle of interdepartmental conflict by allowing it to occur under the veil of anonymity.

Reactions to the trial oscillated between distress over the sanctity of journalistic confidentiality and concern that journalist–unnamed source relationships too often failed to serve the public. While these were both protective stances struck by journalists, they varied roughly according to a division between the form and content of the trial. With regard to form, the irreducible result of this incident was the parading of journalists, under duress, on the witness stand to publicly divulge their methods—a violation of journalistic autonomy first and foremost. The second view took account of the content of the trial and its exposure of less-than-ideal dynamics that threatened the worth of unnamed sources in news discourse. Put differently, interpretations differed between stressing the need for legal rights protecting journalistic confidentiality and emphasizing the component of public opinion required to deploy anonymity. In the broad view, both elements remain necessary and interdependent to ensuring the continued use of unnamed sources even if, in practice, contradictions abound.

Many in the journalistic community regarded the trial not only as an affront to journalism, but as an assault eradicating previous legal agreements, however tentative, that abetted journalists in evading subpoenas. As Lowell Bergman put it, journalists "have to start understanding that maybe they can't protect their sources."[89] Journalists working with unnamed sources have responded to the perception of increased susceptibility to subpoenas by undertaking new measures—including using disposable phones. More than once, this was viewed as reporters "taking on the characteristics of a drug dealer."[90] Such claims underscored an effort to cast journalists as victims of judicial overstepping.

The case was also viewed as the end of a legal détente in place since the Supreme Court decided *Branzburg v. Hayes* in 1972. Media lawyer Theodore J. Boutrous Jr. identified the ultimate takeaway for the trial as, "Every tenet and every pact that existed between the government and the press has been broken."[91] Similarly, the dean of the University of Richmond Law School interpreted the trial as "undercut[ting] the assumptions that existed for several decades that a reporter's promise of confidentiality is not only sacrosanct as a matter of journalistic ethics but relatively secure as a matter of law."[92] The result is a new vulnerability for journalists at the federal level. Fitzgerald, with his novel approach of procuring waivers of confidentiality from potential sources, opened the door for an increase in subpoenas aimed at journalists. This may have been worsened by the effectiveness of the journalists as witnesses for the prosecution in the Libby trial.[93]

A common theme both with Plamegate and across the incidents in this book has been the consistent attempt to connect unnamed sources with the public good so that any harm to journalistic confidentiality translated into a public harm. Bob Zelnick made this clear: "When reporters are the net losers, then the public is the net loser."[94] The *St. Louis Post-Dispatch* also conflated Libby and other officials leaking information about Plame for their own institutional protection with the idealized vision of the whistle-blower. From this vantage point, "the public loses" because journalists testified.[95] The associate publisher of the *Seattle Post-Intelligencer* also took to this normative stance, arguing: "It is the public that suffers when government wrongdoing, corruption and excesses never come to light."[96] Certainly, journalistic independence deserves support, but such views elided the failure of the reporting to reveal problems with prewar intelligence or the post-invasion blame game even with the copious use of unnamed sources and leaks from officials. At worst, such omissions of the actual record of unnamed sources made normative claims of their defense appear terribly ironic.

Others saw the main threat to journalistic autonomy as not the legal threats of subpoenas but the actions of journalists themselves. The Libby trial, in the words of the Poynter Institute's Roy Peter Clark, "demystified the priestly practices of Washington journalism."[97] The sight of respected journalists in a courtroom forced the larger community to contemplate the "all-too-unsettling nexus between the political and media elite" as one editor put it.[98] This view contradicted the normative indignation expressed above by suggesting that the problems emerged at the level of practice. This latter set of complaints often couched the problems in the language of autonomy. Howard Kurtz, a frequent critic in his *Washington Post* column and CNN program of the journalistic practices underlying the Libby trial, questioned whether the journalists asked to testify had "gotten too close with their high-level sources."[99] As the trial progressed, Kurtz adopted an external view as to the true damage of the trial: "Too many people out there think that this has become an insider's game, and we have been, I think, as a profession too willing to play along with that."[100] While others pushed for increased rights, a second set of voices seemed wary that these rights were undeserved until the journalistic community owned up to problems.

Concerns over the actual execution of unnamed sourcing practices often targeted access as the chief culprit causing harm. For example, Tim Rutten turned to access to explain how ostensibly vaunted journalists made such mistakes: "You have the picture of a number of high-level Washington correspondents from very fine news organizations who were essentially missing the story in the interest of preserving their access."[101] The trap for elite reporters is that to maintain their status in the competitive arena of national affairs reporting, they develop an intense dependence on elite sources. The *Chicago Tribune*'s Jill Zuckman, herself a national correspondent for a major newspaper, summed it up on Kurtz's *Reliable Sources* program: "We spend years trying to develop these close relationships. We need this. But there is always this danger that . . . you're going to feel more concern for your source than for your story."[102] On the same program, Kurtz responded to Russert's revelation that he considered all his conversations with officials to be on background—and therefore not attributable to a name—with disdain: "So this is how far the disease has spread."[103]

The Libby trial, it must be remembered, was not an abstracted assessment of the trade-offs journalists make between access and autonomy. It can only be understood in the context of uncovering the persistence of the Bush administration in seeking to impact public opinion through its relationships with journalists to push a political agenda most visibly resulting in the protracted and unpopular Iraq War. Throughout its tenure, the administration employed strategic leaking as one key weapon to entice reporters. This context returns us back to the beginning of this book to the criticism enveloping major news outlets—and the *New York Times* and *Washington Post* in particular—for quasi-investigative or insider journalism that, in the end, only echoed erroneous claims made on the record. The Libby trial, in this narrative, served as an opportunity to confront this sour legacy in the waning years of the Bush administration. The Republican control of all three federal branches diminished with the midterm election gains of Democrats in November 2006—the power shift corresponding with the start of the Libby trial—and the further loses in the 2008 election. It was in this political atmosphere that the ghosts of the prewar reporting again became a focus for journalists.

Journalists evaluating the Bush administration's ability to manipulate the press often focused on the agency of the administration over that of the reporters assigned to cover it. For example, NPR's media reporter David Folkenflik framed the dynamic this way: "This was the administration pressing a lot of levers in a lot of different ways to get out a line that it wanted."[104] Similarly, a *USA Today* editorial noted that the administration "uses leaks to manipulate public opinion, undermine critics and punish or reward individual reporters."[105]

Evidence for these criticisms emerged during the trial from the testimony of Cathie Martin, the vice president's assistant of public affairs. Martin provided insider details about how the Office of the Vice President managed news accounts, which included dispensing talking points to other officials with both material for attribution and for background use only. When pressed by the prosecution as to how her office secured favorable coverage, Martin replied, "Reporters would like to have the story. And each reporter, they're competing against each other. So if you give it to one reporter, they're more likely to write the story if they think it's news and if they think it has just been given to them. In addition, you can give it to them and do it as a senior administration official."[106] Such testimonial insights indicated the administration's savvy in baiting reporters with exclusive information delivered without full attribution. This glimpse into the actual practices behind unnamed sources further diminished the ability of journalists to so resolutely defend their need for a confidentiality privilege.

Martin's testimony allowed critics vilifying the administration's press practices to drift into blaming journalists. For example, the *St. Petersburg Times* blasted journalists for being "all too willing to be used by senior White House officials."[107] However, as in chapter 1, blame came to be personalized, particularly around the figure of Judith Miller. On MSNBC, Keith Olbermann, in describing her testimony at the trial, noted that she was "blamed more than any other by critics of the Iraq war for helping to make that war possible."[108] During the trial, an image emerged of Miller as a reliable go-to for propagating messages before the war as well as after it had started. Michael Isikoff—coauthor of the retracted *Newsweek* item written about in chapter 3—noted how Libby continued "giving her misleading information even after the war to justify the invasion in the first place."[109] Details of her interactions with Libby had been known since her release from prison in fall 2005 and contributed to the shift in her position from martyr to pariah. Two years later, during the Libby trial, Kurtz narrativized Miller's downfall: "She lost a battle of wills with a special prosecutor, surrendered her job at the *New York Times* and became an unwanted symbol of journalistic coziness with the Bush administration and media missteps in covering an unpopular war."[110]

Beyond the voices of traditional journalists, left-wing bloggers seized on the Libby trial as a telltale example of problems plaguing elite journalism. Bloggers at the site firedoglake.com worked together to liveblog the entire trial, providing a stream of real-time updates from a media room set up in the courthouse with a closed-circuit television feed. With no cameras allowed to cover the trial, this blog feed provided the most thorough account of the trial.

Aside from this reporting, bloggers also offered commentary that, in many ways, exceeded the critical tones struck by journalists by more stridently linking the reporters to the administration. One firedoglake.com blogger worked to imbue the trial with symbolic importance: "The Libby case is like an ice core sample of the Bush Administration's incestuous, manipulative, and deeply disingenuous relationship to the media and how they played the press like a concert violin in the run up to the catastrophic set of errors that is the War in Iraq."[111] On her Website huffingtonpost.com, Arianna Huffington also suggested that the Libby trial transcended its subject to become an assessment of journalistic performance: "The media's role in Plamegate—and, by extension, the war in Iraq—. . . will be decided by the court of public opinion. . . . [The Libby trial] has already demonstrated the gulf between the principles those in the press theoretically live by and reality."[112]

Elsewhere, Dan Froomkin, writing in a blog on the *Washington Post* Website, suggested that journalists tried to avoid the Libby trial out of fear of it exposing the divide that Huffington suggested: "Washington's media elites have been against this case from the beginning, seeing Fitzgerald and Wilson as unwelcome interlopers threatening the cozy relationship between the city's top political journalists and their sources."[113] Blogs on the left contained a broader vision of a systematic problem encircling both the administration and journalists. The Libby trial, while a unique spectacle in its own right, epitomized a normal set of flawed relations in which journalists did not resemble the independent crusader so central to their self-definition.

Conclusion: Reconsidering Constraints on Autonomy

While the long and complicated duration of the Plame leak case produced many twists, concerns within the journalistic community converged around a crisis of autonomy befalling unnamed sourcing practices. Time and again, journalists have based their authority to present the news on an occupational independence that emphasizes freedom from other societal institutions, whether governmental or corporate. Yet faced with disparities arising in their actual reporting practices, journalists continuously confronted difficulties in their efforts to enact normative ideals of autonomy. Discussions of unnamed sources encountered tensions over claims of autonomy arising from all sides.

Initially, the issue of autonomy arose with questions of journalism's ability to operate free of government interference following the subpoenaing of journalists over their unnamed sources. In response to efforts by the government to compel Miller and Cooper to testify, journalists staged a normative defense of the right to journalistic confidentiality. Pressing for greater legal protections of journalist–unnamed source relations, these arguments portrayed journalists as surrogates acting on behalf of the public to enable a representative democracy. In so doing, anonymity became inextricable from their ability to provide information about the actual practices of society's institutions. Questions around independence also accounted for the consternation aimed at Time Inc. for turning over Cooper's notes. In shifting scrutiny from government to media owners, journalists and other critics accused the magazine of placing corporate concerns above journalistic ones. The problem of autonomy moved from the separate entity of the government to the problematic linkage of news outlets adhering to a set of journalistic norms to their revenue-driven parent companies. Here, conflicting and competing priorities of contemporary news outlets raised concern among journalists over whether their practices were being compromised from within.

While the interpretive community of journalists backed this view of their democratic role as underpinning their claims to journalistic authority, the actual events of the Plame leak case complicated calls to legally codify a federal-level confidentiality privilege. Instead of a clear-cut rallying point, the case increasingly came to be viewed as a problematic foundation for seeking greater journalistic protections. This culminated in the Libby trial, where the practices brought to light raised many questions regarding whether an elite cadre of Washington journalists maintained proper distance from their sources. On the flip side, questions arose over whether these journalists possessed too much internal autonomy as stars within their news organizations. This was especially true for discussions of Judith Miller. Largely lauded before and during her time in jail, Miller faced scrutiny for her sourcing practices in the Plame leak case, including her apparent closeness to Scooter Libby. Meanwhile, Bob Woodward, while undoubtedly among the pantheon of U.S. journalists, was deemed to be more self-interested in transforming access into bestselling books than in informing his employer about background actions undertaken by the Bush administration.

While not revolution-inducing by any means, the Libby trial did encourage a shift from a generalized need to protect journalistic confidentiality to specific scrutiny of how unnamed sources were actually used both before and after the 2003 invasion of Iraq. Against ideal claims of unnamed sources benefiting the public, the Plame leak case demonstrated how anonymity could be used to attack whistle-blowers. Even Patrick Fitzgerald, the prosecutor in the Libby trial, justified his pursuit of journalists' testimony by differentiating between whistle-blowers and less socially valuable leakers: "We do not think that what Mr. Libby was telling reporters was whistle-blowing."[114]

Instead, the actions of these sources were seen as the inverse of the norms expressed earlier, which shifted the question of autonomy toward the question of whether journalists—who strive to meet deadlines, find novel stories, and prop up their own status—operated at the mercy of their sources. Nicholas Lemann summed up the lesson of the Plame leak case: "In the end, the chummy imperatives of Washington trumped the press's independent self-conception."[115] Thus, a vision of journalism's dependence on news sources overtook the discourse of independence that earlier dominated the case. Ultimately, the Plame leak case moved from a collective stand against government interference to an example of journalists failing to be transparent so as not to lose access and accompanying status. In response, journalists and other critics publicly showed their frustration at seeing unnamed sources stray so far from the whistle-blower ideal to becoming manipulative leakers benefiting from the lack of accountability inherent in anonymity.

The various internal and external challenges to unnamed sources in the Plame leak case connected to a larger concern over the status—or even the continued relevancy—of journalism in contemporary culture. Commentators continually connected the Plame leak case to deeper concerns relating to social perceptions of journalism's credibility and its cultural role. This was clear even as attention oscillated between advocating for legal protections of journalistic confidentiality, condemning inappropriate relationships between journalists and their sources, and questioning the emphasis of corporate values over journalistic ones. In this context, the ability of journalists to deploy anonymity connected to the credibility afforded to them by news audiences as well as to legal and corporate support. Journalists expressed concern over their status through focusing on their autonomy, a notion that figured prominently in journalism's justification for its authority to convey adequately, accurately, and uniquely the happenings of the world. The Plame leak case made salient internal and external tensions that complicated news work and especially the use of unnamed sources, including the question of where underlying allegiances lie and whom they benefit—questions central to efforts to address, repair, and improve the use of anonymity.

6

Rethinking Anonymity:
Problems and Solutions

> So where do these high-profile incidents leave
> the readers? In the cold, that's where. They don't know
> what to think. . . . This goes to the heart of the biggest issue
> facing American media today: credibility.
>
> —Terence Smith on NPR's
> *All Things Considered*

As the dust clears from a string of struggles over unnamed sources at elite news outlets, the inevitable question arises: how did the *New York Times, Washington Post,* CBS News, *Time,* and *Newsweek* all become embroiled in controversies involving unnamed sources? This was not a single story or an isolated wayward reporter, but an overlapping series of incidents united through their use of source anonymity, elite journalists, and focus on Bush administration actions.

To start to untangle this mess, it is useful to first return to the discussion of unnamed sources offered at the outset of this book. While volumes of scholarly work have usefully dissected less than ideal relationships between journalists and their sources, little attention has been paid to unnamed sources as a particular case. Anonymity is a tool taken up by journalists to provide certain information deemed otherwise unattainable. As with all tools, the question best lies in how it is used.

When journalists turn to anonymity, two potentials emerge—unnamed sources as promising and as perilous. The promise is that by shaking off attribution, journalists can break free of relations with sources that all too often appear routinized and unchallenging. Anonymity, in this vision, disrupts circuits of power and legitimation flowing through patterns of news sourcing that ordinarily—but not absolutely—privilege elite sources while leaving out other voices. Anonymity gives journalists a way to combat structural constraints that hinder its normative mission. By contrast, a perilous vision sees unnamed sources as only exacerbating the already entrenched problems of news sources by hiding even such basic information as the name of a source. Absent identification, unnamed sources can really only be heard and not judged—the judging, ostensibly, having already been built into the arrangement by the journalist. The public may recognize this perilousness only at the moment it becomes a problem for journalism—the moment when facts become challenged, motives appear suspect, and arguments for trust fall under fire.

The events detailed in this book make clear the prevalence of this latter view—the image of unnamed sources as perilous—in discussions surrounding the journalistic use of anonymity. Time after time, the use of unnamed sources came across as flawed, sloppy, and, at worst, corroborating officials' claims undeserving of any journalistic legitimation. But any such conclusion needs to be explored in more depth to understand both the issues and responses that persisted throughout discussions of the incidents covered in this book. The goal is not merely to catalog the wreckage recounted in the previous chapters or advocate for the banishment of anonymity, but to carefully pick through this discourse to figure out how the promise of unnamed sources may be activated as part of a larger and much-needed reconception of journalism in these early years of the twenty-first century.

Defining Journalism While Defining Controversy

Before turning to patterns in the persistent squabbling around journalistic uses of unnamed sources, we need to revisit an argument central to this book: journalism is an inconstant, evolving, culturally constructed practice. Journalists may present their role to be obvious, historically mandated, stable, self-defining, and, above all, autonomous. However entrenched these claims may be, treating journalism as an institution somehow existing outside of the social context in which it operates severely limits any analysis of its problems or attempt to craft potential solutions. For this reason, the view here is of journalism as a form of cultural production, a complex amalgam of practices existing alongside—and constantly overlapping—with other institutions and cultural forms.[1] Journalism is an embedded institution, intersecting with fields of political, economic, and cultural power at every turn.

What we gain by not treating journalism as an isolated entity is sensitivity to the ways in which journalism comes to be culturally negotiated. It is not unusual to see, whether explicitly stated or thinly implied, such questions as what is good journalism or bad journalism? What should journalism do? Who is a journalist? These questions lack definitive answers. Instead, they serve as public sites of struggle in which many disparate parties make sense of journalism in the face of ever-changing conditions. This muddled public discourse shapes both the conditions of news work and broader cultural conceptions of the news and what it should do.

Many voices have spoken on the issue of anonymity and what they say needs to be taken seriously. Just as important, the positions of the speakers within competing interpretive communities need to be recognized. Journalists sought to maintain their cultural authority while confronting contradictions raised by the inclusion of unnamed sources in news texts. The Bush administration sought to protect its interests by molding news reporting into favorable forms using authorized unnamed sources while stamping out unauthorized whistle-blowers. Conservative media critics sought to alter news practices according to their political views. Academics, along with many left-leaning critics, sought to promote their critical perspective of constraints faced by journalism. While trying not to overstate the cohesiveness of these interpretive communities, in broad strokes, each group worked to have its voice heard and to counter assertions by other groups. This was always a competition; no single community has the power of interpretive closure over the entire public. No one, it should be clear, is able to define for all what went wrong, why it went wrong, and what should be done.

Debates over unnamed sources are not simply conceptual struggles freed from any real consequences. Heated arguments, normative pleas, professional introspection, and wrathful condemnation are all part of a struggle to define the appropriate political and cultural role of journalism. After all, their purveyors target the actual practices and content of the news we receive. For these reasons, this discourse must be assessed as meaningful and purposive, weighed here against the author's own position of promoting journalistic practices that work to benefit the public first and foremost.

JOURNALISTS RESPOND TO CONTROVERSY

When faced with controversy, the journalistic community has often turned to the strategy of paradigm repair in which the community attaches blame to the individual journalist to deflect away from a deeper questioning of news practices. Attention coalesces around a journalist or small band of journalists cast as deviant for straying from the dictums of acceptable journalism. This strategy deflects potential questions from the dominant paradigm to which journalists ascribe—objectively delivered, neutrally voiced, source-reliant news. Individual ostracism overtakes institutional introspection.

While several studies have demonstrated this process in action,[2] the cases in this book reveal the limits of this strategy. It is one thing to isolate a lone reporter; it is quite another to attempt to marginalize the *New York Times, Washington Post*, CBS News, *Newsweek*, and *Time* within a short span of time. That a sizable number of national news outlets entered into an ongoing drama linked to the deployment of anonymity necessitates a different view—the "critical incident" approach—to provide an analytical framework guiding us through often directly competing assertions made about the incidents.[3] As critical incidents, the discussions of unnamed sources often moved from the level of individualized practice to consider deeper structural issues of which the incidents were symptomatic. Although this expansiveness does signal a more thorough engagement with the problems plaguing journalism, it should not be confused with the abandonment of long-held paradigms—a point revisited below.

In trading the deviant isolationism of paradigm repair for the symptomatic expansionism of critical incidents, the journalistic community responded to unnamed source controversies by portraying journalism as under siege in a number of directions. While individual reporters did get chastised, journalists generally confronted the incidents by publicly enumerating barriers preventing them from being able to properly execute their work in accordance with the norms they so vociferously draw on to undergird their cultural authority. What emerged was a combination of shared anxieties and rallying points as well as professional schisms that extended well beyond the practices of anonymity to comment on the turbulent state of journalism.

The interpretive shift from isolation to contemplation is well illustrated in the efforts by journalists and other critics to connect problems affecting unnamed sourcing practices to the economic imperatives accompanying a largely corporatized, for-profit news system. Discussions of the Killian memos story, the Plame leak case, and prewar intelligence reporting reviews linked problems with unnamed sources to the constant competitive demands journalists confront in their work. Amidst other news outlets vying for exclusive reports in the lead up to the Iraq War, the *New York Times* and the *Washington Post* as elite news sources faced pressures to continually produce original material. Similarly, journalists attributed improper fact-checking in the *60 Minutes*–Killian memos story to a combination of competition in covering the 2004 presidential campaign, a concern over prime-time ratings, and reductions in news gathering resources.

Competition was not the only economic-related hurdle for journalists using anonymity. News outlets balancing journalistic and business interests had to confront the enormous expense necessary to mount a legal defense protecting reporters from revealing their unnamed sources in court. In particular, when *Time*'s Matt Cooper was subpoenaed in the Plame leak case, many in the journalistic community accused Time Inc. of privileging economic factors at the expense of journalistic appropriateness in its decision to surrender Cooper's notes to the grand jury. By contrast, remembrances of the role of Deep Throat highlighted the commitment of the *Washington Post* to protect its reporters seeking to unravel the Watergate scandal.

Anxiety over the priorities of news organizations has long marked the complex relationship between the operations of journalists according to one set of norms and the business interests of media organizations in the historically for-profit dominated U.S. media system.[4] Yet, increasingly, concerns over waning audiences and changes in advertising have made the economic risk associated with unnamed sources appear ever more untenable—regardless of the journalistic contribution. As a result, competitive demands too often encourage the routine use of unnamed sources to attain exclusive reports while discouraging their use for potentially controversial stories to avoid costly legal fees or negative publicity.

The economic concerns expressed by journalists in the preceding chapters were closely linked to apprehension concerning the growth of online sites for news, information, and criticism straying from the paradigms underlying traditional journalism. For example, journalists elevated the role conservative bloggers and message boards played in stoking the Killian memos controversy at CBS News to symbolize the new challenges faced by traditional news outlets. This was not merely a right-wing phenomenon; criticisms of the *New York Times*'s prewar reporting occurring through the Web site *Slate* and the online version of the *New York Review of Books* bubbled up to the mainstream when the newspaper undertook a review of its coverage. But beyond providing scrutiny, these new expressive forms offered textual rules and customs that sharply contrasted what had been done before. While traditional journalistic modes faced competing ideas in the past—literary journalism, for example—this new media world portended potent competition from sites with different ways of doing things. In this environment, the opaque practices behind attributing information to unnamed sources faced fundamental suspicion and calls for openness.

A third set of recurring constraints rose up around governmental actions as journalists balked at both the excessive secrecy of the Bush administration and the legal uncertainty plaguing journalistic confidentiality. With the latter concern, journalists used the opportunity created by controversies over unnamed sources to advocate for the codified recognition of journalist-source confidentiality at the federal level, a movement discussed below. Couched in democratic normative rhetoric portraying government incursion into journalistic affairs as socially harmful, journalists urged the passage of a law extending their rights. While this argument arose through praise of Mark Felt with calls to better protect future whistle-blowers, it became quite prominent in response to the vocal resistance of Matt Cooper of *Time* and Judith Miller of the *New York Times* to a federal subpoena in the Plame leak case. With the threat of jail hovering above Cooper and Miller, journalists came together to criticize the special prosecutor's subpoena through heated televised discussions and emotional newspaper editorials. One newspaper editorial labeled the subpoenas "a systematic attack on the checks and balances inherent in this nation's republican form of government."[5] Such allegations wrote journalism into democratic functioning while stirring up outrage at its hindrance—often without any attempt to look into how unnamed sources were really being used.

JOURNALISTS AS VICTIMS

By constantly presenting contextual constraints preventing their sovereign functioning, journalists situated their work squarely within narratives of victimization. Throughout the cases in this book, journalists reacted to controversies around the use of unnamed sources by enumerating the negative constraints originating outside the control of the newsroom, reasserting the divide between editorial and business functions at news outlets, reavowing their political neutrality, defending the viability of their news forms against competing forms, advocating for increased legal protections, and redoubling efforts to stave off waning credibility. This frame of victim implied that if such constraints could only be avoided, journalists would be better able to realize their normative claims in practice. In doing so, this view separated out the apparent victims—journalists—from a host of perpetrators: press-control-obsessed officials, profit-hungry owners, partisan media critics, overly scrutinizing bloggers, zealous prosecutors, unsympathetic judges, critical academics, and so on.

It is hard to argue against claims that journalistic practice is embedded within a structure that, in many ways, negatively impacts news reporting. The actual circumstances in which news is created should not be ignored for fear of treating news organizations as disconnected from larger trends and, therefore, operating without constraints. However, it would be a mistake to take the opposite perspective of blaming problems only on contextual and structural constraints while ignoring how journalists create problems through their use of unnamed sources. In other words, even if journalists could attain the autonomy they seek, would this really alleviate problems with unnamed sources?

While it is clear that the discussions above moved beyond the confining tactics of paradigm repair to embrace broader issues, the focus on attributing culpability to extrajournalistic causes largely occluded a thorough self-critique. Agency shifted away from the deviant individual to a constellation of forces, but in a manner that still allowed for protecting the underlying paradigm from reconsideration and attack. Given this similarity in these two approaches, the former may be relabeled as "first-order paradigm repair" while the latter may be understood as "second-order paradigm repair." If first-order paradigm repair stops at the individual to protect enduring journalism practices from scrutiny, second-order paradigm repair stops at external constraints to do the same.

What each form of paradigm repair shares is the attempt to halt discussions of news controversies from exposing problems at the core of journalistic practice. The ideology of journalism remains protected by blaming first individual reporters and second the environment in which journalists work. At the same time, both strategies seek to protect the image of journalism by casting blame elsewhere. This may serve the journalistic community by shoring up its claims to cultural authority and relevancy, but it does not necessarily serve the wider public. In other words, second-order paradigm repair problematically conflates the interests of journalists with the interests of the public without considering where interests diverge.

Throughout the incidents in this book, the impact of journalists participating in second-order paradigm repair could be seen in the relative lack of attention surrounding such issues as the power dynamics between unnamed sources and journalists, the reproduction of official perspectives without attribution, and the responsibilities of journalists to the public. Certainly, these issues did arise at times and from particular voices, but far too often such considerations of unnamed sources were left out. Attempts to understand how unnamed sources lead to controversies must recognize not just contextual pressures facing journalism, but also the choices made by journalists in how they allocate and regulate anonymity. With attention directed to agency—although not at the omission of contextual conditions—the narrative of victimization faces limits as a strategy for confronting challenges to journalistic authority. To move forward in addressing problems concerning anonymity, attention to structural constraints must be augmented with an awareness of the actual practices that allow unnamed sources into the news.

THE MECHANICS OF ANONYMITY

The raft of problems elite news outlets experienced with unnamed sources may be confronted through a different approach that avoids the protectionism underlying first- and second-order paradigm repair so often endorsed by journalists. Shifting the perspective to consider the mechanics of unnamed sourcing practices opens up another view that highlights the relationship between unnamed sources and journalists. Far from the antagonistic pledges the interpretive community of journalists makes in setting its work apart from other institutions, the deployment of anonymity too often connects to a set of arrangements between journalists seeking to maintain access and sources wanting to make public statements without attribution. Instead of breaking from news-sourcing routines in which journalists appear beholden to their sources,[6] it is clear from the preceding chapters that the invisibility introduced in the use of unnamed sources too often reproduces these patterns—if not making them worse.

Throughout the incidents examined in this book, scrutiny of unnamed sources led the veil of anonymity to be lifted, revealing relationships deviating from normative claims underpinning journalistic defenses of anonymity. In diverging from the whistle-blowing model held up to represent all of unnamed sources, journalists regularly appeared more concerned with maintaining access to bolster their individual or organizational status than in uncovering otherwise unavailable information for the benefit of audiences. The status motive resulted in the collapse of distance between journalists and sources, as one journalism professor argued: "When reporters become celebrities and trade on their own recognition as news makers, instead of news hounds, bad things happen. Identities of outsiders and insiders commingle. News is put into the blender with camaraderie between source and reporter."[7]

Similar complaints appeared frequently in charges that Judith Miller and Bob Woodward cultivated insider sources for their own benefit above all else, granting anonymity to ensure their continued status as top Washington journalists. On CNN, Geneva Overholser connected Woodward's actions with "public concerns about whether or not reporters are mostly focused on serving the public's need to know, or cozying up with sources."[8] Such charges transcended individual journalists to function as a general critique of the Washington press corps. Critics, educators, and journalists at subnational news outlets regularly chastised national news outlets for using unnamed sources only to exhibit access to high-placed insider sources. This was seen as a dangerous practice, epitomized by the reliance on top government sources by the *New York Times* and the *Washington Post* in their erroneous prewar intelligence reporting. In allowing top government sources to speak anonymously while ignoring other sources with differing views, these newspapers gave credence to intelligence claims later proven to be false.

While journalists do face a host of pressures that constrain their work, the focus on sourcing mechanics makes journalists too often appear less like victims and more like perpetrators. To return to a concept invoked in the introduction, criticisms of access-obsessed journalists misapplying anonymity can be understood through the contradictions of "disobedient dependence," or the tension journalists encounter in balancing the demands of their authoritative self-image with a reliance on news sources for a continued stream of material and for their individual status needs.[9] Journalism must negotiate these two needs: the need to appear independent and the need to placate sources. The inconsistency between these needs renders the watchdog model underpinning journalistic authority as always problematic. It also indicates that beyond the structural and contextual constraints described above, journalists face internal constraints over their need for access and their need to demonstrate their autonomy from these sources. This creates a bind. By being more resistant to the demands of sources, journalists risk losing access to a supply of insider information making news stories possible. Yet, conversely, practices leading to the continual questioning of autonomy destabilize claims underpinning journalistic authority.

Given the tension raised by disobedient dependence, two fundamental ironies impede journalists' efforts to reconcile norms supporting their authority and the realities of unnamed sourcing practices. First, to counter secretive institutional practices, journalists employ secretive news practices. That is, in order to hold officials accountable on behalf of the public by exposing their actions, journalists hide their own. The resulting opacity surrounding unnamed sourcing practices eliminates accountability, leading to a need for trust at the individual level of the journalist, the organizational level of the news outlet, and the institutional level of journalism generally. In this paternalistic dynamic, journalists use their authority to justify their execution of anonymity based on the assertion that this arrangement benefits audiences.

At the same time, journalists face limits in their ability to defend their work against the scrutiny that envelopes unseen practices. Once they reach the limit of disclosure without exposing the source's identity, their only option is to ask to be trusted. Absent definite knowledge of how a story has been reported, struggles to define a controversy involving unnamed sources leave room for competing interpretations. This occurred with the reporting on prewar intelligence, Bush's National Guard record, and Koran abuse by the military. With these incidents, each news organization defended its reporting and admitted to certain mistakes while being challenged with competing interpretations tendered by critics. Because of their pledge to protect their sources' identities, journalists have only limited recourse in countering the claims of others without revealing too much information about their unnamed sources.

A second irony arising in the use of unnamed sources is that a practice situated within the watchdog role of the news actually makes officials *less* accountable by allowing them to make public statements without attribution and accompanying responsibility. A practice based on ensuring accountability at a normative level often functions in the exact opposite manner in practice. This was most visible with the Plame leak case where administration officials used the cloak of anonymity to attack a White House critic. In such incidents, journalists appear beholden to their sources, which suggests that the granting of anonymity originates with the interests of the source rather than on behalf of the audience/public. To the public, journalists may seem more dependent than disobedient.

These core ironies, which emerge in dissections of controversies involving unnamed sources, call into question whether the current constellation of journalistic norms can be realized in practice with any consistency. Too often they give rise to charges that the actual use of anonymity leads to a subversion of journalistic intentions by putting reputational and source interests ahead of the public. Importantly, it is not only the context in which journalistic work occurs, but how practices are employed that creates a key tension for journalism that Peter Dahlgren identifies as "the growing gap between the realities of journalism and its official presentation of self."[10] Specifically of interest here, the undesirable dynamics revealed through controversies involving unnamed sources hampered the ability of journalists to restate their existing arguments for journalistic authority. This being the case, journalism could stand to revisit its presentation of self.

A Way Forward: Repairing Unnamed Source Use

Even with its endemic problems, we cannot look past the good enabled by the schizophrenic practice of journalistic anonymity. This chapter cannot conclude with calls for an outright ban or the evasion of what good comes from withholding identities in some circumstances. Anonymity, at times, is the only way to know and circulate information we want known and circulated. And with no easy patch available, any effort to improve unnamed sourcing practices necessitates a wider reconception of journalism. To fix unnamed sources, journalism must fix its argument for sustaining cultural authority.

BEYOND THE SHIELD

Beset by the parade of controversies described in this book, many in the journalistic community argued for the immediate need to pass a federal shield law protecting journalists from having to disclose their unnamed sources. This was not an unfamiliar request. A slew of congressional efforts, particularly following the *Branzburg v. Hayes* decision in 1972, have aimed to enact such a law, only to fail. Meanwhile, since 1896, thirty-five states and the District of Columbia have passed statutes shielding reporters—with seventeen coming in 1973 or after.[11]

With Democrats taking control of Congress in 2006 and the election of Barack Obama in 2008, efforts to enact a federal shield law gained new momentum. The House of Representatives passed the bipartisan Free Flow of Information Act of 2009 on March 31, 2009, on a voice vote. On the other side of the Capitol, the Senate, while pursuing its own bill, faced apprehension by Obama administration officials as to whether the shield would adversely impact their ability to protect national security interests.[12] After a compromise, the Senate's version moved out of committee on December 10, 2009, but at the time of this writing has not yet received a spot on the official calendar of business. While similar in many ways, the House has adopted a more restrictive definition by reserving protection only for individuals who do journalism "for a substantial portion of the person's livelihood or for substantial financial gain," while the Senate has left room for covering nontraditional journalists, such as bloggers.[13] Nonetheless, the prospects of a federal shield law appeared more promising than ever before.

The question then becomes what will be the outcome of a federal-level reporter's privilege? In the abstract, it is easy to argue on behalf of a shield law in that it seems to so straightforwardly synch with the unassailable value placed on ensuring an independent press. It becomes one more tool freeing reporters to dig deeper into the hidden workings of public institutions. Yet, however enthusiastic the journalism community may be toward a shield law, we should be cautious as to the ability of enhanced legal protections to improve the state of unnamed sources. If reserved only for professionals, a

federal shield law would merely accord the community of professional journalists with a set of rights differentiating them from other citizens. Viewed
from this perspective, shield laws mark out the profession's "jurisdiction"
against would-be intruders.[14] Such restrictions are particularly worrisome
when part of the problem is a lack of journalists willing to break from a small
circle of elite sources.

James Carey cautioned some decades ago that professionalism can too
often become a means for establishing and maintaining social standing for
the sake of privilege instead of its ostensible sake of benefitting the public.[15]
Carey especially bristled at the defense of secrecy as a professional preroga-
tive. While he did admit the occasional need for anonymity, he noted that
"secrecy and journalism are contradictions in terms."[16] Indeed, the call for
legally codified confidentiality advocated within the journalistic community
both in the 1970s when Carey delivered his pronouncement and during the
first decade of the twenty-first century seeks to extend the cultural authority
of journalism by adding to its professionally held rights. What is often absent
is a well-articulated case for how this privilege truly and directly benefits the
public. Certainly an independent press should be sought. But it would be a
disservice to pass a law fending off aggressive prosecutors while doing nothing to prevent collusion—wanton or not—among socially elite journalists
and sources through thinly attributed news stories.

The problems of anonymity cannot be solved simply through enacting a
shield law. This is not to dismiss legislative efforts to protect journalists, but
to critique its alleged panacean powers. There is no simple solution to problems arising when journalists withhold a source's identity because these are
not simple problems. Rather, these are issues bound up in the very fabric of
journalism in its political, economic, technological, competitive, professional,
and organizational context. Given the combination of structural and agentic
barriers at play, any attempt to repair the use of unnamed sources must firmly
address problems at the level of practice. Doing so affords a better view as
to when and how source anonymity can serve the public. It allows us to go
beyond legal advocacy to assemble a set of journalistic principles governing
unnamed sourcing practices that ties together the needs of the public with
the work of journalists.

REMAKING JOURNALISM

Evidence for the complexity of issues related to source anonymity can be
spied in how interpretations of the cases regularly swelled to become more
about the state of journalism than about individualized incidents. That is why

these episodes have been analyzed as interconnected critical incidents. They are not isolated events, understood inter alia, irrelevant outside of themselves and their time. Instead, they congeal to form a rich interpretive struggle at the very heart of what journalism is. Optimistically, the extensive considerations of unnamed sources detailed in the previous chapters and summarized above supply the depth necessary to confront the confounding, risky, and indispensable practice of withholding a source's identity in exchange for information. One characteristic of a critical incident is that it cannot be ignored, which necessitates tackling problems of practice with an eye toward better functioning in the future.

Of course, the word "better" in that last sentence begs the question: with what criteria could we assess the better use of unnamed sources? The evasion of controversy is not enough; unnamed sourcing practices demand careful, public examination firmly grounded in a sense of what journalism we want to have. Put differently, controversies involving unnamed sources require journalists to rethink strategies for maintaining their cultural authority. Many roads lead to authority—that amalgam of legitimacy, relevancy, credibility, and self-determination necessary for institutions to operate successfully within the social order. For journalism, authority is what gives it power to tell society's story to society. However, journalistic authority should never be supported abstractly for its own sake. Instead, it must be judged on the degree to which it benefits the public.

Journalistic authority has long been based on loyalty to a particular professionalized mode of journalism that stresses objectivity and the need for distance.[17] The journalist-as-professional possesses a set of learned skills, an allegiance to a normative democratic worldview, a set of shared ethics, and a mode of self-presentation that implies detachedness from nonjournalists. While this mode of authority making may have functioned well during its ascension in the early years of the twentieth century, we now find doubters at every door. While the ethos of postmodernism has led to a questioning of solid truths, journalists still cling to objectivity, even while admitting to its problems. While the ethos of "Web 2.0" has blurred boundaries between consumers and producers, journalists continue to emphasize their special standing in society. While critics on the left and the right challenge news frames, journalists dismiss these claims as evidence of their ability to rile up all sides. While news sources improve their abilities to promote their messages through the news, journalists blame their lack of resources for preventing in-depth reporting. And while credibility declines and news audiences wane, journalists fret that a constellation of new technologies has doomed their work.

With arguments for journalistic authority so assailed, it is time for journalists to jettison their defensive stance and instead adopt new terms underlying journalistic authority. It is time to go beyond second-order paradigm repair and instead seek to alter the news paradigm to better confront the problems journalism faces.

THE PROBLEMS OF STRUCTURE

Before turning to principles, problems arising from the structural context of journalism need to be revisited and emphasized. As active agents, journalists make choices about their work that impacts the final product audiences receive. In the realm of anonymity, these choices are often hidden, revealed to audiences only retroactively in the unfolding of controversy. But this is not to lose track of the context in which journalists operate. A rich literature examining the political economy of news has tracked tensions between journalists and employers who emphasize profits, advertisers who fund much of their labor, sources who provide sought-after access, and a government that enacts legal policies impacting how news gets made.[18] It is impossible to study the news outside of this context or to present journalism as autonomous and independent. Instead, the problems of structure must be recognized along with problems derived from journalistic agency.

In fact, structure and agency are quite closely aligned. Structure impacts behaviors and, reciprocally, individual behaviors accumulate to reproduce structures.[19] In terms of confronting problems with unnamed sources, structural issues deserve attention alongside suggestions for how journalism can alter its paradigmatic obligations. Public conversations should take place to question constraints placed on news, such as the upsurge of criticism and attention to media ownership laws in 2003 in the face of deregulatory proposals.[20] Sites such as freepress.net offer a centralized location to educate and organize the public around such issues, and this should be applauded and expanded. At the same time, changing the conditions of news work requires dedicated effort and openness within the journalistic community to rethink how the news gets done.

RULES AND PRINCIPLES

Addressing problems accompanying the use of unnamed sources requires a rethinking of journalistic paradigms linked closely to practice. We must avoid espousing abstract normative pledges divorced from news mechanics. Instead, conversations about journalistic authority require close attention to how the news is made. At the same time, it should be acknowledged that, outside of approved style guides, journalism stubbornly resists uniform directives; it is too varied and situational to impose steadfast rules.

In lieu of proposing a mechanical fix, I will draw from the literature on financial accounting standards. While on the surface this may appear to be a non sequitur, it is not difficult to find analogs with journalism. Both involve the activity of "reporting"—financial reporting and news reporting. Corporations are expected to render their financial condition accurately and openly through publicly circulated texts (e.g., balance sheets and annual reports). Likewise, journalists are expected to render happenings in the world accurately through publicly circulated news texts. The question of fidelity matters for each, but in neither case can fidelity be the final measure. After all, there is no greater epistemological minefield than claims to representing truth and reality.

More relevant to the discussion at hand, both accounting and journalism share a dubious track record in recent years. Journalism has been plagued by controversies—only a few of which this book examines. Accounting, too, has suffered through such public controversies as the collapse of Enron. Why do these controversies occur? In accounting, the debate has been between rules and principles. Rules "attempt to tell you what to do,"[21] but are often inadequate because they "allow for technical compliance with the standard while evading the intent of the standard."[22] A company may follow the rules for disclosure, but manipulate the system to avoid disclosing negative information that shareholders and others would want to know. In contrast, principles instruct accountants "not what to do, but how to decide what needs doing."[23] Advocates of this view start by identifying the principles underlying the purpose of financial reporting in the first place—to provide the public with an understanding of a corporation's financial situation—and then match this goal with appropriate techniques.

The rules/principles debate illuminates the debate over unnamed sources. Rules are, by themselves, inadequate. Reporters may follow rules set forth regarding unnamed sources, but, in fact, manipulate them to their own or their source's advantage. In addition, creating new rules governing the application of confidentiality, while a seemingly straightforward fix, cannot account for the complexity of unnamed sourcing practices or their necessity. Instead, I advocate for a principles-based approach that recognizes, at the top level, the purpose of using unnamed sources to be the ability to bring otherwise unattainable information about society's public institutions to the public.

At the same time, this principles-based approach transcends the limited case of unnamed sources to offer a wider path for journalists to reconstruct their argument for journalistic authority. After all, many of the problems associated with anonymity are extensions of other problems enveloping the relationship between journalists and sources as well as journalists and their audiences. Clinging to the worn paradigm of "objectivity above all" only permits too many holes in which problems arise. Although some may be hesitant to accept change, it is worth noting that the idea of journalism is a fluid and dynamic one across time. Journalism has always been forced to adapt and react to its changing context, and the present is no exception. Nor are the changes recommended here radical or unfamiliar—rather, they promote a refocusing on a core set of principles that offer a foundation for rethinking routine news practices.

Through a privileging of three principles—contingency, transparency, and aggressiveness—the journalistic community can work toward reinvigorating its claims to cultural authority. These principles allow journalists to circumvent the self-preservational discourse of paradigm repair to present to the public the benefits of a strong, vibrant journalism. But an avowal to principles must coincide with the recognition that many of journalism's current claims are tainted. Objectivity, on its own, fails when the distance of the reporters obscures the story. The reproduction of official voices, particularly without attribution, may be objective, but it is often not desirable. Likewise, the concept of autonomy lies at the heart of journalism's arguments for its authority, but it elides the complicated ways in which journalism is woven into the very culture it strives to cover from a distance. Journalism cannot attain its goals of objectivity and autonomy, but must instead face constraints originating both inside and outside of newsrooms.

For these reasons, turning to contingency, transparency, and aggressiveness as guiding principles not only for unnamed sourcing practices but for news practice in general offers a way to break from the patterns that have hampered journalists' efforts to achieve the cultural authority they so desire. Most vitally, these principles privilege the needs of the public over the needs of journalists to erect professional boundaries distancing them from the rest of society. Each of the three principles—contingency, transparency, and aggressiveness—requires its own explanation, but it must be stressed that none of them is sufficient in and of itself.

CONTINGENCY

Throughout the discussions of the incidents, a number of commentators expressed dismay at the sheer volume of unnamed sources appearing in the news, especially with Washington-based reporting. One newspaper editor ridiculed this expansion: "Sources now seek confidentiality agreements when asked directions to the men's room."[24] The culture of unnamed sources has inculcated a sense of anonymity entitlement among sources expecting not to be identified. What's more, these confidentiality promises are often blanket statements expected to be maintained even in the event of public or legal pressures pushing for disclosure. As a result, this pledge indemnifies the source from repercussions while overburdening journalists with added accountability.

In reaction to undesirable consequences arising with blanket pledges, several commentators called for the recognition of anonymity as a conditional agreement journalists offer to sources. The justification of this perspective rests on a view that unconditional issuances of autonomy weaken the power of journalists. It suggests journalists give up too much control over their practices to procure information from sources. In response, journalists should reserve the right to annul their agreement when faced with situations where unnamed source–journalist relations lead to problems. Advocating for contingency, Bob Garfield, cohost of NPR's *On the Media,* suggested journalists might regain power over sources by dispensing with an absolutist stance on anonymity. Continued protection extends only to sources deemed worthy to have their identity protected. Following the jailing of Judith Miller, Garfield made this point: "The moral of this story is that not every anonymous source is himself or herself a principled participant. Some of them are simply Machiavellian scoundrels, and we should take care about whom we make professional commitments to, and equal care about what commitments we are making. The solution is simple contingency, a promise of confidentiality with strings attached, each string specified in advance."[25]

This proposal did not specify the knotty question of where the line should be drawn between appropriate and inappropriate anonymity, but it did seek to shift the balance of power away from the source and closer to the journalist. Similarly, criticizing the prewar coverage, Russ Baker insisted journalists should enforce contingencies to stop sources from using anonymity to avoid accountability: "Sources should not be allowed to remain unnamed when the information they are imparting serves to directly advance their own and their employers' objectives."[26] Baker attempted to separate out legitimate uses of anonymity from its undesirable application as a cover for officials.

Both Garfield and Baker usefully sought ways to activate contingency in a meaningful way that quelled critics' complaints by empowering journalists. Reporters would gain standing vis-à-vis their sources by dictating when and on what grounds confidentiality can be broken—heretofore a right solely possessed by sources. In addition, instilling the fear of public disclosure would reduce the ability of sources to take advantage of their anonymity in purely self-serving ways.

Beyond altering the ground rules governing anonymity, the emphasis on contingency abets efforts to reestablish journalistic authority by redistributing power within journalist-source relationships. Journalists gain a tool of resistance to limit the ability of sources to take advantage of their quest for original stories. Ideally, this would counter the power of sources while enhancing journalists' allegiance to their audience. This links back to authority by swapping an image of journalists as objective recorders for a view of them as active agents capable of adjudicating and offering assessments of claims offered up by sources.

The empowerment made possible through contingency works to curtail misapplications of anonymity and the power of sources, but its tenability faces uncertainty given the general ambiguity surrounding unnamed sources. By itself, this principle does not address the problem of journalists granting anonymity out of access and status concerns rather than the public interest. Individual journalists and their outlets continue to find incentives to sustain the system currently in place. Anonymity can be doubly self-serving, benefiting sources who wish to anonymously distribute information through the news and benefiting journalists by granting them access to the type of stories that raise their prominence and support their reputation for having insider sources. In some cases, the continuation of confidentiality, even when problematic, may protect both the journalist or her outlet from scrutiny as well as the source. Contingency also raises problems when would-be whistleblowers, for whom anonymity is an essential precondition, choose not to talk to reporters for fear of eventual disclosure. These qualms are not meant to invalidate contingency, but to signal its limitations and, therefore, the need for concurrent principles.

TRANSPARENCY

Critical incidents arise when taken-for-granted practices become visibly problematic. What had been unexamined draws the light of public attention, which requires prying into usually unseen organizational practices. As with other institutions, such scrutiny proves to be uncomfortable for journalism. This is not to deny that transparency has become a buzzword for news organizations in recent years. To varying degrees, the inclusion of public editors, newsroom blogs, and reporter contact information have all sought to bring audiences closer to the workings of news. Yet for the most part, journalistic authority is built around a *lack* of transparency into news practices—quotes appear without full disclosure of how they came to be, unknowns are rarely acknowledged, and the history of a story's origin goes undiscussed. In many ways, journalism's authoritative apparatus depends on news stories hiding what is tentative and incomplete to declare instead their trustworthy factuality. The news voice comes across with a stern assuredness, not as surmised or approximate. By staking its authority on this voice, journalism perpetually leaves itself open to charges of overstating its certainty. This is especially the case for unnamed sources. Journalists deploying anonymity incur risk by placing themselves at odds with transparency.

Confronting the vulnerability arising from opaque news practices is no easy task, but greater transparency is possible through shedding light on how journalists develop stories, verify source claims, and reach their conclusions.[27] Such suggestions popped up periodically in response to the controversies. The *New Yorker*'s Ken Auletta chastised CBS News for its inability to convincingly explain the practices behind the Killian memos story: "I think one of the things news organizations have to do is be more transparent. I think they have to open themselves up, as CBS failed to do."[28] Similarly, the president of the Society of Professional Journalists recommended telling readers "not just what the news is, but how we're finding it."[29] Both authors suggested journalists do more to describe the processes behind stories instead of merely hiding their deficiencies and uncertainties.

The notion of transparency also encompasses the need to engage with the context in which the news is created and circulated. The editor of the *Indianapolis Star* articulated this extension of transparency to self-reflection in the aftermath of prewar reporting reconsiderations: "Ours is a very subjective business. The play we give stories, the kinds of stories we pursue, and the sources we use involve decisions that aren't dictated to us by a precise formula."[30] Envisaging transparency as a form of reflection helps journalism confront its professionally ingrained resistance to openness. It allows for conversation about the news to be woven into news discourse, and especially encourages such interaction in the face of thorny topics lacking the clarity and order routinely imposed in news stories. In doing so, transparency accommodates complexity without the need for reductionism. Some journalists will dismiss such suggestions to alter the tone of news discourse as dangerously relativistic, uselessly incomplete, or, at the very least, thoroughly unfamiliar. However, emphasizing transparency serves journalism by sharing with the public how the news gets made and allowing the unknown its place alongside the known.

Like contingency, transparency proves insufficient on its own. Inevitably, transparency encounters an uneasy fit with unnamed sources. Confidentiality pledges by definition prevent journalists from disclosing the full details of a story's reporting. The incongruity between transparency and anonymity can be seen in changes at the *New York Times* and the *Washington Post* in the wake of their erroneous prewar reporting. The *Post* required reporters to get "a publishable reason for concealing the source's identity" to explain to readers specifically why sources have been granted anonymity.[31] The *Times* took a similar tack in its revised guidelines.[32] While these are attempts to increase transparency, the published reasons cannot reconcile the intrinsic lack of transparency accompanying unnamed sources. Instead, the printed explanations of why a source receives anonymity regularly come across as ambiguous or tautological—a source goes unnamed because she wants to be unnamed. In the worst case, these attempts to give the reader some background actually make news stories *more* misleading when the identifier used is disingenuous. Consider Judith Miller's agreement to identify Scooter Libby, the vice president's chief of staff, as a "former hill staffer." The insistence on essentially deceptive attribution by a source coupled with the reporter's desire for access renders efforts to increase the transparency of unnamed sources ineffective.

Without full attribution, it is impossible to evaluate anonymous attribution. As a result, when it comes to unnamed sourcing practices, journalism cannot hold itself to the standards of openness it advocates for other institutions. With their procedures closed off from audiences, unnamed sourcing practices will continue to create tensions between journalists and their audiences.

Despite room for abuse, transparency deserves greater appreciation and application, particularly in the face of news controversies. Journalism cannot count on its reporting to be treated as factual purely based on the circular assertion that the news, because it is news, is factual. The cultural ground has shifted too much for this authoritative strategy to function effectively. Instead, journalism needs to embrace a new openness; if it does not reveal names, it still should open up formally hidden practices, reveal uncertainties, and explain contradictions. But transparency is not, on its own, a normative guidepost for unnamed sources or for journalism more broadly. More holes need to be filled, and for that, we turn to aggressiveness.

AGGRESSIVENESS

Why have unnamed sources at all? Why support a practice so prone to misuse and criticism—a practice that so often places journalists in a precarious situation? This larger question floating above the incidents recounted in this book demands an answer. It is the basis of the challenge faced by journalists, but also the ground from which to reestablish the very premises of journalistic authority. To answer the question becomes an opportunity for journalism to address why it deserves its cultural power by reestablishing what the public can expect from the news.

This is not an argument for the radical redefinition of journalism, but it is a call for journalists to significantly shift how they understand the foundation for their worth. Journalists have long supported their claims to authority by drawing on interpretations of such diverse cultural materials as the meaning of the First Amendment, the collective memory of reporting successes, and their role in mediating shared cultural moments. Underlying this array is a self-definition of the journalism as a watchdog.[33] Rather than acting as official stenographers, journalists characterize their role as the Fourth Estate or "fourth branch of government"—imputing themselves as an agent into the fabric of representative democracy.

This vision of journalism as watchdog infuses the news with political and social value, but it is often diluted by competing professional obligations. In the United States, the ascension of neutrality and objectivity pose a fundamental contradiction to the image journalism constructs of itself. The watchdog barking on behalf of the public stands at odds with the political insider intent on access and balance. This is the lasting takeaway of Stuart Hall and colleagues in their analysis of crime news: journalists favor elite sources not due to sinister motives, but because of a combination of professional impartiality and routinized reporting practices.[34] Sources gain the upper hand when journalists place their neutral stance above their watchdog pledge. The problem is all too often made even more acute when journalists grant anonymity to elite sources without adjudicating the claims that are being relayed. Addressing this problem begins with recognizing that this normative contradiction between being a watchdog and being objective damages claims to journalistic authority. A reshuffling is needed.

One way forward is to promote aggressiveness as a key journalistic principle. This is not to lionize aggressiveness for its own sake, but to construct an ideal of aggressiveness as a quality of a journalism that works on behalf of the public. The term is meant to connote the favoring of activity over passivity, public disclosure over private access, and reportorial persistence over acceptance. As a normative basis for journalistic authority, aggressiveness provides a guiding principle for journalism's continued vigilance of government and other social institutions. It eschews the debate over objectivity by supplanting the fear of political slant with an acknowledged popular grounding. In this way, aggressiveness does not require or condemn partisan journalism; rather, it sets the goal at making public institutions accountable and transparent.

Most vitally, this commitment to aggressiveness moves the originating force behind issuing anonymity away from the source and toward the journalist. It roots anonymity in a vision of journalism working as an agent of audiences, not sources. This spurs attempts to address issues of power head on to find a route around persistent problems plaguing all manner of news sources—unnamed and otherwise. After all, journalism can never attain the autonomy it so often expresses because it is bound up with other institutions. Aggressiveness helps by offering a way to think through what journalism should be doing regardless of the structures in which it falls. Again, this is not to ignore the serious problems posed by the structural situation journalism finds itself in. But it does aim to present a way to circumvent some of these problems while reconstructing a public argument for continued cultural relevance.

Aggressiveness deserves specific attention because it so often becomes the chief topic of scrutiny and disagreement. Throughout this book, aggressiveness lies at the heart of the public competition to establish the dominant way of imagining journalism. Questions of appropriate journalistic aggressiveness occurred in all the incidents. With the prewar intelligence reporting, critics cast journalists as inadequately aggressive—antonymically, they were cast as passive—in their coverage of governmental intelligence claims supporting the invasion of Iraq. Journalists were viewed as overly concerned with access and too close to their sources—a charge that would resurface in the Plame leak case around Judith Miller and Bob Woodward. With the Killian memos story, charges of passivity arose from a handful of journalists decrying the suspension of reporting on President Bush's service record in the final months before an election in which military service had already been an issue. What's more, *60 Minutes* shelved a segment critical of the Bush administration out of fear of being further branded as biased. With the Mark Felt revelation, several journalists openly wished for another Deep Throat within the Bush administration, which signaled frustration with ongoing investigative news work and the administration's ability to manage its media messages. With the *Newsweek* Koran abuse story, some questioned whether any reporting on Guantanamo Bay was acceptable or harmful to the nation.

Taken together, these examples tell us that aggressiveness is often contested and difficult. It leads to scrutiny from critics and scorn from sources. It takes time and resources. It may be uncomfortable for journalists unaccustomed to its tone. But, in the end, the resurgence of journalistic authority requires journalists to assume a more assertive reporting style that—inevitably and occasionally—uses unnamed sources.

Aggressiveness requires audiences to be critical as well. In endowing journalism with a mandate to act aggressively on behalf of a public lacking the ability and access to know the activities of our public institutions, vigilance remains a necessary condition. Michael Schudson notes: "Everyone in a democracy is a certified media critic, which is as it should be."[35] The need for watchfulness was made clear early in this study through the consequences of errant reporting preceding the Iraq War. Citizens lacking the capability of gathering knowledge firsthand had to turn to the news to make sense of the government's case for war. What they often found was an echoing of official pronouncements through unnamed sources. While journalists claimed to be constrained by the monitorial environment in which they work, vigilance remains too important to leave journalism unattended. We, the public, should let it be known what principles we expect journalists to follow if we are to recognize the authority of journalism. After all, if notions of appropriate practices, norms, and expectations of journalism are socially constructed, real weight attaches to discussions of what kind of journalism we want to have.

FIXING UNNAMED SOURCES

With so many problems stemming from so many origins, journalistic anonymity if allowed to continue unchecked and unaltered will only spawn further controversies and embarrassments, lead to policy misunderstandings, result in reporting mistakes, and rightfully drain the vitality of journalism's arguments for authority. Instead, a sustained, well-informed discussion of how to fix the practice should accompany and inform a shift in application. Any effort to rethink and improve unnamed sourcing practices must start by recognizing anonymity as entangled in larger structural forces impacting journalism. In this way, the competition to identify faults and merits in unnamed sources extends to a larger struggle over ideas of what forms of news are desirable and which do not work. This is a competition to define the cultural and political roles of journalism by outlining collective notions of what journalism should be in our social imagination. For this reason, any proposal to alter the use of unnamed sources should stick close to the following question: In the end, does it serve journalists, sources, or the public?

Contingency, transparency, and aggressiveness provide an interlinking trio of principles that show promise for finding a way around lingering predicaments. When working in concert, contingency, transparency, and aggressiveness shift the dynamic underlying journalist–unnamed source relations by empowering the journalist with more control over confidentiality while at the same time creating expectations of openness between the journalist and news audiences. By accenting these principles, journalists can judge, in particular situations, the utility of deploying anonymity, how much to identify unnamed sources, and when, if necessary, to restrict or terminate pledges of confidentiality.

Rethinking anonymity around the three principles of contingency, transparency, and aggressiveness is not an easy proposition. Sources will balk at the insistence of limits to their confidentiality agreements, journalists will balk at the insistence of opening up news practices to self-reflection, and stakeholder individuals and institutions will balk at an aggressive journalism with a renewed mission to use unnamed sources for the sake of accountability rather than unattributed assertions. At the same time, the old strategies preserving journalistic authority face new tests in the changing economic, political, and media world in which journalism exists, which necessitates a close look at a new way forward. Ultimately, the interpretive community of journalists, through their many discursive means, must articulate the basis for their continued relevancy as a central mode of cultural production in public life. In these times, journalistic change is complicated, yet inevitable—just like the need for unnamed sources.

Notes

Introduction

Epigraph. "Jailing journalists," *Chicago Tribune*, July 1, 2005, A26.

1. See Pierre Bourdieu, "The Political Field, the Social Science Field, and the Journalistic Field," in *Bourdieu and the Journalistic Field*, ed. Rodney Benson and Erik Neveu (Cambridge, UK: Polity, 2005), 29–47; Pierre Bourdieu, *On Television*, trans. P. Parkhurst Ferguson (New York: The New Press, 1998).

2. This last point is well demonstrated in chapter 6 of Herbert Gans, *Deciding What's News: A Study of CBS Evening News, NBC Nightly News, Newsweek, and Time* (New York: Pantheon Books, 1979).

3. David L. Eason, "On Journalistic Authority: The Janet Cooke Scandal," in *Media, Myths, and Narratives: Television and the Press*, ed. James W. Carey (Beverly Hills, CA: Sage Publications, 1988), 207.

4. Barbie Zelizer, *Covering the Body: The Kennedy Assassination, the Media, and the Shaping of Collective Memory* (Chicago: University of Chicago Press, 1992), 8.

5. The research on sourcing has consistently shown official sources to dominate news discourse: Dan Berkowitz, "TV News Sources and News Channels: A Study in Agenda-Building," *Journalism Quarterly* 64 (1987): 508–13; Jane Delano Brown, Carl R. Bybee, Stanley T. Wearden, and Dulcie Murdock Straughan, "Invisible Power: Newspaper News Sources and the Limits of Diversity," *Journalism Quarterly* 64 (1987): 45–54; Maria Elizabeth Grabe, Shuhua Zhou, and Brooke Barnett, "Sourcing and Reporting in News Magazine Programs: 60 Minutes Versus Hard Copy," *Journalism and Mass Communication Quarterly* 76 (1999): 293–311; Robert A. Hackett, "A Hierarchy of Access: Aspects of Source Bias in Canadian TV News," *Journalism Quarterly* 62 (1985): 256–65, 277; Verica Rupar, "How Did You Find That Out? The Transparency of the Newsgathering Process and a Meaning of News: A Case Study," *Journalism*

Studies 7 (2006): 127–43; Leon V. Sigal, *Reporters and Officials: The Organization and Politics of Newsmaking* (Lexington, MA: D.C. Heath, 1973); D. Charles Whitney, Marilyn Fritzler, Steven Jones, Sharon Mazzarella, and Lana Rakow, "Geographic and Source Biases in Network Television News 1982–1984," *Journal of Broadcasting and Electronic Media* 33 (1989): 159–74.

6. Jay G. Blumler and Michael Gurevitch, "Politicians and the Press: An Essay on Role Relationships," in *Handbook of Political Communication,* ed. Dan D. Nimmo and Keith Sanders (Beverly Hills, CA: Sage, 1981), 469. Classic studies by Walter Gieber include Walter Gieber and Walter Johnson, "The City Hall 'Beat': A Study of Reporter and Source Roles," *Journalism Quarterly* 38 (1961): 289–97; Walter Gieber, "News Is What Newspapermen Make It," in *News: A Reader,* ed. Howard Tumber, (Oxford, UK: Oxford University Press, 1999), 218–23.

7. Edward S. Herman and Noam Chomsky, *Manufacturing Consent* (New York: Pantheon, 1988).

8. Stuart Hall, Chas Critcher, Tony Jefferson, John N. Clarke, and Brian Roberts, *Policing The Crisis: Mugging, the State and Law and Order* (London: Macmillan, 1978).

9. Todd Gitlin, *The Whole World Is Watching* (Berkeley: University of California Press, 1980).

10. Steve Chibnall, *Law and Order News* (London: Tavistock, 1977), 37.

11. Alison Anderson, "Source Strategies and the Communication of Environmental Affairs," *Media, Culture and Society* 13 (1991): 459–76; Aeron Davis, *Public Relations Democracy* (Manchester, UK: Manchester University Press, 2002); Oscar H. Gandy, *Beyond Agenda Setting: Information Subsidiaries and Public Policy* (Norwood, NJ: Ablex, 1981).

12. Simon Cottle, "Rethinking News Access," *Journalism Studies* 1 (2000): 437. Also, Philip Schlesinger, "Rethinking the Sociology of Journalism: Source Strategies and the Limits of Media-Centrism," in *Public Communication: The New Imperatives,* ed. Marjorie Ferguson (London: Sage, 1990), 61–83; Philip Schlesinger and Howard Tumber, *Reporting Crime: The Media Politics of Criminal Justice* (Oxford, UK: Clarendon Press, 1994); David Miller, "Official Sources and 'Primary Definition': The Case of Northern Ireland," *Media, Culture and Society* 15 (1993): 385–406; Zvi Reich, *Sourcing the News* (Cresskill, NJ: Hampton Press, 2009).

13. Gans, *Deciding What's News,* 81.

14. For an overview of research in this area, see John Eldridge, "News, Truth and Power," in *Getting the Message: News, Truth and Power,* ed. John Eldridge (London: Routledge, 1993), 3–33. Key works include W. Lance Bennett, *News: The Politics of Illusion* (New York: Longman, 1983); Todd Gitlin, *The Whole World is Watching* (Berkeley: University of California Press, 1980); Glasgow University Media Group, *Bad News* (London: Routledge and Kegan Paul, 1976).

15. Sigal, *Reporters and Officials,* 27–28.

16. Brian McNair, *The Sociology of Journalism* (London: Arnold, 1998), 6. See also Steven E. Clayman, "From Talk to Text: Newspaper Accounts of Reporter-Source Interactions," *Media, Culture and Society* 12 (1990): 79–103; Mats Nylund, "Quoting in Front-Page Journalism: Illustrating, Evaluating and Confirming the News," *Media, Culture and Society* 25 (2003): 844–51; Barbie Zelizer, "'Saying' as Collective Practice: Quoting and Differential Address in the News," *Text* 9 (1989): 369–88; Sigal, *Reporters and Officials.*

17. Mark Fishman, *Manufacturing the News* (Austin: University of Texas Press, 1980).

18. Richard V. Ericson, Patricia M. Baranek, and J. B. Chan, *Negotiating Control: A Study of News Sources* (Toronto: University of Toronto Press, 1989), 395.

19. Eason, "On Journalistic Authority," 221.

20. Some exemplary stories involving unnamed sources are discussed in chapter 5.

21. These negatives and positives were particularly debated and discussed following the Janet Cooke scandal at the *Washington Post* in 1981. Cooke fabricated her unnamed source and was only discovered after winning the Pulitzer Prize. See Douglas A. Anderson, "How Newspaper Editors Reacted to Post's Pulitzer Prize Hoax," *Journalism Quarterly* 59 (1982): 363–66; National News Council, *After "Jimmy's World": Tightening Up in Editing* (New York: National News Council, 1981); National News Council, *Who Said What?* (New York: National News Council, 1983); Byron St. Dizier, "Reporters' Use of Confidential Sources, 1974 and 1984: A Comparative Study," *Newspaper Research Journal* 6 (1985): 44–50; K. Tim Wulfemeyer, "Use of Anonymous Sources in Journalism," *Newspaper Research Journal* 4 (1982): 43–50.

22. Daniel C. Hallin, Robert Karl Manoff, and Judy K. Weddle, "Sourcing Patterns of National Security Reporters," *Journalism Quarterly* 70 (1993): 759.

23. Taegyu Son, "Leaks: How Do Codes of Ethics Address Them?" *Journal of Mass Media Ethics* 17 (2002): 170.

24. Thomas Kaminski, "Congress, Correspondents and Confidentiality in the 19th Century: a Preliminary Study," *Journalism History* 4 (Autumn 1977): 83–87, 92; Donald Ritchie, *Press Gallery: Congress and the Washington Correspondents* (Cambridge, MA: Harvard University Press, 1991).

25. Richard Kielbowicz, "The Role of News Leaks in Governance and Law of Journalists' Confidentiality, 1795–2005," *San Diego Law Review* 43 (2006), 433–34.

26. Ibid., 436.

27. Ibid., 441; Kaminski, "Congress, Correspondents and Confidentiality."

28. Kielbowicz, "The Role of News Leaks," 444.

29. Daniel Boorstin, *The Image: A Guide to Pseudo-Events in America* (Boston: Athenium, 1961), 30.

30. David Rudenstine, *The Day the Press Stopped; A History of the Pentagon Papers Case* (Berkeley: University of California Press, 1998).

31. James Goodale, "*Branzburg v. Hayes* and the Developing Qualified Privilege for Newsmen," *Hastings Law Journal* 26 (1974–75): 709–43.

32. Although it can be argued the glorification of Woodward and Bernstein has had an adverse effect on journalism, a topic described in chapter 4.

33. Allan Bell, *The Language of News Media* (Oxford, UK: Blackwell, 1991), 193.

34. Barbie Zelizer, "On Communicative Practice: The "Other Worlds" of Journalism and Shamanism," *Southern Folklore* 49 (1992): 25.

35. David E. Boeyink, "Anonymous Sources in News Stories: Justifying Exceptions and Limiting Abuses," *Journal of Mass Media Ethics* 5 (1990): 237.

36. Ibid., 238.

37. Sigal, *Reporters and Officials*, 144.

38. Ibid., 189.

39. Aeron Davis, "Whither Mass Media and Power? Evidence for a Critical Elite Theory Alternative," *Media, Culture and Society* 25 (2003): 669.

40. Reich, *Sourcing the News.*

41. Stephen Hess, *News and Newsmaking* (Washington, DC: The Brookings Institution, 1996), 70–71.

42. Son, "Leaks," 155–73.

43. Gaye Tuchman, *Making News: A Study in the Construction of Reality* (New York: Free Press, 1978), 69.

44. Stephen Hess, *The Washington Reporters* (Washington, DC: The Brookings Institution, 1981), 20.

45. Wulfemeyer, "Use of Anonymous Sources."

46. Hugh M. Culbertson, "Veiled Attribution: An Element of Style?" *Journalism Quarterly* 55 (1978): 465.

47. Herbert Strentz, *News Reporters and News Sources,* 2nd ed. (Ames: Iowa State University Press, 1989).

48. Sherrie L. Wilson, William A. Babcock, and John Pribeck, "Newspaper Ombudsmen's Reactions to Use of Anonymous Sources," *Newspaper Research Journal* 18 (Summer/Fall 1997): 141–53, 150.

49. Hugh M. Culbertson, "Leaks: A Dilemma for Editors as Well as Officials," *Journalism Quarterly* 57 (1980): 402–8, 535; Charles N. Davis, Susan D. Ross, and Paul H. Gates, "How Newspaper Editors Feel About Confidential Sources in Wake of *Cohen v. Cowles,*" *Newspaper Research Journal* 17 (Summer/Fall 1996): 88–97; Hess, *The Washington Reporters;* Angela Powers and Frederick Fico, "Influences on Use of Sources at Large US Papers," *Newspaper Research Journal* 15 (Fall 1994): 87–97; Wulfemeyer, "Use of Anonymous Sources."

50. ABC News/*Washington Post* survey, iPOLL Databank, The Roper Center for Public Opinion Research, University of Connecticut, May 18–22, 2005, http://www.ropercenter.uconn.edu/data_access/ipoll/ipoll.html (accessed December 19, 2006).

51. Pew Research Center, *Online Newspaper Readership Countering Print Losses* (Washington, DC: Pew Research Center, 2005), 17.

52. Ibid.

53. Ibid., 27.

54. Robert S. Billings, Thomas W. Milburn, and Mary Lou Schaalman, "A Model of Crisis Perception: A Theoretical and Empirical Analysis," *Administrative Science Quarterly* 25 (1980): 306.

55. This topic is dealt with superbly in James Carey, *Communication as Culture: Essays on Media and Society* (London: Unwin Hyman, 1989).

56. Pew Research Center, *Trends 2005* (Washington DC: Pew Research Center, 2005), 49.

57. Gallup Organization survey, iPOLL Databank, The Roper Center for Public Opinion Research, University of Connecticut, September 13–15, 2004, http://www .ropercenter.uconn.edu/data_access/ipoll/ipoll.html (accessed March 1, 2007). A year later in September 2005, the divide had evened out to 50 percent trusting and 49 percent not trusting. Ibid., September 12–15, 2005 (accessed March 1, 2007).

58. According to the Pew Research Center, of those respondents able to rate each outlet, the percent believing all or most of *Newsweek* declined from 85 percent in 1985 to 69 percent in 2006. *Time* magazine experienced a sharper decline from 84 percent to 59 percent. With television, CBS News also experienced a steep decline in believability from 85 percent in 1985 to 59 percent in 2006. *60 Minutes* fell from 74 to 64 percent. The *New York Times* was not measured in 1985, but in 2006, only 54 percent of survey respondents said they believed all or most of what the newspaper published. This was less than the Fox News Channel, with 58 percent. Pew Research Center, *Maturing Internet News Audience—Broader Than Deep* (Washington DC: Pew Research Center, 2006), 121–23.

59. Project for Excellence in Journalism, "State of the News Media 2006," http:// www.stateofthenewsmedia.com/2006/chartland.asp?id=211&ct=line&dir=&sort=& co11 box=1.

60. *Editor & Publisher Online*, "US and Canadian Multi-Newspaper Cities," http:// www.editorandpublisher.com/eandp/images/pdf/US%20&%20Can.%20Multi%20 Cities.pdf.

61. Project for Excellence in Journalism, "State of the News Media 2006."

62. Pew Research Center, *Trends 2005*, 42.

63. While newspaper revenues rebounded somewhat following the end of the technology boom in 2000 and the terrorist attacks of September 11, 2001, they have struggled to maintain traditional sources of income including from classified advertising. The broadcast evening news has also experienced turbulent economics. Project for Excellence in Journalism, *State of the News Media 2006*.

64. The subject of media ownership has been carefully analyzed by Ben Bagdikian and Robert McChesney. Their latest works include Ben Bagdikian, *The New Media Monopoly* (Boston: Beacon Press, 2004); Robert McChesney, *The Problem of the Media: U.S. Communication Politics in the 21st Century* (New York: Monthly Review Press, 2004).

65. Eric Klinenberg, *Fighting for Air* (New York: Metropolitan Books, 2007).

66. The amazing outpouring of public support against further deregulation is described in detail in McChesney, *The Problem of the Media,* chapter 7.

67. Project for Excellence in Journalism, *State of the News Media 2006.*

68. This shift has been borne out in survey research. At the time of the incidents in this book (2004), the percentage of people regularly getting news online stood at 29 percent and cable news at 25 percent (Pew Research Center, *Trends 2005,* 42).

69. Several authors have usefully taken up the topic of intermedia battles emerging around the introduction of new media. Three excellent analyses are Samuel P. Winch, *Mapping the Cultural Space of Journalism* (Westport, CT: Praeger, 1997); Jane B. Singer, "Who Are These Guys? The Online Challenge to the Notion of Journalistic Professionalism," *Journalism* 4 (2003): 139–63; Gwenyth L. Jackaway, *Media at War* (Westport, CT: Praeger, 1995).

70. Gillmor offers an impassioned argument for citizen journalism in Dan Gillmor, *We The Media: Grassroots Journalism by the People, for the People* (Sebastopol, CA: O'Reilly Media, 2004), 24.

71. Matthew Klam, "Fear and Laptops on the Campaign Trail," *New York Times Magazine,* September 26, 2004, 42–49, 115–23.

72. Matt Carlson, "Blogs and Journalistic Authority: The Role of Blogs in US Election Day 2004 Coverage," *Journalism Studies* 8 (2007): 264–79.

73. Pew Internet and American Life Project. "Usage Over Time," http://www.pewinternet.org/trend-data/usage-over-time.aspx.

74. Matt Carlson, "Order Versus Access: News Search Engines and the Challenge to Traditional Journalistic Roles," *Media, Culture and Society* 29 (2007): 1014–30; Singer, "Who are These Guys?"; Jane B. Singer, "The Political J-Blogger: 'Normalizing' a New Media Form to Fit Old Norms and Practices," *Journalism* 6 (2005): 173–98.

75. I use the terms "conservative" and "liberal" according to their use within popular political discourse in the United States during the time of the cases. While these labels are problematic and loaded with baggage, they are useful for grouping individuals around their ideological interests relative to one another. Thus, "conservative" will be used synonymously with "the right" and "liberal" with "the left" as points on the ideological spectrum of U.S. society. They are used to signify loose affiliations rather than homogenous and totalizing entities.

76. Lawrence C. Soley, *The News Shapers* (New York: Praeger, 1992).

77. McChesney, *The Problem of the Media,* 111.

78. Pew Research Center and Princeton Survey Research Associates International survey, iPOLL Databank, The Roper Center for Public Opinion Research, University of Connecticut, October 15–19, 2004, http://www.ropercenter.uconn.edu/data_access/ipoll/ipoll.html (accessed March 1, 2007).

79. Pew Research Center, *Online Newspaper Readership,* 26.

80. Ibid., 25.

81. Barbie Zelizer, "Journalists as Interpretive Communities," *Critical Studies in Mass Communication* (1993): 224.

82. Ronald Bishop, "From Behind the Walls: Boundary Work by News Organizations in Their Coverage of Princess Diana's Death," *Journal of Communication Inquiry* 23 (1999): 90–112; Russell Frank, "'These Crowded Circumstances': When Pack Journalists Bash Pack Journalism," *Journalism* 4 (2003): 441–58; Winch, *Mapping the Cultural Space of Journalism.*

83. The question of journalism as a profession has been examined over many decades. See John Wallace, Claire Johnstone, Edward J. Slawski, and William W. Bowman, *The News People: A Sociological Portrait of American Journalists and Their Work* (Urbana: University of Illinois Press, 1976); Thomas C. Leonard, *The Power of the Press* (New York: Oxford University Press, 1986); Jeremy Tunstall, *Journalists at Work* (Beverly Hills, CA: Sage, 1971); David Hugh Weaver and G. Cleveland Wilhoit, *The American Journalist* (Bloomington: Indiana University Press, 1986).

84. Michael Schudson, *Discovering the News: A Social History of American Newspapers* (New York: Basic Books, 1978), 9.

85. Pierre Bourdieu, *The Field of Cultural Production,* ed. Randal Johnson (New York: Columbia University Press, 1993), 42, original emphasis.

86. The term originally was used by Fish to address differences arising in readings among literary theorists. In a literary example, different theorists interpret a text—they "write" the text, in Fish's terminology—according to the strategies of their interpretive community. Stanley Fish, *Is There a Text in This Class?* (Cambridge, MA: Harvard University Press, 1980).

87. Dan Berkowitz and James V. TerKeurst, "Community as Interpretive Community: Rethinking the Journalist-Source Relationship," *Journal of Communication* 49 (September 1999): 125–36, 127.

88. Zelizer, "Journalists as Interpretive Communities," 233.

89. Peter Dahlgren, "Introduction," in *Journalism and Popular Culture,* ed. Peter Dahlgren and Colin Sparks (London: Sage, 1992), 1–23, 2.

90. Ibid., 4.

91. Throughout this book, discourse is viewed not simply as a marker of opinions or a discussion of sourcing practices, but as an active process through which shared meanings and definitions are created. Fiske describes discourse as "structured and structuring, for it is both determined by its social relations and affects them." John Fiske, *Media Matters: Everyday Culture and Political Change* (Minneapolis: University of Minnesota Press, 1994), 3.

92. W. Lance Bennett, Lynne A. Gressett, and William Haltom, "Repairing the News: A Case Study of the News Paradigm," *Journal of Communication* 35 (1985): 50–68; Dan Berkowitz, "Doing Double Duty: Paradigm Repair and the Princess Diana What-A-Story," *Journalism* 1 (2000): 125–43; Elizabeth Blanks Hindman, "Jayson Blair, The *New York Times,* and Paradigm Repair," *Journal of Communication* 55 (2005):

225–41; Stephen D. Reese, "The News Paradigm and the Ideology of Objectivity: A Socialist at the *Wall Street Journal*," *Critical Studies in Mass Communication* 7 (1990): 390–409.

93. Thomas S. Kuhn, *The Structure of Scientific Revolutions*, 3rd ed. (Chicago: University of Chicago Press, 1996).

94. Robert A. Hackett, "Decline of a Paradigm? Bias and Objectivity in News Media Studies," *Critical Studies in Mass Communication* 1 (1984): 229–59.

95. Bennett, Gressett, and Haltom, "Repairing the News," 50–68.

96. Reese, "The News Paradigm," 390–409.

97. Berkowitz, "Doing Double Duty," 125–43.

98. "Institutional" here refers to journalism broadly as an institution with its set of practices, history, and interinstitutional relations. This is contrasted with "organizational," used throughout to refer to the level of individual news outlets with their own practices, traditions, and identities. For a discussion on this topic, see Timothy E. Cook, *Governing with the News* (Chicago: University of Chicago Press, 1998), chapter 4.

99. John C. Flanagan, "The Critical Incident Technique," *Psychological Bulletin* 51 (1954): 338.

100. George Gerbner, "Cultural Indictors: The Third Voice," in *Communications Technology and Social Policy*, ed. George Gerbner, Larry P. Gross, and William Harry Melody (New York: John Wiley & Sons, 1973), 555–73, 562.

101. Cited in Stuart Hall, "The Question of Cultural Identity," in *Modernity: An Introduction To Modern Societies*, ed. Stuart Hall, David Held, Don Hubert, and Kenneth Thompson (Malden, MA: Blackwell, 1996), 595–634, 597.

102. To capture the array of narratives developing in each chapter, a broad search for mediated content was conducted for each incident. The data collected for this book came from many media sources, including newspapers (news articles, columns by media critics/public editors/ombudsmen/reader representatives, editorials, columnists, and op-eds), news magazines, cable television news (especially the prime time talk shows), network television news (including PBS's *NewsHour* and the Sunday morning talk shows), online news sites, blogs, National Public Radio, books, the journalism and media trade press, academics and media think tanks, and media watch groups. Broad searches were conducted to amass a census of available materials. The primary source for data was the Factiva database, which was supplemented with further searches using the LexisNexis Academic and NewsBank databases. While these databases do not provide a complete record, their collections are thorough enough to capture most prominent news sources as well as many smaller ones.

Chapter 1: Media Culpas

Epigraph. Michael Getler, "A Parting Thought on Iraq, Again," *Washington Post*, October 9, 2005, B6.

1. Deborah Howell, "Covert Question, Open Controversy," *Washington Post,* February 25, 2007, B6.

2. Project for Excellence in Journalism, "Before and After: How the War on Terrorism Has Changed the News Agenda," November 19, 2001, http://journalism.org/node/289.

3. Pew Research Center, "American Psyche Reeling from Terror Attacks," September 19, 2001, http://people-press.org/report/3/american-psyche-reeling-from-terror-attacks.

4. According to Gallup/*USA Today* poll results, http://pollingreport.com/BushJob1.htm (accessed May 27, 2009).

5. Gallup/*USA Today* poll results, http://pollingreport.com/CongJob1.htm (accessed May 27, 2009).

6. Robert McChesney, "September 11 and the Structural Limitations of US Journalism," in *Journalism After September 11,* ed. Barbie Zelizer and Stuart Allan (London: Routledge, 2002), 91–100.

7. Michael Massing, "Now They Tell Us," *New York Review of Books,* February 26, 2004, http://www.nybooks.com/articles/16922 (accessed February 26, 2007). The visibility of Massing's critique was increased by the posting of the lengthy article online and its eventual transformation into a book.

8. In many ways, this environment fit with the classic study by Timothy Crouse: Timothy Crouse, *The Boys on the Bus* (New York: Random House, 1973).

9. W. Lance Bennett, Regina G. Lawrence, and Steven Livingston, *When the Press Fails: Political Power and the News Media from Iraq to Katrina* (Chicago: University of Chicago Press, 2007); Eric Boehlert, *Lapdogs: How the Press Rolled over for Bush* (New York: Free Press, 2006); Susan D. Moeller, *Media Coverage of Weapons of Mass Destruction* (College Park, MD: Center for International and Security Studies at Maryland, 2004).

10. Steve Ritea, "Going It Alone," *American Journalism Review* (August 2004), 16–17.

11. Given the concerns over unnamed sources, it is no coincidence that Landay and Strobel's editor in the Knight Ridder Washington Bureau, Clark Hoyt, would later serve as the public editor of the *New York Times.*

12. One notable exception was a pair of articles by *Washington Post* media writer Howard Kurtz scrutinizing Judith Miller's ties with Iraqi defectors and her actions as an embed: Howard Kurtz, "Intra-Times Battle Over Iraqi Weapons," *Washington Post,* May 26, 2003, C1; Howard Kurtz, "Embedded Reporter's Role in Army Unit's Actions Questioned by Military," *Washington Post,* June 25, 2003, C1.

13. Massing, "Now They Tell Us."

14. Ted Gup, "Useful Secrets," *Columbia Journalism Review* 14 (March 2003): 14–16.

15. Tom Wicker, "On the Presidential Power to Wage War," *Editor & Publisher,* March 10, 2003.

16. John R. MacArthur, "The Lies We Bought," *Columbia Journalism Review* 42 (May 2003): 62–63.

17. Joe Strupp, "Asking Questions, Well After the Fact," *Editor & Publisher,* June 9, 2003, 20.

18. Nicholas von Hoffman, "Times Readers Need a New Decoder Ring," *New York Observer,* June 16, 2003, 4.

19. Glenn Greenwald, "The Ongoing Journalistic Scandal at the New York Times," *Salon,* July 9, 2007, http://www.salon.com/opinion/greenwald/2007/07/09/hoyt/index.html (accessed July 17, 2007).

20. Charles Layton, "Miller Brouhaha," *American Journalism Review* 30 (August 2003): 30–35; Rivera had been removed from the field for revealing the positions of troops with whom he was traveling.

21. William E. Jackson, Jr., "Now It's Miller Time," *Editor & Publisher,* June 16, 2003, 33.

22. Shafer wrote about Judith Miller sixteen times in his Press Box column between April 21, 2003, and the eve of *Times*'s editor's note in May 2004.

23. Jack Shafer, "Reassessing Miller," *Slate,* May 29, 2003, http://www.slate.com/id/2083736/ (accessed November 1, 2006).

24. See ibid.; Russ Baker, "'Scoops' and Truth at the Times: What Happens When Pentagon Objectives and Journalists' Needs Coincide," *The Nation,* June 23, 2003, 18; Layton, "Miller Brouhaha," 30–35; MacArthur, "The Lies We Bought," 62–63; and Massing, "Now They Tell Us."

25. Michael R. Gordon and Judith Miller, "U.S. Says Hussein Intensifies Quest for A-Bomb Parts," *New York Times,* September 8, 2002, A1.

26. Judith Miller and Michael R. Gordon, "White House Lists Iraq Steps to Build Banned Weapons," *New York Times,* September 13, 2002, A13.

27. MacArthur, "The Lies We Bought," 62.

28. Judith Miller, "Iraq Said to Try to Buy Antidote Against Nerve Gas," *New York Times,* November 12, 2002, A1.

29. *New York Times* (July 21, 2005), *Washington Post* (July 1, July 7, 2005), *Boston Globe* (July 8, 2005), *Houston Chronicle* (June 30, 2005), *St. Petersburg Times* (June 29, July 8, July 24, 2005), *Denver Post* (June 29, 2005), Cleveland *Plain Dealer* (July 6, 2005), *San Francisco Chronicle* (September 20, 2005), *Indianapolis Star* (July 8, 2005), *Tampa Tribune* (February 17, June 28, 2005), *Rocky Mountain News* (February 17, 2005), Portland *Oregonian* (February 18, July 25, 2005), *Oakland Tribune* (July 3, 2005), *Salt Lake Tribune,* (July 7, 2005), New Orleans *Times-Picayune* (July 8, 2005), *San Diego Union-Tribune* (October 1, 2005), *Columbus Dispatch* (July 9, July 26, 2005), *Seattle Post-Intelligencer* (July 22, 2005), *Pittsburgh Post-Gazette* (July 25, 2005), Albany *Times Union* (February 17, 2005), *Orlando Sentinel* (July 8, 2005), *Kansas City Star* (July 9, 2005), and Nashville *Tennessean* (July 9, 2005), along with a number of other smaller newspapers.

30. Rem Rieder, "Say It Isn't So, Bob," *American Journalism Review* 27, no. 5 (2005), http://www.ajr.org/Article.asp?id=3995 (accessed April 20, 2007).

31. Romenesko's blog can be found at http://www.poynter.org/column .asp?id=45.

32. Poynter Ethics Journal, "The Washington Post's Policies on Sources, Quotations, Attribution, and Datelines," Poynter Online, February 20, 2004, http://www .poynter.org/column.asp?id=53&aid=61244 (accessed November 1, 2006).

33. Ibid.

34. Leonard Downie, Jr., "The Guidelines We Use to Report the News," *Washington Post,* March 7, 2004, B1.

35. This point was made three decades earlier by Tuchman: Gaye Tuchman, "Objectivity As Strategic Ritual," *American Journal of Sociology* 77 (1972): 660–79.

36. Eric Boehlert, "How the New York Times Helped Railroad Wen Ho Lee," *Salon,* September 21, 2000, http://archive.salon.com/news/feature/2000/09/21/nyt/index .html (accessed February 6, 2009).

37. Seth Mnookin, *Hard News: the Scandals at the New York Times and Their Meaning for American Media* (New York: Random House, 2004).

38. Lucinda Fleeson, "A Reporter Under Fire," *American Journalism Review* 22 (November 2000): 28.

39. Robert Scheer, "No Defense: How the New York Times Convicted Wen Ho Lee," *The Nation,* October 5, 2000, http://www.thenation.com/doc/20001023/scheer (accessed January 26, 2010); Lucinda Fleeson, "Rush to Judgment," *American Journalism Review* 22 (November 2000): 20–29.

40. Fleeson, "Rush to Judgment," 20.

41. Paul Farhi, "U.S., Media Settle with Wen Ho Lee," *Washington Post,* June 3, 2006, A1.

42. New York Times Company, "Confidential News Sources," February 25, 2004, http://www.nytco.com/company/business_units/sources.html.

43. Quoted in Howard Kurtz, "N.Y. Times Cites Defects in its Reports on Iraq," *Washington Post,* May 26, 2004, C1.

44. Bill Keller, "The Times and Iraq," *New York Times,* May 26, 2004, A10.

45. Quoted in Liz Halloran, "Times: Iraq Coverage Flawed," *Hartford Courant,* May 27, 2004, D1.

46. For example, the Downing Street Memo was largely ignored in the U.S. media. See Douglas Bicket and Melissa Wall, "Circling the Wagons: Containing the Downing Street Memo Story's Impact in America," *Journal of Communication Inquiry* 31 (2007): 206–21.

47. Raines became executive editor of the newspaper in September 2001, a week before the terrorist attack on New York. He resigned in June 2003 in the wake of the Jayson Blair scandal and criticism of his management style. During this period, Keller wrote a column for the newspaper in which he expressed his personal support

for the invasion of Iraq. See Bill Keller, "The I-Can't-Believe-I'm-a-Hawk Club," *New York Times,* February 8, 2003, A17.

48. Keller, "The Times and Iraq," A10.

49. Massing, "Now They Tell Us."

50. Keller, "The Times and Iraq," A10.

51. Daniel Okrent, "Weapons of Mass Destruction? Or Mass Distraction?" *New York Times,* May 30, 2004, 2.

52. Ibid.

53. Seth Sutel, "Times Finds Faults in Its Iraq Coverage," *Associated Press Newswires,* May 26, 2004; Grant McCool, "Times Says It Fell for Iraq Misinformation," *Reuters News,* May 26, 2004.

54. Sutel, "Times Finds Faults,"; McCool, "Times Says It Fell,"; Don Wycliff, "An Unusual Revelation of Self-Examination," *Chicago Tribune,* May 28, 2004, 31; Eric Slater, "Paper Criticizes Own Reporting on Iraq," *Los Angeles Times,* May 26, 2004, A18; "A Times Apology," *Bangor Daily News,* June 8, 2004, 8.

55. Mark Jurkowitz, "Times Acknowledges Iraq Coverage Flaws: Note from Editors Answers Questions about Reporting," *Boston Globe,* May 27, 2004, E1; "Premise for War: Original Assumptions No Longer Are Clear," *Dallas Morning News,* May 27, 2004, A24; Leon Lazaroff and Mike Dorning, "Rare Admission, Then Tough Scrutiny," *Chicago Tribune,* May 27, 2004, 1; James C. Moore, "Not Fit to Print," *Salon,* May 27, 2004, http://archive.salon.com/news/feature/2004/05/27/times/ (accessed November 1, 2006).

56. Michael Arrietta-Walden, "Partisanship, CBS Fiasco Erode Readers' Trust," *Oregonian,* September 26, 2004, F1.

57. Edward Wasserman, "A Victory of Professionalism," *Miami Herald,* May 31, 2004, A19.

58. Keith J. Kelly, "NYT Whispers Apology for WMD Stories," *New York Post,* May 27, 2004, 37.

59. Halloran, "Times: Iraq Coverage Flawed," D1.

60. Paula Zahn, *Paula Zahn Now,* CNN, May 26, 2004.

61. The oldest article ran on October 26, 2001.

62. Howard Kurtz, *Newsnight with Aaron Brown,* CNN, May 26, 2004.

63. Wycliff, "An Unusual Revelation," A26.

64. James Bandler, "New York Times Criticizes Its Own Iraqi-Weapons Coverage," *Wall Street Journal,* May 27, 2004, B1.

65. Margaret Carlson, *Capital Gang,* CNN, May 29, 2004.

66. Raised by Michael Massing in Bandler, "New York Times Criticizes."

67. Michael Getler, *Reliable Sources,* CNN, May 30, 2004.

68. Moore, "Not Fit to Print."

69. Michael Getler, "Looking Back Before the War," *Washington Post,* June 20, 2004, B6.

70. Howard Kurtz, "The Post On WMDs: An Inside Story," *Washington Post*, August 12, 2004, A1.

71. Ibid.

72. Ibid.

73. "Reflections on the Post's Self-Evaluation," *Washington Post*, August 15, 2004, B6.

74. Howard Kurtz, "Ultimately, Newspapers Can't Move the Earth," *Washington Post*, August 22, 2004, B1.

75. Randy Dotinga, "This Just In: The Factors Behind Newspapers' Rush to Contrition," *Christian Science Monitor*, August 24, 2004, 2.

76. Howard Kurtz, *NBC Nightly News*, September 21, 2004.

77. Paul Krugman, "To Tell the Truth," *New York Times*, May 28, 2004, A21.

78. Jacques Steinberg, "Washington Post Rethinks Its Coverage of War Debate," *New York Times*, August 13, 2004, A14.

Chapter 2: "Blogs 1, CBS 0"

Epigraph. Joanne Ostrow, "CBS Proves Medium Is Still the Message," *Denver Post*, September 23, 2004, F1.

1. *NBC Nightly* News, September 10, 2004; Michael Dobbs and Mike Allen, "Some Question Authenticity of Papers on Bush," *Washington Post*, September 10, 2004, A1.

2. Quoted in Brooks Barnes, "CBS Defends Report Critical of Bush Service," *Wall Street Journal*, September 13, 2004, B6.

3. *CBS Evening News*, September 13, September 15, 2004; *60 Minutes*, September 15, 2004.

4. *60 Minutes*, September 15, 2004. CBS considered this information to corroborate the overall story while critics viewed it as a smoking gun due to Killian's lack of typing skills.

5. Dan Rather, *CBS Evening News*, September 20, 2004.

6. Burkett had appeared on MSNBC's *Hardball* on February 12 claiming Bush's Guard records had been purposefully destroyed.

7. See Mary Mapes, *Truth and Duty* (New York: St. Martin's Press, 2005) for a full explanation of how Burkett came into possession of the memos.

8. James Pinkerton, "Rather Deserved to Be Fired Too," *Cincinnati Post*, January 13, 2005, A12.

9. Jessica Mintz, "When Bloggers Make News: As Their Clout Increases, Web Diarists Are Asking: Just What Are the Rules?" *Wall Street Journal*, January 21, 2005, B1.

10. Quoted in Howard Kurtz, "After Blogs Got Hits, CBS Got a Black Eye," *Washington Post*, September 20, 2004, C1.

11. Matt Carlson, "Blogs and Journalistic Authority: The Role of Blogs in US Election Day 2004 Coverage," *Journalism Studies* 8 (2007): 264–79.

12. Jeff Greenfield, *News from CNN,* September 20, 2004.

13. Keith Olbermann, *Countdown,* MSNBC, September 20, 2004.

14. Tom Costello, *NBC Nightly News,* September 21, 2004.

15. Dave Kopel, "Citizen Journalists Bring CBS to Heel; Balance of 'Information Power' Shifting After Bloggers Pounce on Memo Fiasco," *Rocky Mountain News,* September 25, 2004, C14.

16. Howard Kurtz, *Larry King Live,* CNN, September 21, 2004.

17. Jonathan Klein, *O'Reilly Factor,* Fox News Channel, September 10, 2004.

18. Carlson, "Blogs and Journalistic Authority."

19. Kathleen Parker, "Bad Bias Carried Dan Rather, CBS into Phony Story on George Bush," *Grand Rapids Press,* September 22, 2004, A10. Emphasis added.

20. John Podhoretz, "CBS Forges Ahead; Dan Rather, Deep in Denial," *New York Post,* September 14, 2004, 29.

21. Quoted in Mark Jurkowitz, "Lockhart Contacted Memo Scandal Figure; Says CBS Official Suggested Talk," *Boston Globe,* September 22, 2004, A9. Emphasis added.

22. Eric Fettmann, "Eye on CBS's Mess: It Is Watergate," *New York Post,* September 22, 2004, 31.

23. Rather was also pilloried by critics on the left who did not view his work as challenging conservatives or advocating for progressive causes. In response to charges that Rather only coddled Democrats, the liberal media watch group Fairness and Accuracy in Reporting detailed examples of Rather's lauding of conservatives: Fairness and Accuracy in Reporting, "Rather's Retirement and Liberal Bias," March 2, 2005, http://www.fair.org/index.php?page=2460 (accessed April 23, 2007).

24. Joseph Perkins, "Abandoning Neutrality at CBS News," *San Diego Union-Tribune,* September 24, 2004, B9.

25. Pat Buchanan, *Scarborough Country,* MSNBC, November 23, 2004.

26. Andrea Peyser, "A Sorry Apology at CBS," *New York Post,* September 21, 2004, 8.

27. Matt Carlson, "Media Criticism as Competitive Discourse," *Journal of Communication Inquiry* 33 (2009): 258–77.

28. Kevin Johnson, Dave Moniz, and Jim Drinkard, "CBS Had Source Talk to Kerry Aide," *USA Today,* September 21, 2004, A1.

29. Lawrence Kudlow, *Kudlow and Cramer,* CNBC, September 23, 2004.

30. Sean Hannity, *Hannity & Colmes,* Fox News Channel, September 21, 2004.

31. Charles Krauthammer, "Rather Biased," *Washington Post,* January 14, 2005, A19.

32. Mike Barnicle, *Scarborough Country,* MSNBC, September 22, 2004.

33. Sean Hannity, *Hannity and Colmes,* Fox News Channel, January 10, 2005.

34. Cal Thomas, "The Media's Trust Problem," *Tulsa World,* October 1, 2004, A18.

35. Tina Brown, "Breaking the News, Then Becoming It," *Washington Post*, September 23, 2004, C1.

36. Steven Levy, "Memo to Bloggers: Heal Thyselves; Taking the Low Road Is a Well-Trodden Path to Big Readership, Just As It Is in Old Media," *Newsweek*, October 4, 2004, 15.

37. Hunter, "TANG Typewriter Follies; Wingnuts Wrong," *DailyKos.com*, September 10, 2004, http://www.dailykos.com/story/2004/9/10/34914/1603 (accessed on February 11, 2009).

38. Debra J. Saunders, "Love Thy Newspaper," *San Francisco Chronicle*, September 21, 2004, B9.

39. "Dark Days, and Bright Ones, for American Journalism," *Virginian-Pilot*, September 23, 2004, B8.

40. Corey Pein, "Blog-Gate: Yes, CBS Screwed Up Badly in 'Memogate'—But So Did Those Who Covered the Affair," *Columbia Journalism Review* 43 (January 2005): 30.

41. The day the *60 Minutes* story ran, the *Boston Globe* also carried a front page story criticizing Bush's military record: Walter V. Robinson, "Bush Fell Short on Duty at Guard; Records Show Pledges Unmet," *Boston Globe*, September 8, 2004, A1.

42. Hunter, "TANG, revisited," *DailyKos.com*, January 7, 2005, http://www.dailykos.com/storyonly/2005/1/7/214951/9910 (accessed February 6, 2009).

43. Bob Steele, *All Things Considered*, NPR, September 20, 2004.

44. Howard Kurtz, "Document Experts Say CBS Ignored Memo 'Red Flags,'" *Washington Post*, September 15, 2004, A10.

45. "60 Minutes' Memos: Self-Inflicted Black Eye," *Seattle Post-Intelligencer*, September 21, 2004, B6.

46. "Old Story, New Problem," *Palm Beach Post*, September 22, 2004, A14. The alternative judgment that CBS erred by recklessly pursuing a scoop resonated across newspaper editorials, including "Failing Journalism 101," *St. Petersburg Times*, September 23, 2004, A16; "CBS' Goof," *Tulsa World*, September 23, 2004, A18; "Rather Embarrassing," *Winston-Salem Journal*, September 23, 2004, A8; "CBS' Black Eye," *Buffalo News*, September 23, 2004, A8.

47. The "Journalism 101" phrase appeared in several editorials or columns, including *New York Times* (September 23, 2004), *Wall Street Journal* (January 11, 2005), *Washington Post* (January 13, 2005), *St. Louis Post-Dispatch* (September 23, 2004), *St. Petersburg Times* (September 23, 2004), *Pittsburgh Post-Gazette* (January 11, 2005), and *Bangor Daily News* (January 15, 2005).

48. "Poor Judgment at CBS," *Washington Post*, September 22, 2004, A30.

49. Phil Rosenthal, "Rather Sorry," *Chicago Sun-Times*, September 21, 2004, 49.

50. Quoted in Tim Cuprisin, "Four Fired for '60 Minutes' Report; Examination of Piece on Bush's Service Shows CBS Rushed It to Air," *Milwaukee Journal Sentinel*, January 11, 2005, A1.

51. Dusty Saunders, "Rather Remains in Hot Seat," *Rocky Mountain News*, September 23, 2004, D2.

52. Quoted in Brooks Barnes and Joe Flint, "CBS Controversy Comes as Network Nightly News Shows Are Losing Clout," *Wall Street Journal*, September 22, 2004, A19.

53. Bill Carter, "Courage, CBS News," *New York Times*, November 24, 2004, C1.

54. Tom Rosenstiel, *Morning Edition*, NPR, September 21, 2004.

55. Howard Kurtz, Michael Dobbs, and James V. Grimaldi, "In Rush to Air, CBS Quashed Memo Worries," *Washington Post*, September 19, 2004, A1.

56. Dusty Saunders, "Midweek Edition of '60 Minutes' Gone," *Rocky Mountain News*, May 19, 2005, A45.

57. Bob Zelnick, *Reliable Sources*, CNN, September 26, 2004.

58. The tension between a competitive desire for generating scoops and standards of verification is well examined by Bill Kovach and Tom Rosenstiel in *Warp Speed: America in the Age of Mixed Media* (New York: The Century Foundation Press, 1999).

59. Robert P. Laurence, "CBS Must Can Dan to Regain Credibility," *San Diego Union-Tribune*, September 23, 2004, E1.

60. Marvin Kalb, *All Things Considered*, NPR, September 20, 2004.

61. Peter Ames Carlin, "'Rather-gate' Isn't About Fake Papers; It's Fake News," *Oregonian*, September 21, 2004, E1.

62. "At CBS, A Parable on Haste," *Denver Post*, January 12, 2005, B8.

63. Dick Thornburgh and Louis D. Boccardi, *Report of the Independent Review Panel*, January 5, 2005, http://wwwimage.cbsnews.com/htdocs/pdf/complete_report/CBS_Report.pdf, 4 (accessed May 6, 2008).

64. Richard Thornburgh, *Nightline*, ABC, January 10, 2005.

65. Richard Thornburgh, *NewsHour*, PBS, January 10, 2005.

66. Newspapers devoting editorials to the independent panel report between January 11 and 14, 2005, included the *New York Post, New York Daily News, Wall Street Journal, USA Today, St, Petersburg Times, Orange County Register, Tampa Tribune, Denver Post, Oregonian, Columbus Dispatch,* Cleveland *Plain Dealer, Virginian-Pilot, Buffalo News, San Diego Union-Tribune, Knoxville News-Sentinel, Atlanta Journal-Constitution, Pittsburgh Post-Gazette, St. Louis Post-Dispatch,* and *Palm Beach Post.*

67. Pein, "Blog-Gate," 30.

68. Jonathan V. Last, "The CBS Whitewash," *Weekly Standard*, January 24, 2005, 22.

69. Quoted in Rob Owen, "CBS Fires 4 for Putting Faulty Bush Story on Air," *Pittsburgh Post-Gazette*, January 11, 2005, A1.

70. John Podhoretz, "Boxed In By Bias—Why CBS Let Flawed Bush Report Air," *New York Post*, January 11, 2005, 29.

71. Pat Buchanan, *Hardball*, MSNBC, January 10, 2005.

72. Jaques Steinberg and Bill Carter, "Rather Quitting as CBS Anchor in Abrupt Move," *New York Times*, November 24, 2004, A1.

73. Nancy Franklin, "Anchor Away," *The New Yorker,* May 26, 2008, 86.

74. Jaques Steinberg, "CBS Is Sued by Rather Over Ouster," *New York Times,* September 20, 2007, A1.

75. Peter Johnson, "Rather Sues Ex-Boss CBS for $70 Million; Says He's 'Scapegoat' for Memogate Scandal," *USA Today,* September 20, 2007, D1.

76. As further evidence of corporate and governmental influence on news, Rather cited CBS News's decision to hold its 2004 story breaking the Abu Ghraib scandal at the request of the U.S. military. See Carlson, "Media Criticism as Competitive Discourse."

77. Dareh Gregorian, "Judge: Dan Can Have an Eyeful—CBS Must Show & Tell," *New York Post,* January 10, 2008, 5. See also David Barron, "Can This Man Be Saved?" *Houston Chronicle,* January 20, 2008, 10.

78. Jaques Steinberg, "Rather's Lawsuit Shows Role of G.O.P. in Inquiry," *New York Times,* November 16, 2007, B1.

79. Dareh Gregorian, "Dan's Bad News Day—Half of Suit vs. CBS Tossed," *New York Post,* September 23, 2008, 13.

80. "Dan Rather and the Bloggers; That Pesky Accountability Thing," *Philadelphia Inquirer,* September 23, 2007, C6.

81. Said by former CBS News executive Rome Hartman on *Reliable Sources,* CNN, September 23, 2007.

82. Tucker Carlson, *Tucker with Tucker Carlson,* MSNBC, September 21, 2007.

83. *Reliable Sources,* CNN, September 23, 2007.

84. "Conventional Wisdom Watch," *Newsweek,* October 1, 2007, 8.

85. Bill O'Reilly, *The O'Reilly Factor,* Fox News Channel, September 19, 2007.

86. Bill O'Reilly, *The O'Reilly Factor,* Fox News Channel, September 20, 2007.

87. Ibid.

88. Daniel Schorr, *Morning Edition,* NPR, September 20, 2007.

89. Daniel Schorr, *Weekend Edition,* NPR, September 23, 2007.

90. Eugene Robinson, "Some Bad News to Break," *Washington Post,* September 24, 2007, A19. Robinson did acknowledge Rather's normative claims, asking "When the next set of Pentagon Papers comes down the pike, how will our corporatized news media react?"

91. "Mistakes: Political Forces on the Left and the Right and a Media Legend Diminish Themselves," *Houston Chronicle,* September 25, 2007, 8.

92. See Kimberly Meltzer, "The Hierarchy of Journalistic Cultural Authority," *Journalism Practice* 3 (2009): 59–74.

93. Steinberg, "Rather's Lawsuit Shows Role," B1.

94. "Dan Rather and the Bloggers," C6.

95. Brown, "Breaking the News," C1.

96. Robert Thompson, *Today,* NBC, September 21, 2004.

Chapter 3: Journalists Fight Back

Epigraph. Clark Hoyt, "Anonymous Sources Erode Media, Government Credibility," *St. Paul Pioneer Press,* May 19, 2005, B12. Hoyt became the public editor of the *New York Times* in 2007.

1. Pew Research Center, *Online Newspaper Readership Countering Print Losses* (Washington, DC: Pew Research Center, 2005), 26.

2. Douglas McCollam, "The Crowded Theater," *Columbia Journalism Review* 44 (July 2005): 24.

3. Joe Strupp, "Losing Confidence," *Editor & Publisher,* July 2005, 32.

4. Ibid., 34–35.

5. Joe Hagan, "Newsweek Flap Stirs Debate Over Sources," *Wall Street Journal,* May 17, 2005, B1.

6. Frank Stasio, *Talk of the Nation,* NPR, May 16, 2005.

7. "Preserving Our Readers' Trust," *New York Times,* May 2, 2005, http://www .nytco.com/pdf/siegal-report050205.pdf (accessed March 5, 2007).

8. Bill Keller, *On the Media,* NPR, May 13, 2005.

9. Strupp, "Losing Confidence," 32–39.

10. Lorne Manly, "Big News Media Join in Push to Limit Use of Unidentified Sources," *New York Times,* May 23, 2005, C1.

11. Ibid.

12. The issue was available both in print and online by May 1.

13. Michael Isikoff and John Barry, "Guantanamo: A Scandal Spreads," *Newsweek,* May 9, 2005, 4.

14. Isikoff made this claim on the *Charlie Rose Show* (PBS, May 23, 2005). A search using the Factiva database did not reveal any reporting on the *Newsweek* story in U.S. news outlets until after it was tied to the Afghan riots.

15. "Pakistan's Imran Demands US Apology Over Koran Report," *Reuters,* May 6, 2005.

16. "Afghans Protest Over U.S. Abuse of Koran Report," *Reuters,* May 10, 2005.

17. "Pentagon Says It Is Reviewing Allegation Koran Was Desecrated at Guantanamo," *Agence France Presse,* May 11, 2005.

18. "US Says Koran Abuse 'Abhorrent' in Bid to Ease Muslim Anger," *Agence France Presse,* May 12, 2005.

19. Stephen Graham, "Afghan President Blames Unrest on Opponents of U.S. Ties, Taliban Reconciliation," Associated Press, May 14, 2005.

20. "Afghan Anti-US Protests Spread to Kabul," *Agence France Presse,* May 12, 2005.

21. Charlie Savage, "Newsweek Backs Off Guantanamo Article," *Boston Globe,* May 17, 2005, A1.

22. *CBS Evening News,* May 15, 2005.

23. Joe Garofoli, "Newsweek's Gaffe—Damage Is Done," *San Francisco Chronicle,* May 17, 2005, A1.

24. Peter Johnson, "Even a Few Sentences Can Have a Huge Effect," *USA Today,* May 17, 2005, D6.

25. Toni Locy, "Detainees' Lawsuits Also Allege Sacrilege," *USA Today,* May 17, 2005, A7.

26. Cited in Katharine Q. Seelye and Neil A. Lewis, "Newsweek Says It Is Retracting Koran Report," *New York Times,* May 17, 2005, A1.

27. Isikoff had initially uncovered the Lewinsky scandal for *Newsweek,* but editors held the story pending corroboration. It was then picked up by Matt Drudge and referred to on his Web site, drudgereport.com. Bill Kovach and Tom Rosenstiel, *Warp Speed: America in the Age of Mixed Media* (New York: The Century Foundation Press, 1999), 11.

28. Michael Isikoff, *Uncovering Clinton: A Reporter's Story* (New York: Crown Books, 1999).

29. Joan Walsh, "Newsweek Isn't the Problem," *Salon,* May 18, 2005, http://archive.salon.com/opinion/feature/2005/05/18/newsweek/print.html (accessed January 19, 2007).

30. Mark Whitaker, *NewsHour,* PBS, May 16, 2005.

31. Kathleen Hall Jamieson and Joseph Capella, *Echo Chamber: Rush Limbaugh and the Conservative Media Establishment* (New York: Oxford University Press, 2008).

32. Bill O'Reilly, *The O'Reilly Factor,* FOX News Channel, May 16, 2005.

33. Bill O'Reilly, *The O'Reilly Factor,* FOX News Channel, May 17, 2005.

34. Bill O'Reilly, "Newsweek, Others Should Be Careful What They Wish For," *Chicago Sun-Times,* May 23, 2005, 53.

35. Bill O'Reilly, *The O'Reilly Factor,* FOX News Channel, May 18, 2005.

36. Bill O'Reilly, *The O'Reilly Factor,* FOX News Channel, May 19, 2005.

37. Bill O'Reilly, *The O'Reilly Factor,* FOX News Channel, May 23, 2005.

38. Brent Bozell, *Hannity & Colmes,* FOX News Channel, May 16, 2005.

39. Brent Bozell, *Scarborough Country,* MSNBC, May 16, 2005.

40. Cal Thomas, *Fox News Watch,* May 21, 2005.

41. Paul Gigot, *Fox News Sunday,* May 22, 2005.

42. "Journalists and the Military," *Wall Street Journal,* May 17, 2005, A12.

43. "Nobles and Knaves," *Washington Times,* May 21, 2005, A12.

44. "Newsweek Takes It Back," *Boston Herald,* May 17, 2005, 28.

45. John Podhoretz, "Unfit to Print: Newsweek's Real Mistake," *New York Post,* May 17, 2005, 31.

46. Rich Lowry, "Media Want to Believe Worst about Military," *Seattle Post-Intelligencer,* May 18, 2005, B7.

47. Michelle Malkin, "Newsweek Just the Latest," *Baton Rouge Advocate,* May 20, 2005, B8.

48. "Newsweek's Malfeasance," *New York Post,* May 17, 2005, 32.

49. See Matt Carlson, "Media Criticism as Competitive Discourse," *Journal of Communication Inquiry* 33 (2009): 258–77.

50. "It Seems to Us . . . ; There's More Than One Kind of Roundabout, and a Sudden Horror at 'Wrong' Information," *Buffalo News,* May 21, 2005, A6.

51. W. Lance Bennett, Lynne A. Gressett, and William Haltom, "Repairing the News: A Case Study of the News Paradigm," *Journal of Communication* 35 (1985): 50–68.

52. Stephen D. Reese, "The News Paradigm and the Ideology of Objectivity: A Socialist at the *Wall Street Journal,*" *Critical Studies in Mass Communication* 7 (1990): 400–2.

53. Tom Rosenstiel, *World News Tonight,* ABC, May 16, 2005.

54. Jack Shafer, "Down the Toilet at *Newsweek,*" *Slate,* May 17, 2005, from http://www.slate.com/id/2118826/ (accessed January 18, 2007).

55. "A Journalistic Blunder Triggers Riots Abroad," *Tacoma News Tribune,* May 17, 2005, B6.

56. Database searches turned up eighty-four editorials and sixteen editor columns confronting the story. See the introduction for more information about database searches.

57. "A Huge Mistake; An Inflammatory Story Handled Carelessly," *The Record,* May 18, 2005, L8.

58. "Credibility," *Lansing State Journal,* May 20, 2005, A12.

59. Richard Foster, "Newsweek's Deadly Story," *Milwaukee Journal Sentinel,* May 17, 2005, 14.

60. Howard Kurtz, "Newsweek Apologizes; Inaccurate Report on Koran Led to Riots," *Washington Post,* May 16, 2005, A1.

61. *The Big Story with John Gibson,* FOX News Channel, May 16, 2005; *Special Report with Brit Hume,* FOX News Channel, May 16, 2005; *Hannity & Colmes,* FOX News Channel, May 16, 2005; and *The O'Reilly Factor,* FOX News Channel, May 17, 2005 and May 18, 2005.

62. *American Morning,* CNN, May 16, 2005; *Crossfire,* CNN, May 17, 2005.

63. *Hardball,* MSNBC, May 16, 17, and 19, 2005; *Scarborough Country,* MSNBC, May 16, 2005.

64. "Power of the Press Misused," *Hartford Courant,* May 17, 2005, A8.

65. Katharine Q. Seelye and Neil A. Lewis, "Newsweek Says It Is Retracting Koran Report," *New York Times,* May 17, 2005, A1.

66. Howard Kurtz, "Painted with Horns that Won't Retract," *Washington Post,* May 23, 2005, C1.

67. Robert L. Jamieson, Jr., "Press Is Doing Its Worst to Erode Trust," *Seattle Post-Intelligencer,* May 18, 2005, B1.

68. Ibid.

69. Quoted in Michael McGough, "Journalism Scholars Criticize Newsweek Magazine Faulted for Failing to Check Facts, Sources," *Pittsburgh Post-Gazette,* May 18, 2005, A9.

70. Project for Excellence in Journalism (n.d.), "Circulation Among the Big Three News Magazines," http://journalism.org/node/1187 (accessed August 12, 2008).

71. "A Case of Shoddy Journalism," *Des Moines Register,* May 18, 2005, A14.

72. Paul Tash, "Why the Times Avoids Using Anonymous Sources," *St. Petersburg Times,* May 22, 2005, P3.

73. Gil Smart, "Speak No Evil, See No Evil, What About the Evil Itself?" *Lancaster Sunday News,* May 22, 2005.

74. Audit Bureau of Circulation report, September 30, 2006.

75. Tom Berger, "Newsweek Acted Timidly, Late in Retraction," *Marshfield News-Herald,* May 23, 2005, A4.

76. Gary Sawyer, "Say No to Anonymous Sources," *Decatur Herald & Review,* May 22, 2005, B4. This was also expressed by the editor of the *Lafayette* (Indiana) *Journal and Courier:* Julie Doll, "Accountability, Anonymous Sources and the Other Guy," *Journal and Courier,* May 22, 2005, A8.

77. Audit Bureau of Circulation report, September 30, 2006.

78. Editorial, *Lancaster Eagle-Gazette,* May 21, 2005, A4.

79. Outside of the executive branch, several congresspersons attacked *Newsweek,* including Representative Robert Ney, who said, "*Newsweek*'s behavior is not merely unfortunate, it is criminal" (*ABC World News Tonight,* May 16, 2005).

80. Quoted in Marda Dunsky, "Credibility on the Koran: Blame the Messenger!" *Chicago Tribune,* May 22, 2005, 1.

81. Quoted in Paul D. Colford and Corky Siemaszko, "W Orders Koran Flap Fix," *New York Daily News,* May 18, 2005, 14.

82. Elisabeth Bumiller, "White House Presses Newsweek in Wake of Koran Report," *New York Times,* May 18, 2005, A19.

83. Chris Hanson, "The 'Scoop' Heard 'Round the World. Sadly," *Washington Post,* May 22, 2005, B3.

84. Cited in Eric Black, "'Hooked' on Anonymous Sources? Flap Highlights Credibility Hurdles," *Star-Tribune,* May 23, 2005, A4.

85. Lynnell Burkett, "Anonymous Sources Can Trap Journalists," *San Antonio Express-News,* May 22, 2005, H2.

86. Quoted in Joe Hagan, "Newsweek Flap Stirs Debate Over Sources," *Wall Street Journal,* May 17, 2005, B1.

87. "Policy and Practice," *Washington Post,* May 20, 2005, A20.

88. Greg Mitchell, *Countdown,* MSNBC, May 17, 2005.

89. Hendrik Hertzberg, "Big News Week," *New Yorker,* May 30, 2005, 33.

90. Michael Isikoff, *Charlie Rose Show,* PBS, May 23, 2005.

91. Katharine Q. Seelye, "Red Cross Reported Koran Abuses," *New York Times,* May 20, 2005, A22.

92. Carol D. Leonnig, "Desecration of Koran Had Been Reported Before," *Washington Post,* May 18, 2005, A12.

93. "What Really Happened?" *Chicago Tribune,* May 20, 2005, 26.

94. *NBC Nightly News,* May 20, 2005.

95. James Gordon Meek, "Real Gitmo Shame? Report U.S. Soldier Rapped for Koran Abuse at Lockup," *New York Daily News,* May 20, 2005, 15. The controversy around the *Newsweek* story also spurred the U.S. military to conduct an investigation of Koran abuse to counter the *Newsweek* claims. While no incidents of military personnel flushing the Koran were substantiated, the military did issue a report citing thirteen cases of Koran mishandling, which made the front pages of the *New York Times* and the *Washington Post* on May 25. Two days later, five of these cases were substantiated by the U.S. military, again making the front page of the *New York Times* on May 27.

96. Gene Lyons, "A Convenient Furor," *Arkansas Democrat Gazette,* May 18, 2005, 21.

97. Josh Marshall, "Bush Wants Another Rathergate from the Newsweek Flub," *The Hill,* May 19, 2005, 16.

98. Jacob Weisberg, "Abuse Week," *Salon,* May 18, 2005, http://www.slate.com/id/2119055/ (accessed January 18, 2007).

99. Richard Cohen, "Newsweek's Mistakes," *Washington Post,* May 20, 2005, A21.

100. Leonard Pitts Jr., "CBS Bush Story Hurt Journalism," *Houston Chronicle,* September 20, 2004, A4.

101. "Newsweek's Deadly Sins," *San Francisco Chronicle,* May 18, 2005, B8.

102. "A Sudden Taste for Openness," *New York Times,* May 18, 2005, A22.

103. "Selective Outrage," *Los Angeles Times,* May 17, 2005, B12.

104. Other editorial criticisms appeared in large and small newspapers, including the *Newark Star-Ledger* (May 17, 2005), *Tulsa World* (May 17, 2005), *Charleston Gazette* (May 18, 2005), *Chicago Sun-Times* (May 18, 2005), *Palm Beach Post* (May 18, 2005), *Seattle Post-Intelligencer* (May 18, 2005), *Bangor Daily News* (May 19, 2005), *Berkshire Eagle* (May 19, 2005), *Evansville Courier* (May 19, 2005), *Erie Times-News* (May 20, 2005), *Greensboro News & Record* (May 20, 2005), *Charlotte Observer* (May 21, 2005), and the *Toledo Blade* (May 21, 2005).

Chapter 4: Deep Throat and the Question of Motives

An earlier version of this chapter appeared as Matt Carlson, "Embodying Deep Throat: Mark Felt and the Collective Memory of Watergate," *Critical Studies in Media Communication* 27, no. 3: 235–50.

Epigraph. Daniel Roddy, "Glory and Honor," *Pittsburgh Post-Gazette,* June 5, 2005, J1.

1. Edward Jay Epstein, *Between Fact and Fiction: The Problem of Journalism* (New York: Vintage Books, 2005).

2. Barbie Zelizer, "Journalists as Interpretive Communities," *Critical Studies in Mass Communication* 10 (1993): 219–37.

3. Michael Schudson, *Watergate in American Memory* (New York: Basic Books, 1992), 124.

4. Bob Woodward and Carl Bernstein, *All the President's Men* (New York: Simon & Schuster, 1974).

5. John D. O'Connor, "I'm the Guy They Called Deep Throat," *Vanity Fair,* July 2005, 86–89, 129–33.

6. Roddy, "Glory and Honor," J1. Felt did partially recover from his stroke and was able to make some media appearances months after the initial disclosure. He also authored a book, although largely through relying on his past memoir and the help of John O'Conner: Mark Felt, *A G-Man's Life: The FBI, Being "Deep Throat," and the Struggle for Honor in Washington* (New York: Public Affairs, 2006).

7. CNN (*Anderson Cooper 360,* May 31 and June 1, 2005; *Crossfire,* June 2, 2005; and *Inside Politics,* June 1, 2005), MSNBC (*Hardball,* May 31, 2005, and *Scarborough Country,* June 1, 2005), and the Fox News Channel (*Special Report with Brit Hume,* May 31 and June 1, 2005).

8. Johanna McGeary, "Inside Watergate's Last Chapter," *Time,* June 13, 2005, 28.

9. Nina J. Easton, "Insiders' Parlor Game Takes Surprising Twist," *Boston Globe,* June 1, 2005, A6.

10. "It's Still Nixon's America; Deep Throat Brings It All Back—With a Vengeance," *Arkansas Democrat Gazette,* June 5, 2005, 12.

11. "Now We Know," *Raleigh News & Observer,* June 2, 2005, A10.

12. Anderson Cooper, *Anderson Cooper 360,* CNN, June 1, 2005.

13. While reporting on Felt's disclosure often included praise and criticism from sources, journalists were able to adopt a subjective voice supporting Felt through columns and op-ed pieces.

14. Charles Colson, *NBC Nightly News,* May 31, 2005.

15. Robert Novak, "Felt's Motivation Might Not Have Been So Noble," *Chicago Sun-Times,* June 1, 2005, 3.

16. Mary Laney, "Deep Throat Was a Craven Opportunist, Not a Hero," *Chicago Sun-Times,* June 13, 2005, 47.

17. "The Men Who Really Brought Nixon Down," *New York Post,* June 2, 2005, 34.

18. Andrew Napolitano, *O'Reilly Factor,* Fox News Channel, June 2, 2005.

19. John Gibson, *The Big Story with John Gibson,* Fox News Channel, June 1, 2005.

20. William F. Buckley, "A Foul From Felt; "Deep Throat" Advanced His Own Drama; Now He Wants to Cash In," *Grand Rapids Press,* June 7, 2005, A9.

21. Jack Shafer, "Why Did Deep Throat Leak? Hint: It Wasn't Out of a Sense of Patriotism," *Slate,* June 2, 2005, http://www.slate.com/id/2120148/ (accessed February 20, 2007).

22. Eileen McNamara, "Throat Soreness," *Boston Globe,* June 1, 2005, B1.

23. Colbert I. King, "Deep Throat's Other Legacy," *Washington Post,* June 4, 2005, A17.

24. Joan Felt, *Lou Dobbs Tonight,* CNN, May 31, 2005.

25. Quoted in Katharine Q. Seelye, "Felt is Praised as a Hero and Condemned as a Traitor," *New York Times,* June 2, 2005, A18.

26. McGeary, "Inside Watergate's Last Chapter," 28.

27. Carl Bernstein, *Larry King Live,* CNN, June 2, 2005.

28. Bob Woodward, *Dateline,* NBC, July 6, 2005.

29. Bob Woodward, "How Mark Felt Became Deep Throat," *Washington Post,* June 2, 2005, A1.

30. Bob Woodward, *The Secret Man* (New York: Simon and Schuster, 2005).

31. "Felt, Finally; High-Ranking FBI Official Who Doubled as 'Deep Throat' Deserves Praise for Helping to Reveal Nixon's Corruption," *Plain Dealer,* June 2, 2005, B8.

32. "The Ultimate Source, Deep and Historic," *Seattle Times,* June 2, 2005, B6.

33. "Moral Minority—Our Stand: Deep Throat Paid a Price, and Deserves Thanks," *Arizona Republic,* June 2, 2005, B8.

34. "Brave Decision Shaped History," *Kansas City Star,* June 2, 2005, B6.

35. "A Mystery Solved," *Rochester Democrat and Chronicle,* June 2, 2005, A8.

36. "Mark Felt: If Not a Hero, He's Definitely a Patriot," *San Antonio Express-News,* June 2, 2005, B6.

37. Tom Brokaw, *Today,* NBC, June 1, 2005.

38. Bob Woodward, *Today,* NBC, June 2, 2005.

39. Ben Bradlee, *NBC Nightly News,* June 1, 2005.

40. Neil Steinburg, "For Young Readers, Watergate 101: Ousting Nixon from Office Was Good," *Chicago Sun-Times,* June 3, 2005, 22.

41. George Arnold, "The Usual Suspects," *Arkansas Democrat Gazette,* June 7, 2005, 16.

42. Tom Brokaw, *NBC Nightly News,* May 31, 2005.

43. Daniel Schorr, *All Things Considered,* NPR, June 1, 2005.

44. Searches for newspaper opinion pieces of Felt found over 100 editorials and 137 separate columns on Felt.

45. "Deep Throat Speaks," *Boston Globe,* June 2, 2005, A10; "A Source of Inspiration for Protecting Free Press," *Chicago Sun-Times,* June 2, 2005, 37; "Confidentiality Matters," *San Diego Union-Tribune,* June 2, 2005, B10; "Deep Throat Takes a Bow," *Commercial Appeal,* June 3, 2005, B4; "Watergate: Secret Source of Secrets," *Seattle Post-Intelligencer,* June 2, 2005, B6.

46. "The Mystery Unravels," *Austin American-Statesman,* June 1, 2005, A10. Other newspapers labeling Felt a reminder of the importance of unnamed sources included *Dallas Morning News* (June 1, 2005), *Charlotte Observer* (June 2, 2005), *Houston Chronicle* (June 2, 2005), *Louisville Courier-Journal* (June 2, 2005), *Orlando Sentinel* (June 2, 2005), *St. Louis Post-Dispatch* (June 2, 2005), and *Wall Street Journal* (June 2, 2005).

47. Fred Brown, "The Two Faces of Anonymity," *Denver Post,* June 5, 2005, E6.

48. "Get Out Your Notebooks, Again," *Indianapolis Star*, June 2, 2005, A14.

49. Amy White, "Out of One Shadow; Into Another," *St. Louis Post-Dispatch*, June 2, 2005, B7.

50. Lucy Morgan, "Informers in Shadows Can Bring Truth to Light," *St. Petersburg Times*, June 11, 2005, B1.

51. Quoted in Todd S. Purdum, "'Deep Throat' Unmasks Himself: Ex-No. 2 at F.B.I.," *New York Times*, June 1, 2005, A1.

52. Richard Cohen, "A Brave Friend," *Washington Post*, June 1, 2005, A19.

53. Leonard Garment, *Paula Zahn Now*, CNN, May 31, 2005.

54. Pat Buchanan, *Today*, NBC, May 31, 2005.

55. Chuck Colson, *CBS Evening News*, May 31, 2005.

56. Alexander Haig, *Special Report with Brit Hume*, Fox News Channel, June 1, 2005.

57. David Gergen, *NewsNight with Aaron Brown*, CNN, May 31, 2005.

58. William Kristol, *Fox News Sunday*, June 5, 2005.

59. Gary Aldrich, "Deep Throat Uncut; FBI Official Remains Untouched," *Washington Times*, June 3, 2005, A21.

60. Toni Locy, "FBI Veterans Reflect on Ethics and Obligations," *USA Today*, June 2, 2005, A6.

61. Dan Eggen, "At FBI, Reflections on Felt and Loyalty," *Washington Post*, June 2, 2005, A21; Stacy Finz, "Former FBI Agents Debate Felt's Ethics," *San Francisco Chronicle*, June 2, 2005, A3.

62. Daniel Schorr, *All Things Considered*, NPR, May 31, 2005.

63. Quoted in Alex Ben Block, "Shielding the Truth," *Television Week*, June 13, 2005, 8.

64. Bob Woodward, *Reliable Sources*, CNN, July 17, 2005.

65. Elizabeth Sullivan, "Anonymous Sources: Endangered Necessity," *Plain Dealer*, June 2, 2005, B9.

66. Quoted in James Rainey, "Journalists See More to Story Than Secret Source," *Los Angeles Times*, June 1, 2005, A14.

67. See Epstein, *Between Fact and Fiction*.

68. Even Woodward and Bernstein seemed to not have lived up to their earlier success. Woodward, in particular, became an accomplished book author, but has been badgered by charges of being too close to sources. See, for example, Joan Didion, "The Deferential Spirit," *New York Review of Books* 43 (1996): 14–19.

69. Howard Kurtz, *Paula Zahn Now*, CNN, May 31, 2005.

70. Loren Steffy, "It's Not About the Big Break; It's About Doing a Job Well," *Houston Chronicle*, June 5, 2005, 1.

71. Quoted in Anne E. Kornblut, "The News Media Is Still Recovering from Watergate," *New York Times*, June 5, 2005, 4.

Chapter 5: "Journalism on Trial"

Epigraph. Rudi Bakhtiar, *Anderson Cooper 360,* CNN, July 6, 2005.

    1. Woodward suggested the idea on *Larry King Live,* CNN, July 11, 2005.

    2. Lou Dobbs, *Lou Dobbs Tonight,* CNN, August 9, 2005.

    3. Arthur Sulzberger, *All Things Considered,* NPR, February 15, 2005.

    4. This narrow frame for understanding unnamed sources follows a trend prevalent in discussions of Mark Felt's role as Deep Throat (described in chapter 4).

    5. Matt Cooper, *On the Record with Greta Van Susteren,* Fox News Channel, February 15, 2005.

    6. "And Strikes a Blow at a Strong Press," *New York Times,* June 28, 2005, A22.

    7. "Prosecuting the Messenger," *Seattle Times,* July 1, 2005, B6.

    8. Bill Keller, "Remarks by Times Editor and Magazine Reporter," *New York Times,* July 7, 2005, A18.

    9. The negative result of the subpoenas for journalism was labeled a "chilling effect" or "chilling" on CNBC (*Capital Report,* August 10, 2004); CNN (*Wolf Blitzer Reports,* February 15, 2005; *American Morning,* June 30, 2005; *Reliable Sources,* July 3, 2005; *Lou Dobbs Tonight,* July 6, 2005; *Live Today,* September 30, 2005); Fox News (*Special Report with Brit Hume,* August 10, 2004 and July 6, 2005); MSNBC (*Hardball,* July 6, 2005; *The Situation with Tucker Carlson,* July 6, 2005); and NPR (*All Things Considered,* June 27, 2005). For newspapers, the phrase "chilling effect" appeared in the *Rocky Mountain News* (February 17, 2005), *New York Times* (June 28, 2005), *Miami Herald* (June 29, 2005), Newark *Star-Ledger* (July 3, 2005), *San Diego Union-Tribune* (July 4, 2005), *USA Today* (July 5, 2005), *Toledo Blade* (July 11, 2005), *Arkansas Democrat-Gazette* (July 12, 2005), and *Christian Science Monitor* (September 15, 2005), among others. The *San Francisco Chronicle* called Miller's incarceration a "chilling message" (July 7, 2005) while the *Indianapolis Star* identified its "chilling impact" (July 3, 2005). Newspapers calling the investigation "chilling" included the *Las Vegas Review-Journal* (July 10, 2005), *USA Today* (July 14, 2005), *Washington Post* (August 16, 2004), and the *Kansas City Star* (November 30, 2005). The term "chill" appeared in the *New York Post* (February 16, 2005), *Tampa Tribune* (February 17, 2005), *Hartford Courant* (June 29, 2005), Raleigh *News & Observer* (June 29, 2005), *Orange County Register* (July 10, 2005), and the Portland *Oregonian* (July 25, 2005). An editorial in the *San Diego Union-Tribune* wrote that Miller's jailing "chills the spine" (July 9, 2005).

    10. Bob Dole, "The Underprivileged Press," *New York Times,* August 16, 2005, 15.

    11. Quoted in "Shield Laws Protect Public's Right to Know, Too," *Dayton Daily News,* July 26, 2005, A9.

    12. "Need for Shield is Clear," *Columbus Dispatch,* July 9, 2005, A10.

    13. Matthew Cooper, Massimo Calabresi, and John F. Dickerson, "A War on Wilson?" *Time,* July 17, 2003, http://www.time.com/time/nation/article/0,8599,465270,00 .html (accessed January 16, 2009).

14. Joe Hagan, "*Time* Says It's Not Above Law; Will Obey Court," *Wall Street Journal*, July 1, 2005, B1.

15. Criticism was directed at *Time* magazine for giving away Cooper's notes—with the exception of an editorial in the Albany *Times-Union* calling Cooper's actions "clumsy and self-serving." "A Chilling Effect," *Times-Union*, July 8, 2005, A10.

16. James Bandler, "Contempt Orders Are Upheld on Reporters in CIA Leak Case," *Wall Street Journal*, February 16, 2005, A2.

17. Quoted in Hagan, "*Time* Says It's Not Above Law," B1.

18. Ibid.

19. Norman Pearlstine, *Off the Record* (New York: Farrar, Strauss and Giroux, 2007).

20. Frank Rich, "We're Not in Watergate Anymore," *New York Times*, July 10, 2005, 12.

21. Ben Bagdikian, *Marketplace*, Minnesota Public Radio, June 30, 2005.

22. "Who Has Your Back? Journalism in the Corporate Age," *Columbia Journalism Review* 44 (September 2005): 7.

23. "If the Next Deep Throat Clams Up," *Oregonian*, July 1, 2005, E6.

24. "Plame Probe Heats Up, But Effects Are Chilling," *USA Today*, July 14, 2005, A12.

25. "*Time* Sells Out," *Salt Lake Tribune*, July 1, 2005, A14.

26. David Ignatius, "Bad Case for a Fight," *Washington Post*, July 8, 2005, A23.

27. Nicholas Kristof, "Missing In Action: Truth," *New York Times*, May 6, 2003, A31.

28. Joseph Wilson, "What I Didn't Find in Africa," *New York Times*, July 6, 2003, 9.

29. Stuart Karle, "In Defense of a Press Shield Law," *Wall Street Journal*, October 24, 2005, A15.

30. Nicholas Lemann, "Telling Secrets," *New Yorker*, November 7, 2005, 48.

31. Howard Kurtz, *Reliable Sources*, CNN, August 15, 2004.

32. Quoted in Howard Kurtz, "A Case Most Clearly Defined by Its Shadows," *Washington Post*, July 7, 2005, A12.

33. Joe Strupp, "Here Is an E&P Countdown of the Newspaper Biz Stories of the Year, with Hopes That 2006 Will Prove a Bit Calmer (and More Prosperous)," *Editor & Publisher*, December 23, 2005.

34. See Margaret Sullivan, "Why Judith Miller's Jail Term Matters to You," *Buffalo News*, July 10, 2005, B1.

35. Margaret Sullivan, "On Buffalo's Future, and Judith Miller's Past," *Buffalo News*, November 6, 2005, B1.

36. Brook Gladstone, *On the Media*, NPR, September 30, 2005.

37. Seth Mnookin, "Unreliable Sources," *Vanity Fair*, January 2006, 132.

38. Don Van Natta Jr., Adam Liptak, and Clifford J. Levy, "The Miller Case: A Notebook, a Cause, a Jail Cell and a Deal," *New York Times*, October 16, 2005, A1.

39. Judith Miller, "My Four Hours Testifying in the Federal Grand Jury Room," *New York Times,* October 16, 2005, A31.

40. Maureen Dowd, "Woman of Mass Destruction," *New York Times,* October 22, 2005, A17; Byron Calame, "The Miller Mess: Lingering Issues Among the Answers," *New York Times,* October 23, 2005, 12.

41. Van Natta, Liptak, and Clifford, "The Miller Case."

42. "Fixing the New York Times Starts with Miller's Departure," *Tampa Tribune,* October 19, 2005, 14.

43. Tina Brown, "Seeing Right Through the Times's Transparency," *Washington Post,* October 20, 2005, C1.

44. Miller, "My Four Hours."

45. Steve Roberts, *Reliable Sources,* CNN, November 13, 2005.

46. "Miller, Libby Talks Too Cozy," *Denver Post,* October 18, 2005, B6.

47. "Source of Frustration," *Los Angeles Times,* October 18, 2005, B10.

48. Quoted in Lynne Duke, "The Reporter's Last Take," *Washington Post,* November 10, 2005, C1.

49. "Little Credit in Miller Case," *Oregonian,* October 18, 2005, B8. Also, see Gina Lubrano, "Reporters Deal with Difficult Sources," *San Diego Union-Tribune,* November 21, 2005, B7.

50. Shafer questioned whether Miller's support for Bush administration actions colored her reporting: Jack Shafer, "Defending General Judy," *Slate,* June 27, 2003, http://www.slate.com/id/2084992/ (accessed November 1, 2006).

51. Amy Goodman, *Hardball,* MSNBC, October 17, 2005.

52. Quoted in Michael Massing, "Now They Tell Us," *New York Review of Books,* February 26, 2004, http://www.nybooks.com/articles/16922 (accessed February 26, 2007).

53. Jack Shafer, "The *Times* Scoops That Melted," *Slate,* July 25, 2003, http://www.slate.com/id/2086110/ (accessed November 1, 2006).

54. Jack Shafer, "Miller Time (Again)," *Slate,* February 12, 2004, http://www.slate.com/id/2095394/, original emphasis (accessed November 1, 2006)

55. Massing, "Now They Tell Us."

56. "Seduced by Access," *Brattleboro Reformer,* October 19, 2005.

57. Jack Shafer, "Deep Miller," *Slate,* April 21, 2003, http://www.slate.com/id/2081774/ (accessed November 1, 2006).

58. Jack Shafer, "Follow That Story: Deep Miller," *Slate,* April 23, 2003, http://www.slate.com/id/2081905/ (accessed November 1, 2006).

59. Jim VandeHei, and Carol D. Leonnig, "Woodward Was Told of Plame More Than Two Years Ago," Washington Post, November 16, 2005, A1.

60. Leonard Downie, *The Situation Room,* CNN, November 16, 2005.

61. "And the Name of the Star Is Called Woodward," *The Hotline,* November 16, 2005, http://blogometer.nationaljournal.com/archives/2005/11/1116_and_the_na.php (accessed April 20, 2007).

62. Brooke Gladstone, *On the Media*, NPR, November 18, 2005.

63. James Carroll, "The Fall of Bob Woodward," *Boston Globe*, November 21, 2005, A15.

64. "Newsrooms Need Some Sun," *Editor & Publisher*, February 1, 2006, 18.

65. Deborah Howell, "Tough Week for the Post and a Star," *Washington Post*, November 20, 2005, B6.

66. Bob Gabordi, "Confidentiality Can Erode Credibility," *Tallahassee Democrat*, November 20, 2005, E5.

67. See John Soloski, "News Reporting and Professionalism: Some Constraints on the Reporting of the News," in *Social Meanings of the News*, ed. Daniel A. Berkowitz (Thousand Oaks, CA: Sage, 1997), 138–54.

68. Joe Scarborough, *Hardball*, MSNBC, November 16, 2005.

69. Joe Hagan, "Now, Woodward Reveals Learning Plame's Identity," *Wall Street Journal*, November 17, 2005, B1.

70. Kenneth F. Bunting, "Underlying Principles Mired in Scandal," *Seattle Post-Intelligencer*, November 18, 2005, B6.

71. Woodward retained the title of assistant managing editor, but worked out of his home. Quoted in Howard Kurtz, "Woodward Apologizes to Post for Silence on Role in Leak Case," *Washington Post*, November 17, 2005, A1.

72. Howell, "Tough Week," emphasis added.

73. Quoted in Scott Shane and Katharine Q. Seelye, "Post Editor Foresees Possibility of Naming Leak Source," *New York Times*, November 18, 2005, A24.

74. Rem Rieder, "Say It Isn't So, Bob," *American Journalism Review* 27 (October/November, 2005), http://www.ajr.org/Article.asp?id=3995 (accessed April 20, 2007).

75. Quoted in Kurtz, "Woodward Apologizes to Post."

76. Frank Rich, "All The President's Flacks," *New York Times*, December 4, 2005, 13.

77. Joan Didion, "The Deferential Spirit," *New York Review of Books* 43 (1996): 14–19.

78. Arianna Huffington, *Reliable Sources*, CNN, November 27, 2005.

79. Brooke Gladstone, *On the Media*, NPR, November 18, 2005.

80. Dana Priest, "CIA Holds Terror Suspects in Secret Prisons," *Washington Post*, November 2, 2005, A1.

81. James Risen and Eric Lichtblau, "Bush Lets U.S. Spy on Callers Without Courts," *New York Times*, December 16, 2005, A1.

82. The Pulitzer Prizes, "The 2006 Pulitzer Prize Winners: National Reporting," http://www.pulitzer.org/citation/2006-National-Reporting, emphasis added.

83. Steve Roberts, *Reliable Sources*, CNN, November 13, 2005.

84. Scott Johnson, "The Pulitzer Prize for Treason," Powerlineblog.com, April 17, 2006, http://www.powerlineblog.com/archives/2006/04/013571.php.

85. Accuracy in Media, "AIM Report: Treason, Plagiarism and the Washington Post," December 4, 2007, http://www.aim.org/aim-report/aim-report-treason-

plagiarism-and-the-washington-post/. AIM also accused Priest of having duplicated already existing work by a British journalist.

86. See discussion in chapter 1.

87. Quoted in Matt Apuzzo, "In CIA Leak Case, Reporters Will Be Key Witnesses," *Associated Press Newswires*, January 1, 2007.

88. *Reliable Sources*, CNN, February 4, 2007.

89. Lowell Bergman, *Reliable Sources*, CNN, February 11, 2007.

90. Hope Yen, "CIA Leak Trial Prompts Scrutiny of News Reporting Practices," *Associated Press Newswires*, March 7, 2007.

91. Adam Liptak, "After Libby Trial, New Era for Government and the Press," *New York Times*, March 8, 2007, A18.

92. Neil Lewis, "Libby Trial to Display Changed Reporter-Source Relations," *New York Times*, January 22, 2007, A16.

93. Joe Garofoli, "Analysts Say Information Now Could Be Harder to Get," *San Francisco Chronicle*, March 7, 2007, A10.

94. Bob Zelnick, *Morning Edition*, NPR, March 7, 2007.

95. "Shielding Sources," *St. Louis Post-Dispatch*, March 17, 2007, A41.

96. Ken Bunting, "Reporters in Court Can Stifle Whistle-Blowers," *Seattle Post-Intelligencer*, March 9, 2007, B6.

97. Hope Yen, "Libby Trial Prompts Scrutiny on Media," *Associated Press Newswires*, March 6, 2007.

98. Howard Kurtz, "A Case of Bad Ink: Portrait of Media Is Not So Flattering," *Washington Post*, March 7, 2007, C1.

99. Howard Kurtz, *Reliable Sources*, CNN, January 21, 2007.

100. Howard Kurtz, *Reliable Sources*, CNN, February 18, 2007.

101. Tim Rutten, *NewsHour*, PBS, February 7, 2007.

102. Jill Zuckman, *Reliable Sources*, CNN, February 18, 2007.

103. Ibid.

104. David Folkenflik, *Talk of the Nation*, NPR, 3/6/2007.

105. "White House Hates Leaks, Except When It Doesn't," *USA Today*, February 20, 2007, A12.

106. Murray Waas, *The United States v. I. Lewis Libby* (New York: Union Square Press, 2007), 107.

107. "Libby's Fallout," *St. Petersburg Times*, March 8, 2007, 14.

108. Keith Olbermann, *Countdown*, MSNBC, January 30, 2007.

109. Michael Isikoff, *Reliable Sources*, CNN, February 4, 2007.

110. Howard Kurtz, "Journalist Forced to Reveal Her Methods," *Washington Post*, January 31, 2007, C1.

111. TRex, comment on "Why It Matters (Plame Edition)," Firedoglake.com, comment posted February 5, 2007, http://firedoglake.com/2007/02/05/why-it-matters-plame-edition/ (accessed February 20, 2009).

112. Arianna Huffington, "Libby and Russert: Two Trials in the Same Court-

room," *Huffington Post,* February 8, 2007, http://www.huffingtonpost.com/arianna -huffington/libby-and-russert-two-tr_b_40759.html (accessed February 20, 2009).

113. Dan Froomkin, "Some Explaining to Do," Washingtonpost.com, March 7, 2007, http://www.washingtonpost.com/wp-dyn/content/blog/2007/03/07/ BL2007030701183_pf.html (accessed February 20, 2009).

114. Patrick Fitzgerald, *CNN Newsroom,* CNN, March 6, 2007.

115. Lemann, "Telling Secrets," 48.

Chapter 6: Rethinking Anonymity

Epigraph. Terence Smith, *All Things Considered,* NPR, November 28, 2005.

1. See Pierre Bourdieu, "The Political Field, the Social Science Field, and the Journalistic Field," in *Bourdieu and the Journalistic Field,* ed. Rodney Benson and Erik Neveu (Cambridge, UK: Polity, 2005), 29–47; Pierre Bourdieu, *On Television,* trans. P. Parkhurst Ferguson (New York: The New Press, 1998).

2. W. Lance Bennett, Lynne A. Gressett, and William Haltom, "Repairing the News: A Case Study of the News Paradigm," *Journal of Communication* 35 (1985): 50–68; Dan Berkowitz, "Doing Double Duty: Paradigm Repair and the Princess Diana What-A-Story," *Journalism* 1 (2000): 125–43; Elizabeth Blanks Hindman, "Jayson Blair, The *New York Times,* and Paradigm Repair," *Journal of Communication* 55 (2005): 225–41; Stephen D. Reese, "The News Paradigm and the Ideology of Objectivity: A Socialist at the *Wall Street Journal,*" *Critical Studies in Mass Communication* 7 (1990): 390–409.

3. See the introduction for more background on critical incidents.

4. This is well documented by Ben Bagdikian in *The New Media Monopoly* (Boston: Beacon Press, 2004).

5. "Assault on the Media," *Roanoke Times,* May 19, 2005, B10.

6. For key works in this area, see Mark Fishman, *Manufacturing the News* (Austin: University of Texas Press, 1980); Herbert J. Gans, *Deciding What's News: A Study of CBS Evening News, NBC Nightly News, Newsweek, and Time* (New York: Pantheon Books, 1979); Stuart Hall, Chas Critcher, Tony Jefferson, John N. Clarke, and Brian Roberts, *Policing the Crisis: Mugging, the State and Law and Order* (London: Macmillan, 1978); Leon V. Sigal, *Reporters and Officials: The Organization and Politics of Newsmaking* (Lexington, MA: D.C. Heath, 1973).

7. Stephen J. Cimbala, "Bad Things Happen When Reporters Are Newsmakers," *Patriot-News,* November 27, 2005, F5.

8. Geneva Overholser, *Reliable Sources,* CNN, November 20, 2005.

9. David L. Eason, "On Journalistic Authority: The Janet Cooke Scandal," in *Media, Myths, and Narratives: Television and the Press,* ed. J. W. Carey (Beverly Hills, CA: Sage Publications, 1988), 205–27, 221.

10. Peter Dahlgren, "Introduction," in *Journalism and Popular Culture,* ed. Peter Dahlgren and Colin Sparks (London: Sage, 1992), 1–23, 7.

11. Dean Smith, "Price v. Time Revisited: The Need For Medium-Neutral Shield Laws in an Age of Strict Construction," *Communication Law & Policy* 14 (Spring 2009): 235–72.

12. Charlie Savage, "Deal in Senate on Protecting News Sources," *New York Times,* October 30, 2009, A1.

13. HR 985, "Free Flow of Information Act of 2009," sec. 4, cl. (2).

14. Andrew Abbott, *The System of Professions: An Essay on the Division of Expert Labor* (Chicago: University of Chicago Press, 1988).

15. James Carey, "A Plea for the University Tradition," *Journalism Quarterly* 55 (1979): 846–55.

16. Ibid., 851.

17. Michael Schudson, *Discovering the News: A Social History of American Newspapers* (New York: Basic Books, 1978).

18. For an overview, see Vincent Mosco, *The Political Economy of Communication,* 2nd ed. (London: Sage Publications, 2009).

19. See Anthony Giddens, *The Constitution of Society* (Berkeley: University of California Press, 1986).

20. Robert McChesney, *The Problem of the Media: U.S. Communication Politics in the 21st Century* (New York: Monthly Review Press, 2004), chap. 7.

21. David Alexander and Eva Jermakowicz, "A True and Fair View of the Principles/ Rules Debate," *Abacus* 42 (2006): 132–64, 134. See also Christopher Nobes, "Rules-Based Standards and the Lack of Principles in Accounting," *Accounting Horizons* 19 (2005): 24–34.

22. Alexander and Jermakowicz, "A True and Fair View," 151.

23. Ibid., 134.

24. Bob Gabordi, "Confidentiality Can Erode Credibility," *Tallahassee Democrat,* November 20, 2005, E5. Of course, there are reporters who instead request directions to the women's restroom.

25. Bob Garfield, *On the Media,* NPR, July 8, 2005.

26. Russ Baker, "'Scoops' and Truth at the Times: What Happens When Pentagon Objectives and Journalists' Needs Coincide," *The Nation,* June 23, 2003, 18.

27. The suggestion that journalists need to be more transparent is presented cogently in Bill Kovach and Tom Rosenstiel's influential book, *The Elements of Journalism* (New York: Three Rivers Press, 2001). They state that journalists should "be as open and honest with audiences as they can about what they know and what they don't" (80) to simultaneously reduce the ability of sources to take advantage of their access to the news while improving the relationship between journalists and their audiences.

28. Ken Auletta, *NewsHour,* PBS, January 13, 2005.

29. Irwin Gratz, "Don't Just Tell the Story: Tell How the Story Was Done," *The Quill* (June 2005): 4.

30. Dennis Ryerson, "The Media's Duty Is to Ensure All Sides Get Their Due," *Indianapolis Star,* August 15, 2004, E1.

31. Poynter Ethics Journal, "*The Washington Post*'s Policies on Sources, Quotations, Attribution, and Datelines," Poynter Online, February 20, 2004, http://www.poynter .org/column.asp?id=53&aid=61244 (accessed November 1, 2006).

32. New York Times Company, "Confidential News Sources," February 25, 2004, http://www.nytco.com/company/business_units/sources.html.

33. Bennett and Serrin define watchdog journalism around journalistic autonomy, investigative practices, and information provision to the public. W. Lance Bennett and William Serrin, "The Watchdog Role," in *The Press,* ed. Geneva Overholser and Kathleen Hall Jamieson (New York: Oxford University Press, 2005), 169–88, 169.

34. Hall, et al., *Policing the Crisis.*

35. Michael Schudson, *The Power of News* (Cambridge, MA: Harvard University Press, 1995), 3.

Index

MATT CARLSON is an assistant professor of communication at Saint Louis University.

The University of Illinois Press
is a founding member of the
Association of American University Presses.

Composed in 10.5/13 Adobe Minion Pro
with FF Meta display
at the University of Illinois Press
Manufactured by Cushing-Malloy, Inc.

University of Illinois Press
1325 South Oak Street
Champaign, IL 61820-6903
www.press.uillinois.edu